THE ODDS AGAINST US

Peter Townsend

THE ODDS AGAINST US

WILLIAM MORROW AND COMPANY, INC. / NEW YORK

Library of Congress Cataloging-in-Publication Data

Townsend, Peter, 1914–
  The odds against us.

  Bibliography: p.
  Includes index.
  1. Townsend, Peter, 1914–   . 2. Britain, Battle of,
1940. 3. World War, 1939–1945—Aerial operations,
British. 4. World War, 1939–1945—Personal narratives,
English. 5. Great Britain. Royal Air Force—Biography.
6. Fighter pilots—Great Britain—Biography. I. Title.
D756.5.B7T693 1987   940.54′4941   86-28602
ISBN 0-688-04290-2

Printed in the United States of America

First Edition

1 2 3 4 5 6 7 8 9 10

BOOK DESIGN BY VICTORIA HARTMAN

To the memory of my brothers,
Michael and Philip

FOREWORD

This book is a natural sequel to *Duel of Eagles*, in which I described the events culminating in 1940 in the Battle of Britain, the first decisive battle ever fought in the air, when the RAF day fighters defeated the Luftwaffe and thus put an end to Hitler's aim of eliminating Britain from the war and leaving him master of Europe.

The day battle over, the Germans switched to a relentless night bombing offensive whose object was to subdue the British into surrender. Goering, the Luftwaffe chief, announced the "progressive annihilation" of London and British industrial and harbor towns. London itself was bombed night after night, without respite, for two months.

The day-fighter squadron, No. 85, that I had led during the day battle was, in the autumn of 1940, abruptly assigned, as were half a dozen others, the role of a night-fighter squadron. I tell the story here of how we in the night defenses, in the face of formidable technical and weather problems, tried, with little success at first, to help stem the nine-month-long German night onslaught—the "night blitz"—while Britain, alone save for her loyal Commonwealth and a few brave survivors from occupied Europe, kept fighting on at home as well as on many foreign fronts.

I am deeply indebted to the following persons and institutions who helped so readily in my researches:

Air Commodore Henry Probert, head of the Historical Branch, Ministry of Defense, and his staff, notably Sebastian Cox, an expert on the Luftwaffe

Andrew Orgill, librarian of the Adastral Library, and his staff

The Imperial War Museum

The Public Records Office

Oberst Hans-Joachim Weste, German air attaché in Paris, who kindly put me in touch with Herr Berthold Kruger, president of the Kampfgeschwader 2 Comrades Association, who in turn put me on the trail of Herr Martin Mummer, observer of the Dornier 217 I intercepted one dark night in February 1941. My letter to him was apologetic—I felt sorry for the harm I done to Mummer and his companions. No reply was forthcoming.

Patrick and Penny Langrishe, who kindly lent me the wartime diary of their uncle, the late Ronald Horley. It was a source of inspiration, both literary and artistic.

Pat Barnard, director of the Military Gallery, Bath, whose wide connections were invaluable, particularly as he led me to Ray Callow and his brother Johnny, to whom I am grateful for giving me many hours of their time, so that I could form a lively picture of how Londoners "took it" during those long days and nights of the "blitz."

Although the incident occurred after the period covered by this book, Mme. "Dirkie" Kiddley helped my understanding by recalling vividly her memories of the disastrous bombing of Sandhurst Road School, where she was a seven-year-old pupil.

I should like particularly to thank Bruce Lee, senior editor at my publishers, William Morrow, for all his helpful suggestions. To Dana Noye and my daughter Françoise I am grateful for their painstaking work in typing my manuscript.

I feel an undying admiration for the people of London and all the other blitzed cities and towns of Britain. It was they who, bare-handed, did more than we armed men to keep Hitler out of our island.

CONTENTS

They agreed on at least one thing:

Hitler: "The spirit of the British people enables it to carry through to victory any struggle that it once enters upon, no matter how long . . . or however great the sacrifice."

Churchill (visiting bombed-out civilians): "I see the spirit of an unconquerable people."

THE ODDS AGAINST US

1

TROPICAL NIGHTS

Night had fallen on Singapore. In those tropical latitudes the sun, blazing overhead all day, sank swiftly at eventide below the horizon and day changed abruptly into night. In the brief half hour of dusk, I had made a few "circuits and bumps" to get accustomed to the flare path, a row of half a dozen buckets, spaced out over as many hundred yards, containing kerosene in which a kind of wick, like a mop, was immersed. They burned with an orange flame which trailed away in a wispy cloud of black smoke.

Each one of these crude flares was minded by a Tamil boy, as black as the night itself. His job was to stoke the fire. Sometimes an airplane landing too close to the flare path would fan the flares into a wild blaze and send the Tamil boys scurrying off to safety.

Now it was dark, I took off again, this time on my first "night solo," piloting a Vickers Vildebeeste, a big biplane as ugly as its African namesake. In the open cockpit the pilot's sole protection was a small windscreen.

The Vildebeeste's huge propeller, a masterpiece of woodwork carved out of laminated mahogany, churned the air, dragging the aircraft along at a comfortable cruising speed of 100 mph. In a dive you dared not exceed 140 mph; otherwise you were likely to continue diving minus the tail unit. But the Vildebeeste, within its limits, was a trusty friend, for which, though bred as a fighter pilot, I formed a deep affection.

Climbing away into the starry, purple sky, I rejoiced as much in the immense feeling of puissance and solitude as in the smell of the warm night air. In Malay kampongs and Chinese villages, lights flickered;

they were cooking the evening meal, and mixed odors of grilled fish and spices and burning charcoal wafted up until they pervaded my cockpit. Some way south the lights of Singapore twinkled brightly. Above, stars crowded the heavens, their customary brilliance slightly faded in the pale light of the rising moon. I flew on into the midst of the night, marveling at that multitude of celestial bodies and feeling like an extraterrestrial body myself, at one with them.

These were dream conditions for night flying. With the stars above and the lighted earth beneath, you at least could tell that you were the right way up. In those days—and nights—men flew like birds. People sometimes called us birdmen, even intrepid birdmen. That made us laugh, though frankly we preferred to fly as the birds do, with the horizon before us separating earth and sky, rather than concentrate anxiously on the turn-and-bank indicator, a dial in the center of the dashboard whose two needles wobbled uncertainly. This instrument, with your compass and altimeter, graded in hundreds of feet, was supposed to help you, in poor visibility, to fly straight and level. It was a hateful little instrument which perpetually conveyed the impression that your aircraft was erring in every direction but the right one.

But give us the natural horizon and we flew like the birds. That night in Singapore was the first of September 1936. I was twenty-one and supremely happy with my life as a pilot, dangerous though it was and far from home. Singapore was ten days' flying from London. My first night flight, alone at the controls, was a new adventure in flying, the career which, since the age of fourteen, I had firmly decided to follow.

No one could force you to be a pilot; you became one out of love, of a passion for flying. While in the exclusive Tanglin Club or at Raffles Hotel, you might spend a blissful evening in the select company of some well-bred daughter of the British community or, at the Happy World, in the arms of a lissome Chinese hostess, dancing away the hours, your first love was for your ugly Vildebeeste, with its oily reek and the emotions it provided in plenty. A pilot more in love with a girl than with his aircraft grew ''broody'' and lost the taste for the risks of his trade.

Flying was for me pure romance. The technical aspect, though inevitable, was secondary. I took to the working of the engine without too much trouble because it was full of amusing names: big ends and little ends, crankshafts and camshafts, poppet valves and sprockets, splines and pinions and pushrods. They made music, as did the steady rhythm of the Bristol Pegasus engine itself, as its 650 horses turned that great wooden windmill in front.

We trusted the engine implicitly, flying, as we always were, over sea and jungle. Occasionally a spark plug would blow out, but the "Peggy," puffing like a steam engine, would bring us safely home.

The technicalities of radio, on the other hand, were forever to remain beyond my understanding. As an eighteen-year-old pupil pilot, I had listened intently, but comprehending nothing, to our diminutive signals flight sergeant. At the end of one lecture he inquired, "Any questions?" I quickly thought up some unlikely electronic hypothesis and put it to him, asking for an explanation. "That's enough from you, smarty," he snapped. Thereafter, it was only in the most simplistic terms that I could grasp the basics of the intriguing mysteries of radio. Meanwhile, the important thing was to know the right button to push, and thus benefit gratuitously from that marvel of man's inventive genius. I mention this to reassure the reader who may be as ignorant as I am in the field of electronics, which were to become a vital factor in the air war.

Both before and during the German air raids on Britain, both sides were vying with each other in a separate theater of war, the "Wizard War," as Winston Churchill, a self-confessed novice on the subject, called it.

The Vildebeeste did not normally carry a radio set; we could communicate with no one either in the heavens above or on the earth beneath. Only by day could we make hand signs—sometimes rude ones—to a nearby aircraft. By night when we set forth in flight or squadron strength across the sharky waters of the South China Sea for a practice torpedo attack against some complaisant liner or naval vessel, we, the wingmen, still carried no radio. On such special occasions, however, a W/T (wireless telegraphy) set and operator were installed in our flight commanders' aircraft. The "wireless op" could communicate with base in Morse code. Our job, not always an easy one, was to follow the navigation lights (red on the left wingtip, green on the right) of our leader's aircraft.

The target ship located (this, with all its lights burning, was no great problem), an obliging accomplice, specially designated in our formation, would drop a flare, or maybe several. Down went our flight commander, his wingmen following. The torpedo, carried between the wheels of the fixed undercarriage, was fitted of course with a dummy warhead. We would "put her in" at 25 feet above the surface. This somewhat hazardous task accomplished, we would then look up, searching among the myriad stars for two special ones—the red and green lights of our leader. With luck we would join up with him and follow him home. Otherwise we would have to make it back to base alone on a compass course. Fortunately, the lights of Singapore, of the Happy World and other fun spots, burned late and were visible, at least in good weather, from afar. Disregarding our compass, and with a passing thought for an evening off-duty on the morrow, we would steer toward them.

Such was the uncomplicated nature of radio and air navigation in the mid-thirties—at least in that distant outpost of Empire. If not highly technical, it was warmly human.

2

"THIS CURSED, HELLISH INVENTION"

I returned home in mid-1937 to Tangmere, in Sussex—"Sussex by the sea," as Kipling wrote, where the English Channel, there some eighty miles wide, had formed an impregnable defense since William the Conqueror, nine centuries ago, against would-be invaders from the Continent, as Europe was called, not without a trace of disdain. It was at Tangmere, two years earlier, as a twenty-year-old pilot officer, that I had joined No. 1 Fighter Squadron. This time I went to No. 43, No. 1's sister. Both squadrons had shared the base for many years.

Some sixty miles south of London, Tangmere was one of the seven sector headquarters stations in No. 11 Fighter Group. Little appeared to have changed there. The usual crop of hay had been taken off the airfield, a broad meadow unspoiled by any runway, where sheep now peacefully grazed. Grass airfields, some more undulating and uneven than others, were the rule and brought a pleasant pastoral serenity to our otherwise exciting lives, though admittedly they had their practical drawbacks, the hay crop and the grazing sheep among them. Worse, for it was unredeemed by any touch of romance, was mud, which clogged the air intake and radiator of the Rolls-Royce Kestrel engine which powered our Hawker Fury biplane fighters, which were nimble as birds in the air but which on the ground, without brakes, could sometimes make a fool of you. Painted a gleaming silver, top wing and fuselage decorated with the squadron's markings—a flaming red triangle for No. 1, a black-and-white checkerboard for No. 43—they stood, neatly parked, in front of the hangars. These, with their gently curving roofs and wooden beams, gave a delightful old-world feeling to this peaceful place. They were built by German prisoners in World War I; in World War II German airmen would demolish them with bombs.

Yet for all the familiarity of Tangmere, I was struck by one unusual feature. The place was full of new young faces, many more than in the past. Moreover, Tangmere was no longer purely a fighter station; a coastal reconnaissance squadron, No. 217, with twin-motor Avro Ansons, had come to roost there. The RAF's expansion was now urgently under way, in face of the German Luftwaffe's enormous and ever-growing strength. As long ago as 1934, Churchill, then MP for Epping, had warned Parliament, "We are vulnerable as we have never been before. . . . This cursed, hellish invention and development of air power has revolutionized our position." At the time, he had faced jeers and insults: "Medieval baron! Warmonger!" Now people were listening to him. He sat on the Air Defense Research Committee and knew better than anyone Britain's urgent need to modernize and strengthen her air defenses. The most pressing need of all was to devise a scientific method of detecting hostile aircraft approaching our shores. Crude experiments had been made in 1934 with two huge sound locators near the Kent coast, but a year later Dr. Robert Watson Watt, already known as a brilliant physicist, came up with the answer: high-frequency radio beams (actually discovered some four decades earlier). Watson Watt immediately went to work on a system with the cover name of Radio Direction Finding, or RDF, soon to be called radar. The building began of twenty "Chain Home" (CH) radar stations, stretching along the coast from the Orkneys to the Isle of Wight.

It was one thing to detect hostile aircraft at long range, another to guide our fighters to within sighting distance of them. This side of the business was entrusted to Fighter Command's new chief, Air Marshal Sir Hugh Dowding. He set up a telephonic network linking the coastal radar stations with the operations room at Fighter Command headquarters, thence to each of its six group headquarters, and from them down to each of their sector operations rooms. Thus the enemy "plots," first seen on the coastal stations' radar screen and reported by telephone to Fighter Command, could be replotted a few moments later on the operations map at the sector station where the fighter squadrons waited, ready to go, guided to the "hostile" by the sector controller's radio telephony (R/T). Though yet far from complete, the system was unique in the world.

In its embryonic form the air defense system was put to the test during the air exercises on August 5–7, 1937. Although operating with only three radar stations widely spaced on the east and southeast coast and with its meager force of obsolete biplane fighters, Fighter Command was satisfied that the results looked promising.

Yet seven months later, in March 1938, no more than five radar stations were ready on watch when Hitler's Wehrmacht, with the Luftwaffe thundering overhead, invaded Austria. Churchill, the watchdog of Britain's defenses, again loudly voiced his increasing concern. Britain and her allies, he roundly declared in Parliament, must choose either to submit to Hitler or else take effective measures against him.

The measures so far taken in the realm of air defense were ludicrous. Britain possessed but a quarter of her essential coastal radar stations. Her fighter squadrons were too few and were equipped with old-fashioned biplanes. Delivery of modern antiaircraft guns had hardly begun; to fill the gap, out-of-date 3-inch guns were being hastily refurbished —some, it was said, had been commandeered from the Imperial War Museum. Searchlights and barrage balloons were in short supply, as were the trained crews needed to operate them.

Barely six months after Hitler's rape of Austria, Britain and her ally France came to the verge of war with Germany, this time over Hitler's threat to liquidate Czechoslovakia as a political entity. But neither of the Allies, despite their protests, had the stomach for a showdown with the Nazi dictator. The Luftwaffe chief Goering was talking of the English skies being darkened by masses of Luftwaffe bombers as they flew on to deliver the "knockout blow" against London.

British Air Minister Kingsley Wood was predicting half a million civilian casualties in the first three weeks of air attack. Cowed by the menacing Luftwaffe, the British cabinet authorized prime minister Neville Chamberlain to negotiate with Hitler. He and French Prime Minister Edouard Daladier met the Fuehrer at Munich. On landing back at Heston, near London, on September 30, the smiling Chamberlain held aloft a sheet of white paper signed by Hitler. It guaranteed, he told the rapturous crowd, "peace in our time." It also meant, though Chamberlain did not say so, the sacrifice of Czechoslovakia to the rapacious Nazi warlord.

Relief in Britain was heartfelt. From the cabinet down to the man in the street, the fear of air attack was very real, though time would prove that both Kingsley Wood and Goering were wildly exaggerating the effect of aerial bombardment—unless gas were used. This was always a possibility. However, the truth was that our air defenses were in no shape to prevent heavy air raids, had the Luftwaffe launched them.

Barely one hundred AA guns could be found to defend London, let alone our ports and industrial cities. Searchlights were equally poor in numbers and performance; both they and the guns depended for aiming on sound locators which were practically useless against fast-flying aircraft. Balloon barrages were not yet dense enough to dissuade low-flying bombers. The coastal radar chain afforded only partial cover and did not yet perform reliably.

Finally, our fighter force, Britain's first line of defense. Fighter Command possessed 750 fighters. Only ninety of them were Hurricanes—the latest, and redoubtable, model, but its eight guns froze up above 15,000 feet. The Spitfire was not yet ready. The rest of the fighters were a mixed lot of out-of-date biplanes, like our Furies; we ourselves, once part of an elite force of interceptors, could not now even catch the Luftwaffe's more speedy Heinkel and Dornier bombers. Global figures, moreover, are misleading; only about half of that motley force of 750 fighters would be serviceable—fit to fly—at any one time.

And our night fighters? It was by no means sure that the Luftwaffe would not bomb under cover of night (as indeed it was eventually to do). Night fighting was literally as different from day fighting as night is from day. Special radar equipment, both in the fighter aircraft and for the use of ground control, were essential, save for the odd fluke, to successful interception at night. Specially trained pilots were equally necessary. In none of these requirements did any specialized night-fighter force exist. In 43 and 1 squadrons, we joked about night flying. The night was made for love, as the song went, not for flying. Only fools and owls flew at night, and anyway our Furies were declared unsuitable for night flying. So we were not bothered.

3

THIS HAPPY BREED

If the Munich crisis found Britain's (not to mention France's) air defenses still pitifully feeble, the people of Britain, not for the last time, demonstrated their will to defy Germany and, more personally, Hitler. The British public, ourselves included, could not yet believe that "Adolf," who, with his proud strutting, screeching voice, and wild gestures, was taken for a kind of music-hall character, could seriously upset our easygoing, enjoyable way of life. "Adolf" had no lack of imitators who made us rock with laughter. Goering, with his portly figure, comic-opera uniforms, and lavish display of decorations, seemed better suited to vaudeville. But his threats of annihilation from the air did, after all, strike home.

It was the British citizen, the man in the street, his wife and children, who stood to suffer most from the "knockout blow" of explosive, fire, and possibly gas, promised by that other Nazi warlord, with his dreaded Luftwaffe. At no time did the British feel more that their home was their castle, nor were they ever more determined to defend it. In the six months between Austria and Munich, half a million men and women came forward as volunteers for the Civil Defense Service, as air-raid wardens, firemen, ambulance drivers, dispatch riders, telephonists, rescue workers, and the like.

The appeasement of Hitler at Munich, humiliating as it was, gave Britain nearly a year, the "Year of Salvation," to press forward ever more urgently with her defenses, including civil defense (Air Raid Precautions, as it was simply called) against attack from the air. The Munich crisis, when Hyde Park and other pleasant London parks and commons were disfigured by hastily dug trenches and the thirty-five million gas masks were handed out, brought the British people abruptly face to face with the dreadful reality of war—total war, in which the civil population would be in the front line.

Six months after Munich, in March 1939, the armed hordes of the Fuehrer (with the Luftwaffe, as usual, thundering overhead), marched, without opposition, into Czechoslovakia. Hitler declared: "Czechoslovakia has ceased to exist."

In Britain a month later, conscription—always considered an affront to our liberties—compelled twenty-year-olds to join up; their numbers were steadily swelled by volunteers outside the age category who came flocking to the colors. Yet another half-million men and women volunteered for civil defense—"ordinary people" who, in the coming hours of darkness, unarmed save with their courage, were to prove themselves far from ordinary.

One such volunteer was Johnny Callow, a Londoner from Woolwich. Churchill had described London as the biggest target in the world and likened the capital to a fat cow, tethered and awaiting the slaughter. London's number-one military target was Woolwich Arsenal, a huge complex of munitions factories covering ten square miles with its own railway service and even its own little navy, for it was traversed by canals giving on the south bank of the Thames. The Arsenal was six miles, as the crow flies, downstream from that ancient Norman stronghold the Tower of London, which, since Plantagenet times, had served as a depot (and still does) for weapons. Woolwich, originally a fishing village, succeeded the Tower, and well before Trafalgar and Waterloo, it assumed the role and the title of the Royal Arsenal.

Johnny's father, Henry Callow, got his first job driving the pair of horses which pulled, at full gallop, the fire engine of the neighboring borough of Southwark. Then followed a spell as groom to the colonel commanding the Royal Regiment of Artillery, the "Gunners," whose home, like that of the Royal Engineers, the "Sappers," is at Woolwich, the "Garrison Town." In time, Henry forsook the colonel's horses for the white horses of the high seas. He joined the merchant navy as a stoker.

Young marriages and large families were the tradition among Londoners, though they lived, most of them, in extreme poverty. Barely out of his teens, Henry Callow married, and he and his Irish wife, Mary-Anne, began, during Henry's leave ashore, to found their family. By the outbreak of war in 1914, they already had three children, Johnny being one of them. He was four when his father went off to sea again as an engineroom greaser in the Royal Navy. Back from the war, Henry Callow signed on again in the merchant navy. He and Mary-Anne increased their family. Ray, their last and tenth child (two had died in infancy), was born in 1927, about the time I made my first flight as a fourteen-year-old schoolboy and started along the road which would lead me to the Battle of Britain and the night battle which followed— the night blitz.

At that time also, Johnny, now seventeen, was set on becoming a professional ballroom dancer. Though he had the warm heart of his father, he was, physically, the very opposite—short and spare and soft of speech. A natural athlete, he first proved himself during the autumn nights of 1915 when German zeppelins began bombing London, looking like silver sausages floating in the searchlight beams while a few anti-aircraft bursts crackled around them. Johnny's job was to run around shinnying up the lampposts and pulling the little ring on the end of a chain which doused the gaslight. While this impromptu blackout proceeded, a policeman would cycle along the streets, a notice in large letters attached to his back saying "TAKE COVER." There was, in fact, no effective cover to take, other than the occasional basement like the one beneath the Tabernacle Church in Beresford Street. Even then, people were in no hurry to go underground.

Johnny, like all little boys in Woolwich, belonged to a gang—no gang of young criminals, but a little band of friends united in their love of sport and fun, with a harmless dose of mischief thrown in, and ever willing to earn a penny or two for services rendered. Most of the gang were sons of market traders—"squareheads" as they were called, not because they were dim-witted (far from it) but because their stalls were ranged in Beresford Square. Johnny earned more pennies from strapping down the horses of the costermongers who drove their carts up to Covent Garden market, where they bought their produce. So small was he that he had to climb onto a stool to brush the horses' manes, except when it came to old Ben, who obligingly lowered his head.

Johnny, like his Irish mother, was a Catholic. Daily he walked the two miles to St. Peter's Catholic School and another two miles home in the evening; his parents had not the money to buy him a bicycle or a bus ticket. Poverty was the common lot of most Londoners. But they survived, and later triumphed on humor, courage, and mutual help. The Callows' front door, like everyone else's, was left on the latch, and never locked; anyone could lift the latch by pulling on the string which protruded from a hole bored in the door. Few families had the means to maintain their numerous children; many of the kids were boarded out with relatives or friends.

At St. Peter's School, Johnny was better than most at games and bright at his lessons, which, on occasions, would be interrupted by the intrusion of his father, back from the sea. With apologies to the teacher, father Callow would march Johnny out of the classroom down to the nearest fish-and-chips shop, there to buy enough "tuppennies," which stood for fish; and "pennies," for chips, for the whole family. Then off they marched back to the house, which was decorated and hung with "Welcome Home" notices. There they feasted and celebrated the sailor's return.

Johnny left school at fourteen, to earn his own living and contribute a few shillings to the family kitty. His first job was at the local glass-works; on Saturdays, he played football for the Rose Athletic Club. Some months later, he went to work in the Woolwich Borough Council and switched his loyalty to the Footscray football eleven. Then a broken collarbone put him out of the game for some time. His Saturdays were blank and dull until his friend Jim Cassidy took him along to Eltham Drill Hall, leased on weekends for dancing. As Johnny watched the professional couples, he was captivated by their grace and the rhythm of the music. Here was a new kind of sport in which broken collarbones—his was still hurting like the devil—were the exception. It was that evening that Johnny decided to become, in his spare time, a professional ballroom dancer. His girlfriend, Kathleen, now in her early teens, was thrilled when Johnny asked her to partner him. At his dance salon in Bond Street, London, Victor Sylvester, the famous dance-band leader, put them through their paces until they reached competition level. Perfect partners on the dance floor and deeply in love, they decided to become partners for life; in 1934, they married.

Johnny worked on at the council offices, but on weekends the young couple took the floor in competitions all over the country. Rapidly they made a reputation for themselves, though at Cheltenham in 1936, dis-aster nearly overtook them. Johnny had forgotten his evening trousers; he was lent a pair so ample around the waist that the slack had to be gathered up and tied with string. Despite the handicap, he and Kathleen danced into third place to the music of Joe Loss and his band.

With Johnny in his own trousers, they won the national champion-ships. Fox-trot, quickstep, tango, and waltz, they loved them all, but being a romantic young couple, the waltz, more than any other measure, made their own and the spectators' hearts beat fastest. Reaching international level, they took fourth place, in 1937, at the world championships in Blackpool.

A year later, after Austria and Munich, Johnny and his friends, like everyone else, talked much of a coming war. All of Johnny's old gang joined up. His two brothers also—Bert, "Silent Jack" as they nicknamed him, enlisted in the RAF Balloon Command, and Alf, too young for the services, joined the Home Guard.

Johnny and Kathleen danced their last world championship in May 1939, a month or so after Czechoslovakia was heeled under by the Nazi jackboot. Then Johnny discarded his white tie and tails for the heavy blue serge and helmet of a fireman; he joined the Auxiliary Fire Service. His day's work in the office over, he reported at the Eltham substation for training.

Kathleen, an accomplished seamstress, applied for a job at the Arsenal; she was assigned to sewing up bags of cordite destined for the shells of the big guns—a daily stint of twelve hours in the "Danger Buildings."

Ray, the youngest brother, had meanwhile been growing up. Seventeen years separated him from his oldest brother, Johnny. Though Johnny was a Catholic and his mother's favorite, Ray, like his father, was a Protestant and his father's favorite. Yet Johnny and Ray were firm friends, Johnny encouraging his small brother to be kind with others yet hard on himself, honest in all his dealings, and, within his modest limits, a sportsman and adventurer. Many an evening they would race each other dozens of circuits around the block; it was fun and kept them fit. When Ray, diminutive but solid of build, took the field for the Plumstead Imperials, the sleeves of his borrowed shirt were rolled up and up again until his forearms at last protruded; his shorts, borrowed too, came down to his knees, and the football itself came nearly up to them. Ray, like all of his gang, loved cricket too; their pitch was in Helen Street, the lamppost outside Ray's home serving as a wicket.

Ray joined the gang when he was five—their youngest member. They were a dozen or so little street urchins. The streets were their world and their playground, and they knew every bump and crevice and corner by heart. Old man Callow allowed Ray to stay out till midnight, knowing he could trust his boy not to get up to mischief. Ray's gang, as Johnny's had been, was a band of young brothers united in sport and daring, and in good works too.

Today, fifty years later, if you care to look for them, you may find, near the Arsenal station, notched in the brick wall by Ray and his gang, the footholds which enabled them to vault up to the top. One after another, the boys took a run, then one, two, and up. Ray, being so small, could always be sure of a hand-up from the boy before him.

This was one of the gang's meeting places—the White Roofs, they called it; the other was the Green, a tiny patch of grass near the signal box some way down the line, and to which honor obliged that they should walk along the top of the wall, a seven-foot drop on the street side, a precipice of thirty feet on the Arsenal side. Whenever an army draft left for overseas, the soldiers marched down to the Arsenal station, brass bands playing and drummers in tigerskin aprons beating out the measure and twiddling their drumsticks, with Ray and his gang and all the others trailing along behind. Arrived at the station, the soldiers settled down on the platform, lolling among their gear, for the long wait before the train's departure. The gang leaped one by one to the top of the wall. "Anyone want a beer?" they would call down to the soldiers. Having taken their orders, the boys slipped down again into the street to make the round of residents and shopkeepers, collecting pennies. Londoners are always ready to give for a good cause; with their pennies the gang bought the needed beer. Then up again on top of the wall, they lowered the bottles on a length of string down to the thirsty soldiers on the platform below.

Ray, the youngest of the gang, was the poorest too. There was always the problem of raising funds, a few pennies for himself, the rest for his family. He had two systems going. From the "squareheads" in the market, he collected empty wooden crates. Ray would tow them, stacked up, on the end of a rope around the streets and sell them as firewood. This earned him several pennies.

The other system, just as simple, but requiring a little more patience, was to follow, bucket and shovel in hand, a horse-drawn cart. Sooner or later he was sure to gather a harvest of fresh dung, for which he always found a ready market. He took the pennies home, as usual, to his mother.

Ray's good mother, whose first concern was to feed and maintain her large family, appointed Ray as the family shopper. With his sense of economy, he was naturally gifted for the job. He would memorize the items needed, and having rattled them off to the shopkeeper he would invariably add (as his mother had told him), "And me dad's out of work . . ." This would often bring him an extra tidbit.

Ray started school, like his brother Johnny, at St. Peter's. Then one day, in the middle of lessons, his father, once again back from the sea, made one of his unexpected entries. With apologies, as usual, to the teacher, he took Ray gently by the scruff of the neck and marched him off, not to the local fish-and-chips shop but to the Burrage Grove School, a Protestant establishment close to home. As in other schools, the little ones were confined to the ground floor, the middling ones to the second, and the seniors to the top floor. Now Ray could play cricket in the playground. In summertime, the boys paid in a penny a week to save up for a day's outing to Margate. Ray, never having any pennies to spare, would, when the great day came, hang around the bus, hoping. There was hardly an occasion when, once all the fare-paying boys were on board, the teacher would not call to Ray, "All right, Callow, jump in," and Ray would wriggle into some narrow corner.

After Munich, Ray, to keep up with his brothers who were enlisting in the services, himself joined the Boy Scouts—with at first only enough money to buy the "woggle" which held the green scarf (yet to be acquired) in place. Thanks to his assiduous fund-raising with firewood and manure, he was soon able to buy the scarf itself. More weeks of saving and he bought the Boy Scout shirt. Now he was prepared, like a good scout, for anything. Little did he imagine what that would amount to.

Ray dreamed of flying. He began by carving his favorite airplanes out of balsa wood. Then with his earnings he bought kits of Furies, Gladiators, Hurricanes, and Spitfires. His father, impressed by his boy's gift for handicrafts, sometimes brought his friends around to admire Ray's work, pretty sure, as Ray was too, that the visitor would press a sixpenny bit into Ray's hand before leaving.

After Munich, kits of German aircraft appeared in the shops—Dorniers, Heinkels, Junkers, and Messerschmitts. Ray was glad to have them for his model air fleet; at the same time, he got the feeling that this commerce in German aircraft meant that things were warming up. There were other signs too: gangs of Irish workmen were busy digging trenches on Woolwich and Plumstead commons, and bunks were being installed in the Woolwich Equitable Insurance building.

In the months following Munich, on to the Czechoslovakian tragedy of March 1939 and beyond, civil-defense wardens were more and more seen in the streets, with their blue uniforms and white tin hats emblazoned with the initials ARP—Air Raid Precautions.

Air-raid drills and exercises provided good sport to Ray and the gang.

Only too happy to volunteer as "victims," they lay prostrate in the streets feigning death or injury. After first aid and bandages, an ambulance would cart them off to the hospital, where, after smiles and thanks all around, each boy was rewarded with a few candies. It was fun for all, fun which would give way before long to dreadful reality.

Dark clouds were gathering. After Czechoslovakia, people began to brace themselves against the threatening storm. In the Callow family, Amy, the oldest daughter, got a job in the Arsenal, sewing parachutes. Rose, her sister, whose man was in the merchant navy, continued to mind her home and her children. Melve, who worked in a denture factory, stuck to her job, an essential one after all; and Renée, still in her teens, found a place ushering in the Granada Cinema, a useful job, she reckoned, for if war came, she could help in an emergency.

Finally, there was the old man. He signed off from the merchant navy and joined up in the big-gun shop at the Arsenal. There only the strongest men could survive the fierce heat of the foundry and the twelve-hour work day. Henry Callow, during his early days as a naval stoker, had acquired the muscles and the guts for the job.

Thus did the Callow family, like thousands of others in London's boroughs north and south of the Thames and in cities throughout the land, prepare for the war which, they were sure, would hit them in their hearts and their homes. They were to be the mainstay of Britain's night defenses.

4

PREPARING FOR WAR

With Britain redoubling her efforts to defend herself against air attack, Hawker Hurricanes and Supermarine Spitfires, "300-mph-plus" eight-gun fighters, now came streaming off the production lines. In 43 Squadron, we collected, in December 1938, our first "Hurries" from Brooklands, Hawker's airfield, surrounded by the famous racing-car circuit. By the time Hitler had crushed Czechoslovakia in March 1939, the squadron was operational both by day and by night.

Yes, night flying was now on the menu of every day-fighter squadron. No one had yet heard of a night-fighter squadron nor of a night-fighter aircraft, because no such thing existed. So we had to swallow our words about fools and owls and in our day fighters explore the terrors of the night.

In its initial tests the prototype Hurricane was reported to be maneuverable and docile. Maneuverable it certainly was, but in war trim, with ammunition tanks full, radio fitted, and camouflage war paint daubed on, it was not all that docile. It did not forgive errors in flying, particularly when near the stall, as did the gracious, good-tempered Fury, whose conception differed little from the fighters of World War I: an open-cockpit biplane with fixed undercarriage. Its two Vickers machine guns were mounted in the cockpit and fired through the propeller by means of an "interrupter gear." The Hurricane, by contrast, was of entirely different design: a high-performance monoplane which demanded a cockpit covered, in flight, by a sliding roof, a retractable undercarriage, and wing flaps to reduce landing speed. It mounted a powerful battery of eight Browning .303 guns, four in each wing. With its Rolls-Royce Merlin engine of 1,030 horsepower, the Hurricane was over 100 mph faster than the Fury and a redoubtable war machine. Beside it the Fury was a delightful plaything.

Despite its mighty engine, the Hurricane, while sensitive on the controls, was not fitted with a rudder-trimming device that would permit the pilot to counteract the powerful propeller torque. Consequently, in cloud and darkness, when flying on instruments, which included an artificial horizon and sensitive altimeter, you had the impression of pushing harder with one foot than with the other on the rudder bar, and the disconcerting feeling that the aircraft was slithering sideways from under the seat of your pants. In its early career, the Hurricane killed dozens of pilots and earned a bad name for itself.

Another disturbing feature, at night, of this formidable day fighter was the torrent of flame which poured out of the three exhaust ports on each side of the slim pointed nose that housed the V-12 Merlin engine—blue "Bunsen" flame, the sign of perfect combustion. The Hurricane not being designed specifically as a night fighter, no one apparently had realized that the exhaust flames would half-blind the pilot and obscure his all-important view of the horizon. The problem was temporarily solved by screening the flames from the pilot's view with a narrow, horizontal strip of metal. But they still remained visible to an enemy bomber some hundreds of yards away.

Yet another problem with the early Merlins was "surging." Without warning, the blue flames would fade to a feeble yellow, with an alarming decrease of power and a corresponding increase in the pilot's pulse rate; then the blue flames, to the pilot's relief, would reappear.

We played at pretending to be enemy night bombers for the benefit of the searchlight batteries. Not for ours, though; their dazzling silver-blue beams, flooding the cockpit, could so confuse the pilot that he could barely read his blind-flying instruments.

Searchlights, manned though they were by devoted crews, were forever to be the bane of the night fighter, for they too often fixed mistakenly on him, refusing to relax their hold.

A more agreeable exercise was the night sector "recco"—reconnaissance. Given reasonable weather, the lights of Chichester, Horsham, and Brighton glittered reassuringly below, each town recognizable by its particular lighting pattern. The dim lights of villages, hamlets, farms, and baronial manors would wink at us too, reassuring us that in all our loneliness, we were not entirely cut off from the world.

Our radiotelephony provided a more tenuous though no less precious contact. We were almost helpless without the controller's guidance. When he called, "Transmit for fix," we replied into the combined microphone and oxygen mask, "One, two, three, four, five; five, four, three, two, one." Before long, the pilot's voice transmission for a fix was to be superseded by a cunning little box mounted in the aircraft— the "Pipsqueak," or IFF (Identification, Friend or Foe), which automatically transmitted a radio signal. Down below was one of those radio devices, quite simple at this stage, called the Chandler-Adcock homing system, by which our position was duly "fixed." Then a cheery call from the controller like "Vector [steer] 245 and you'll be over base in twelve minutes." The controller guided us everywhere, out to intercept the enemy (so far imaginary) and back to land. The system seldom failed; when it did, it was more often than not a defect in the aircraft's electrical circuit. You headed contentedly for home and, given reasonable weather, picked up the "flashing beacon," a red light parked for the night at a prearranged distance and bearing from the base. It flashed, in Morse, two letters which differed from night to night. The sight of it was always a relief; you were home. But I always told myself, "You may be home, but you've still got to get down."

The old buckets of burning, smoking kerosene, which in Singapore had marked the landing flare path, had now been replaced by "gooseneck" flares—little cans filled with kerosene, with a spout out of which flared a small flame, theoretically invisible to the enemy, and, of course, to us, above about 1,000 feet altitude. At the touchdown end of the flare path stood a mobile floodlight, ironically named, after its manufacturers, the Chance light. Beside it the airfield control officer listened on the radio and watched for the aircraft's wingtip lights. "Switch on," he would order the floodlight crew, and out of the darkness, into the glaring beam, the aircraft would glide, like a moth into the glow of an electric lamp, and touch down. Then the floodlight was extinguished and once again all was darkness, save for the flickering gooseneck flares.

If those last few moments of a night patrol, the approach and landing, were what you were most longing for, they were also moments which demanded all your concentration and judgment: line up on the flare path, then let down at the correct angle and speed—not like poor Charles, who got it all wrong, flew into a tall oak tree, and died. There were others too, alas, who did not survive those last moments.

Navigational "aids" had certainly improved since those nights in Singapore. You could get off safely, be "vectored" anywhere within

R/T range, then "home" back to base and land without undue hazard, given reasonable visibility. We were still living and flying in the last few months of peace and were not expected to go out of our way to risk our lives on account of bad weather. Most nights, the earth below and the heavens above still shone with a million lights.

Yet even when favored by the weather, the problem of intercepting a night raider was still far from being solved. The crews of the two weapons, antiaircraft guns and fighters, capable of downing an unseen raider concealed by cloud or darkness needed to know, in all the hundreds of cubic miles of space in the sky above, the position, within yards, of their target. Searchlights, "aimed" (like the guns) by obsolete sound locators, could help but little. Silvery-blue shafts of light in the dark, they rarely picked up the target. Only radar, as an integral part of the aiming system, could pinpoint with precision the invisible enemy.

The fighter pilot, in the dark, was even worse off; he had to fly in close enough to the "hostile" in order to discern, with his own eyes, its dark, indefinite shape. Searchlights, if only they could illuminate it, could help. But the radical solution was to fit, in the fighter aircraft itself, a radar set which could guide the pilot close enough to sight the stealthy enemy.

Such electronic marvels were now, in Britain, only being dreamed up. The problem was to condense the tons of steel masts and aerials of the coastal radar stations into a small box. The RAF had, as yet, no concrete plans for a specialized night-fighter force.

Only five coastal radar stations had been available to keep watch when Hitler invaded Austria in March 1938. By the end of that year a total of fourteen were operational; six more were still in the building. These "Chain Home" stations with their 300-foot-high steel lattice masts were rooted, immobile, where they stood. From their fixed—and extremely vulnerable—position they could look out across the sea over an arc of 120 degrees; they could detect an aircraft at well over a hundred miles from the coast and read its height (if not too low) and its direction. Inland, however, they were blind; they could see nothing of an aircraft once it crossed the coast.

It was to the Observer Corps (later "Royal") that fell the task of plotting aircraft flying overland. Observer Corps posts covered the country, using their eyes, their ears, and a field telephone; they were at the time a vital link in the aircraft detection system. Meanwhile Winston Churchill, comparing the coastal radar and the Observer Corps as a "transition from the mid-twentieth century to the Stone Age," insisted on the urgent need for inland radar cover; this "ground-controlled interception" (GCI) was, like radar for guns, searchlights, and fighters, still in the embryonic stage. The men of the Observer Corps were to keep faithful watch, in all weathers, for many more a long day and night.

Without knowing much about each other's progress in radar, the British and the Germans had been working on almost parallel lines, the Germans ahead, all the same, in technology. At the time of Munich, they possessed an excellent long-range radar, the Freya. Though it could not tell height, it could detect at a range of seventy-five miles and through a complete circle of 360 degrees. And it was mobile—a boon, the Germans would find, when they came to command the European coastline from Norway to the Pyrenees.

But—and it would prove decisive when the hour of battle struck—the British, whose first thought was the defense of their island, had linked their coastal radar sentinels by telephone and radiotelephone with their defending fighters. The Germans, bent only on aggression and a "lightning war," had done nothing of the kind. British long-range radar, if less refined than German, had been incorporated into a formidable system of air defense.

In short-range radar, the Germans had a clear lead over Britain with their Wurzburg, a small, entirely mobile apparatus which could detect with remarkable accuracy at a distance of twenty-five miles. As such, it was an ideal "seeing aid" for antiaircraft guns and searchlights. Goering, though professing a distaste for radio devices—"boxes with coils, and I don't like them," he once grumbled—was all the same so enthusiastic about Wurzburg that he rashly boasted, "If a single enemy bomber crosses our frontier, you can call me Meier." At the same time, the *Reichsmarschall* was equally impressed with the Luftwaffe's first working model of an airborne radar set. If only the British had possessed such radar devices so that their guns, searchlights, and fighters could strike at the Luftwaffe bombers in the dark! The British, for it was they who were threatened, needed them urgently. The Germans, who already had them, would not need them till later.

Throughout 1939, the British pressed on with the completion of their projected twenty stations of the coastal radar chain. Those lofty masts could not possibly escape the notice of curious eyes, including those of the Germans. They were evidently part of a radio system, and the Germans, wanting to know more, decided to investigate them closely. The huge and stately German airship *Graf Zeppelin*, with eleven years' commercial flying to its credit, was now fitted out with the latest in electronic detection gear. At the end of May, the airship, with the chief of the Luftwaffe signals section, General Wolfgang Martini, aboard, cruised at a leisurely pace up the east coast of England, its technicians, including Martini, quite ignorant that they were being followed every inch of the way by those very radar stations whose secrets they had come to discover. The zeppelin's "plots" were recorded on the operations map at Fighter Command, which watched its progress in silence, even when the great airship transmitted to base its position, wrongly calculated. It may have been a trap, but the controller, at Fighter Command, though sorely tempted to transmit the correct position, wisely refrained. Throughout the *Graf Zeppelin*'s voyage, nothing but a horrible crackling assailed the ears of General Martini and his radio detectives. They returned to the Fatherland without a single clue to enlighten them about British radar.

At midnight on August 2—exactly a month before Britain and Germany were at war—the *Graf Zeppelin* slipped off again into the dark for another try. Not only was it unsuccessful, but the airship was indiscreet enough to reveal itself to coast guards in Aberdeenshire as well as to the astonished eyes of two British fighter pilots sent up to intercept it. On August 4, *Graf Zeppelin* returned once again empty-handed.

Fortunately, the *Graf Zeppelin* was not on the prowl when a couple of days later, on August 6, the RAF's air exercises started. Otherwise she might have picked up the radio chatter between our ground control and fighters, and this could have given away the whole show. Those two days of maneuvers provided a full dress rehearsal for Fighter Command, both in the air and on the ground. Little realizing the Germans' interest in our air-defense system, we had, during the past months, been training intensively for war, with battle climbs to 30,000 feet, mock air combats, gunnery at targets in the sea, and an unpleasant chore—night patrols. We had become skilled with our new aircraft. Our faithful, practiced ground crews could refuel the tanks, rearm the guns, and retune the radio all within a few minutes. Indeed, our Hurricanes had completely transformed our fearful mood of the Munich crisis into one of supreme confidence. Spitfires, too, their early production problems solved, now formed the new equipment of nine squadrons. The coastal radar chain which had been on twenty-four-hour watch since Good Friday 1939 was put to the test during the air exercises and proved its worth. If we pilots did not exactly comprehend its detailed layout, we all knew perfectly well that the giant masts at Poling, a few miles from

Tangmere, were part of it, but so hush-hush we dared not mention them. We appreciated, too, that our sector controller was guiding us to intercept with extreme precision.

The "Wizard War," as Churchill called it, was already fully engaged, an occult and secret war, with only a handful of men on each side who really knew what was going on. An even smaller number, with the instincts of Sherlock Holmes or James Bond, were working diligently, in obscurity, trying, with the help of odd and occasional clues, to penetrate the secrets of the other side.

The scientific war was waged in stealth and silence, on fronts other than radar. For some years, the German Wehrmacht, the Kriegsmarine, the Luftwaffe, and the sinister Schutzstaffel (SS) had been exchanging radio messages in high-grade cipher by means of an automatic enciphering machine called Enigma. In 1928 the British Government Code and Cypher School, code-named Station X, at Bletchley, fifty miles north of London, had managed to "acquire" two German-made enciphering machines identical to Enigma. The British copied and improved them. The modified version was called the RAF Enigma and, later, Typex. The Typex cipher remained unbroken during the war. Not so the original German Enigma. The Germans, too, had their experts, but not such a band of dedicated genii as the cryptographers of Station X. They believed that their own Enigma cipher was unbreakable. But the British cryptographers, despite tantalizing problems, succeeded finally in elucidating the secrets of Enigma.

First, however, the RAF Wireless Intelligence Service (the "Y-Service"), whose monitoring stations were ceaselessly eavesdropping on all German radio traffic, had to record what they had heard. We in the squadrons became in time vaguely aware of their nefarious but highly successful practices through the intelligence reports (much watered-down) which reached us. It was none of our business, however, to know how the system worked, that while the Y-Service operators coped well with low-grade cipher and plain-language messages, the high-grade cipher of Enigma was reserved for specialists at the listening station at Chicksands in Bedfordshire. Once received, Enigma signals were sent on to Station X, whose "wizards" broke down the highly secret cipher messages—a mass of information emanating from the German armed forces, and not least the Luftwaffe (which was the least discreet of all), concerning their future plans and a whole lot more.

Station X then passed on this information, under the name of "Ultra-intelligence," to a small circle including the prime minister and a few top ministers and service commanders. Ultra was the best-kept secret of the war. It was only years later that the public, myself included, came to hear about it.

Toward midnight on August 24, I took off on a night reconnaissance, glad, as usual, to see the dark earth below carpeted with the lights of inland and seaside towns. My next flight would be in the bewildering obscurity of the nationwide blackout. Meanwhile we flew little, nursing our Hurricanes and waiting, alert, for the inevitable.

It came on September 1, when Hitler's armies, with the Luftwaffe in close support, blasted their way into valiant, helpless Poland. This time the allies, France and Britain, acted. On September 3, they declared war against Germany. Lying on the grass beside our Hurricanes we waited, chatting quietly among ourselves, for the Luftwaffe bombers to darken our fair skies, as Goering had promised, and deliver the knockout blow on London. It was not to come for another year—and then many of us would no longer be around.

5

BOFFINS AND OTHERS

During the next ten months until July 1940, when the day battle over our coasts and countryside and towns began in earnest, the Luftwaffe did not molest Britain with anything like the violence expected. Sporadic attacks, mostly by single aircraft, were made against our shipping, and a few heavier raids were launched against the naval bases of Rosyth on the northern shore of the Firth of Forth, not far from Edinburgh, and Scapa Flow, in the Orkneys. In May and June, the Luftwaffe had been concentrating its gigantic strength in helping the Wehrmacht to reduce our allies in Europe—Norway, Denmark, Holland, Belgium, Luxembourg, and France—to vassal states, as well as harassing the retreat of 340,000 Allied troops evacuated from Dunkirk.

In all these operations the Luftwaffe proved that its role was essentially a tactical one, to support the army in the field. Hitler had promised the German people that Christmas 1939 would be the last Christmas of the war; he had no wish to get involved in a long-term war which would require his bombers to make raids on distant, strategic targets—ports, industrial cities, and eventually residential areas. He made it clear that he alone would decide if and when to attack strategic targets in Britain.

The possibility of such bombing operations, however, was by no means excluded. Their success would depend on very accurate navigation. The traditional method of long-distance air navigation, "dead reckoning," was a cumbersome exercise, with its paraphernalia of maps and a table to spread them on, a magnetic compass, and dividers, set-square, and ruler to plot the aircraft's position. It was better suited to the bridge of a naval vessel. With data such as airspeed, "drift" (caused by the wind), a visual fix on some prominent object, or an occasional radio fix from a radio direction-finding (D/F) station, the navigator calculated the correct course to fly. This he passed on to the pilot, who adjusted his compass accordingly.

Dead reckoning was an artisanal craft; its only advantage was its immunity from radio "jamming." But in darkness or in cloud it was seriously wanting in the acute precision required for "blind" bombing.

Since 1933, when Hitler came to power and the "black" (secret) Luftwaffe was born, the Germans had been experimenting with more sophisticated methods of long-range navigation, inspired by their famous Lorenz system of blind approach and landing, which was used not only by themselves but by many airlines and air forces, including the RAF itself. Highly ingenious it was, yet simple for the pilot. A radio beam, like invisible trolley tracks, led him down to the landing path. In his earphones, he heard, when firmly on the tracks, a steady note. If he deviated to the right, he heard Morse dashes, if to the left, dots. The trolley tracks' steady note was always there between the dots and dashes.

Early in 1939, British scientists—"boffins," as they were affectionately known—of the Committee of Scientific Study of Air Defense came to the regrettable but timely conclusion that, if much was suspected, little was known in Britain about German navigational methods. It was wisely decided to let loose a "boffin" among the nonscientific experts of the Directorate of Air Ministry Intelligence. The man chosen was Dr. R. V. Jones, a genial young giant of a man and brilliant physicist from Oxford University. He took up his job soon after the outbreak of war; a couple of months later he had already obtained clues, as astonishing as they were unexpected, concerning the Luftwaffe's radio-beam system of navigation.

On November 4, 1939, an odd-looking parcel addressed to the naval attaché was delivered to the British embassy in Oslo. It contained many pages of text, written in German, referring to a number of German secret weapons. It was signed "From a well-wishing German scientist." It was not long before Dr. Jones, in his office in London, was studying the English version, amazed by the revelations of what became known as the Oslo Report.

Among many other subjects, it mentioned an important research station at Peenemünde, a small island in the Baltic Sea; it described the development there of a rocket-powered gliding bomb and of a supersonic rocket, both to become only too familiar to the British more than four years later respectively as the V-1 and V-2.

Another passage, which particularly intrigued Dr. Jones, explained the details of a new radio-beam device intended to guide long-range bombers. It was able to measure the exact distance of a bomber, flying along a beam fixed on the enemy target, from the transmitting station, which, in turn, had only to tell the bomber pilot the exact moment to release his bombs. The system was a sensational advance on navigation by dead reckoning.

The British were wary of the Oslo Report; it could be a "plant." But Dr. Jones was convinced that at least in his particular field of German radio beams, the evidence was perfectly trustworthy.

At Tangmere, we kept waiting for the knockout blow, basking in the September sun on the grass beside our Hurricanes, sleeping by night in some discomfort in the pilots' room beside the tarmac. At any second we were ready to go, but for all Goering's bombast, Hitler's main wish was to avoid a general war, above all with the British, for whom, although they were later to infuriate him, he felt a positive admiration. A love-hate affair.

The days passed slowly with little doing but routine flights and an occasional false alarm. Night flights were more of a problem. The blackout deprived us of the friendly carpet of lights below us which told us where we were and which way was up. We could rivet our eyes, it is true, on the artificial horizon in the middle of the dashboard, but that soulless little robot was no substitute for the real horizon separating earth from sky.

One night, lined up on the flare path for takeoff, I thanked God for the rising moon, wanly shining out of a blank wall of darkness. So peaceful and lovely it looked, and reassuring too, above. A few moments after takeoff, as I turned left, it reappeared below my right wing, giving the disconcerting impression that I was nearly upside down. Thus ended abruptly that brief, faerie vision of the moon; my eyes darted back to the dashboard and its unromantic artificial horizon.

Another night, on a lone reconnaissance beyond the sector boundary, I flew down moonlit canyons formed by massifs of dark cloud towering heavenward and sometimes obscuring the stars. It was all too easy to feel overawed by these gigantic, eerie mountains which isolated me from the friendly earth. It needed a conscious mental effort to persuade myself that my airplane and I were one, that I was both its brain and its sinews, that it must function according to my will. Lost above all that mass of cloud, I called the controller for a fix. It was David Lloyd that night. As he gave me my position, I detected some concern in his voice, and in his efforts to reassure me as he added, "We'll get you down soon; we've put the kettle on for tea." Between cup and lip there's many a slip. David had no exact information on the margin of clear air between cloud base and earth, except that the 500-foot-high downs to the north of Tangmere were in cloud. But he did the right thing, talking me down until I broke cloud not overland, but 300 feet above a dark waste of sea. I knew I was safe, so far. Steer north by compass and hit the coast. David confirmed my course, telling me, "You will see the flashing beacon, and we've had the floodlight switched on." Five minutes later I touched down. Though the air was our playground and, before long, would be our field of battle too, it was always a relief to feel the good earth beneath our feet. A few moments more and I was drinking the promised cup of tea with David in the ops room. Though we did not say so, we felt grateful to one another. Between us we had succeeded in a rather hazardous landing.

Compared with the Lorenz blind-approach system, fitted in all German bombers and most of our own, the "fighter boy" method was archaic. Yet there was something far more human in David's voice and his promise of a "cupper" than in the irritating dots and dashes of the Lorenz system.

In November, 43 Squadron moved to Acklington, a grass field north of Newcastle-upon-Tyne, one of our biggest shipyards, on the northeast coast. The smoke which the industries of this great city poured into the air did not, when the wind was in the south, make for good visibility. As day fighters our job was to protect, in all weathers, the coastbound convoys. With raging seas and gloomy skies, it was harder for the sailors down below than for us in our snug, though unheated, cockpit.

When darkness fell, we left the convoys, now in relative safety, to perform our secondary role of night flying. "Hideous obscurity," I wrote in my flying logbook after one patrol. After another, intended for test-firing my guns (a spectacular fireworks display), the searchlights, uninvited, held me in a blinding flood of light. "Unable to turn for five minutes. Those *bloody* searchlights," I commented this time in my logbook. Clearly, the searchlights needed help to tell friend from foe. Somebody may have tipped them off, for a week later I flew undisturbed in the dark for an hour, and wrote in my logbook, "No death rays got me tonight."

Foul weather, apart from the artificial kind created by smoke, added to the excitement. During January 1940, heavy falls of snow blanketed the airfield and the surrounding country. Flying through a snowstorm was like flying through heavy gunfire, only the "tracer" was not red but white and there was more of it. Landing on snow was tricky—like flying low above the glassy sea around Singapore. The glazed surface made it difficult to judge height. Happily, though, the snow, with its dangers, repaid us in full with the startling beauty of its white mantle cast upon the earth and glistening under the kindly light of the moon.

One night, in February 1940, while on patrol, confused voices jammed my R/T. From the hubbub I gathered that John Simpson, one of the more skillful pilots in my flight, had crashed on takeoff. I sped back to the airfield, landed, and taxied to the end of the flare path, where fire engines and floodlights were already on the scene. A Hurricane had indeed crashed, scything its way for more than fifty yards through a stand of young fir trees before coming to rest. An ambulance had already carried John, shaken but unhurt, off to the hospital. That blessed Hurricane—apparently the engine had failed—lay there among the fallen trees, still in one piece. So robust was it that were it fir trees or enemy fire, it could take the most brutal punishment.

My impromptu landing was fortuitous, for I badly needed to relieve myself—an untidy operation, when forced upon you in the cramped cockpit of a Hurricane. After inspecting John's crash, I taxied hurriedly to a discreetly dark corner of the airfield and, without stopping the engine, hopped out of the cockpit onto the left wing and down to the ground. The necessary done, back I climbed onto the wing and into the cockpit, strapped myself in, parachute harness first, then the Sutton harness which held you in. A few moments later I was soaring away once more into the darkness. Night flying, for all its dangers, was not without its homely side.

On the morning of February 3, I fought my first combat. The airfields in the Catterick (Yorkshire) sector to the south were snowbound. So was ours at Acklington until we had the bright idea of tearing a door off its hinges and, with six men on it, towing it behind a tractor up and down over a stretch of a thousand yards until the snow was compacted and we had a makeshift runway. This done, we reported to our sector controller that 43 Squadron was operational and ready, if need be, to defend the whole of northern England.

That morning my Blue section was at readiness when the phone rang. "Scramble"—take off. A few minutes later we were airborne and the controller called me. "Blue leader, vector [steer] one-eighty [due south]. Bandit [enemy] attacking trawler off Whitby. Buster! [Full speed!]"

Whitby was seventy miles south, in the Catterick sector. With Flying Officer "Tiger" Folkes and Sergeant Jim Hallowes following, we sped south at wavetop height—wave-chopping, we called it. It gave us the best chance of avoiding detection by low-flying enemy aircraft. We flew thus for twenty minutes, then suddenly I saw it—a twin-engine Heinkel 111 bomber, above and to the right, just beneath the low-lying cloud. "Tallyho!" I shouted over the radio, and swerving up toward it got my sight on and pressed the firing button on the stick (the control column). The shattering salvo from my guns immediately disabled the Heinkel, whose stream of red tracer from the upper-rear-gun position passed me harmlessly by. Folkes and Hallowes came in behind me, sealing the Heinkel's fate. It turned toward the coast and crash-landed in the snow near Whitby. A Heinkel of Kampfgeschwader 26, the "Lion" *Geschwader*. Next day, I traveled to the bedside of one of the two survivors, Unteroffizier Karl Missy. I felt sorry for him, having wounded him so grievously that he was now without a leg. His pilot, Wilms, was unhurt; the two others of the crew were buried next day with a wreath from 43 Squadron.

Three weeks later I caught another Heinkel high up over the North Sea. As it plunged to destruction, its wings were shorn off—a sickening, unforgettable sight. Then at the end of February, the squadron moved to wilder climes on the rugged coast of the northeast tip of Scotland, at Wick. Our new job was to protect the naval base at Scapa Flow, twenty-five miles north. It was there, way out over the sea, that I fought my first night combat. The interception itself was far from a classic affair, to say the least.

In that particular sector the radar was notoriously unreliable; its vagaries could make you laugh. One day, while on a "calibration test" and cruising at a steady 200 mph, I was called up by the genial controller Mac, a World War I pilot. "It may interest you to know," he said, "that according to our radar plots you are cruising at nine hundred mph!"

No wonder, then, that just after nightfall on April 8 I failed to intercept a raid of several bombers heading for the great naval base of Scapa Flow, in the Orkneys, just opposite. Jim Hallowes was with me in open formation. This was a time before fighters were dispatched individually at night. Craning our necks, we searched the sky, now a pale blue in the fading light. In vain. "But you must see them!" Mac called impatiently. "Your plots and theirs are identical." But the sky above was empty. A moment later, over Scapa, it suddenly became alive with bursting antiaircraft shells. So that was where the bombers were. But how to engage them in the midst of that gigantic fireworks display, with lead flying in all directions? I called Hallowes. "You're on your own, do what you can," I said. So I edged towards the barrage, hoping to pick out a bomber. All I got for my pains was a near miss from the AA, which, I discovered on landing, had smashed my taillight and damaged the rudder.

A thought occurred to me. Some weeks before, while chatting with the landlord of a pub in John O'Groats, this worthy had told me how on a previous raid some of the enemy bombers had flown out low over his pub on their way home. So down I went in a steep dive and circled the little town, but spied no bombers—only a few bombs plopping into the waters of the Pentland Firth. Again I looked up searching, and there, high above, were two Heinkels, unmistakable by their wing shape silhouetted against the luminous sky, hurrying home.

The chase was on. Climbing at full throttle, my eyes glued on those fleeing shapes, I began to close on them. Then came the faint voice of Mac in my earphones: "Blue leader, return to base and land." With a passing thought for Admiral Nelson,* I switched off my radio. I was now gaining fast and could clearly make out the dark shape of the hindermost of the two Heinkels. Closing the range still further, I opened fire. Immediately the bomber's undercarriage dropped down, a phenomenon common to Heinkels when badly hit. Streaming oil and vapor from its engines, the bomber was going down, but its rear gunner, seeing me silhouetted against the afterglow in the northwest, was still putting up a desperate fight. I went in again, guns blazing, flying down his cone of tracers until, as I dodged below, I could hear his MG15 still firing just above my head. He was a brave man fighting for his life, as I was for mine; two young gladiators between whom there was no real enmity. It was a pity that one of them—and his comrades—had to die.

As the Heinkel glided down toward the sea, its navigation lights came on. I followed it until I could faintly discern the white furrow it plowed in the sea as it ditched. Then its lights disappeared.

Back at base, I found that my Hurricane had been riddled with the bullets of that brave gunner. Was this again an aircraft of Kampfgeschwader 26? I do not know. It left no trace for the British to investigate.

During the previous month, March, another Heinkel 111 of KG 26 was brought down on English soil. In the wreckage was found a scrap

---

*At the Battle of Copenhagen (1801), when signaled by flag to withdraw, Nelson put his telescope to his blind eye and said: "I see no such signal."

of crumpled paper with a few words written on it: "Beacon Plan A. . . . *Knickebein* from 0600 hours on 315°." What could *Knickebein* mean, other than literally "crooked leg"? Here was a clue for Dr. Jones to solve.

Soon afterward a Luftwaffe prisoner of war provided another vague clue. *Knickebein*, he told the RAF interrogator, was "something like the *X-Geraet*" (X-equipment) mounted in some aircraft to receive signals from *X-Verfahren* (X-system), a very narrow radio beam which could reach London. He thought that the British knew about *X-Geraet*. He thought wrong; the British knew nothing about this top-secret device, which was all the more surprising because ten members, including the commanding officer and technical officer, of the only Luftwaffe unit trained to use it, Kampfgruppe (KGr) 100, were in British prisoner-of-war camps. They had been captured during the Norwegian campaign the month before, and had wisely kept their mouths shut, unlike their compatriot, who had let a fair-sized cat out of the bag, though it would take the British some months to run it down.

In May another of KG26's Heinkels was brought down on dry land. Intelligence experts sifting through the wreckage happened upon a diary belonging to one of the crew. An entry for March 5 recorded: "In the afternoon, we studied *Knickebein*."

With these clues in hand, Dr. Jones deduced that *Knickebein* and *X-geraet* must be directional beams which could be used for navigation and blind bombing. And they seemed to be used exclusively by Heinkels. Dr. Jones recalled an earlier incident, the first Heinkel down in Great Britain; it crashed near Edinburgh. The intelligence men in their minute examination of the aircraft had been struck by its Lorenz blind-approach equipment; it was much more sensitive than the Lorenz apparatus used by the RAF. Had the Luftwaffe adapted it to receive long-range radio beams? That is what Dr. Jones had yet to prove.

6

THE WIZARD WAR

It was on May 10, 1940, a fortnight before the evacuation began of 340,000 harassed British and French troops from Dunkirk, in northern France, that Winston Churchill succeeded Neville Chamberlain as prime minister, thus reaching the summit of a turbulent political career which had begun forty years earlier, in 1900. His first ministerial post, in 1906, was that of colonial undersecretary. In that year, Adolf Hitler, having failed his exams (like Churchill a decade earlier), had just left school with the dream of becoming an artist. Hermann Goering was then a lusty youngster of thirteen. Five years later, in 1911, when Churchill assumed the prestigious post of first lord of the Admiralty (the British navy was then the mightiest in the world), Hitler, having failed this time the entrance exam to the Vienna Academy of Fine Arts, was earning a meager living painting picture postcards. Goering was still in his teens. These were the men who, on the British side and the German, were to oppose each other in the battle for survival thirty years later.

Churchill, as he admits, knew nothing about science; Hitler and Goering knew less than nothing. But Churchill did know something of scientists and in his many previous ministerial posts "had much experience," as he wrote later, "in handling things I did not understand." For four years, during the thirties, as a member of the Defense Research Committee, he had acquired an outline knowledge of the radar problem.

As scientific adviser Churchill had invited Professor Frederick Lindemann, an able scientist but, more important to Churchill, his friend and confidànt of twenty years. The "Prof" possessed, in Churchill's words, the ability to "explain in lucid, homely terms what the issues were." Incidentally, Lindemann had been Dr. Jones's tutor at Oxford.

Winston Churchill, in 1940, was the man of the hour, the man that the British, very soon to find themselves alone in the struggle against Nazi Germany, needed to lead them. Three days after taking office he declared to Parliament, "I have nothing to offer but blood, tears, toil and sweat." Again, on May 22, warning Parliament and the nation of the risk of invasion, he uttered these defiant words for all the world to hear: "We shall go on to the end . . .; whatever the cost may be we shall fight on the beaches, we shall fight on the landing grounds, we shall fight on the fields and in the streets, we shall fight in the hills; we shall never surrender. . . ." The British took Churchill to their heart. They were as determined as he.

The day after that stirring speech I arrived at Debden, north of London. My time with 43 Squadron was over and I had orders to take command of 85 Fighter Squadron. After the fierce fighting in the Battle of France, the squadron, its bases blasted by the Luftwaffe and overrun by the Wehrmacht, was being pulled out to prepare for the next and final battle of Hitler's sweepingly successful European offensive. The Battle of France was over, said Churchill; the Battle of Britain was about to begin.

So swift had been the German advance in France that 85 Squadron had had to leave many of its Hurricanes behind. The pilots arrived at Debden by dribs and drabs, some in Hurricanes they had managed to save, some in trainer aircraft, others by train or private car.

There I awaited them with a welcoming smile and not a little apprehension. No. 85, like No. 43, was a crack squadron. The Canadian airman Major Billy Bishop, VC, had been one of its commanders in World War I; Major Micky Mannock, VC, had been one of its aces.

In the last few weeks in France, the squadron had fought hard and punished the enemy, downing for certain eighty-nine of their aircraft. It had just lost, in the space of a few days, two commanding officers —"Doggy" Oliver, badly wounded, and Michael Peacock, killed. I was third on the list. How would "the boys" take to their new leader, a fighter no less than they, but from the wild and windy wastes of northern Scotland and the barren North Sea?

In the event, we soon became friends. 85 Squadron had lost a number of pilots, missing, killed, or wounded, in France. A dozen new pilots, youths in their teens or early twenties, came to replace them. They had but little experience of flying, far less of flying the swift and powerful Hurricane. Compared with them I was an old hand, already twenty-five, and with seven years of flying behind me; but I had already discovered, and in the coming months was to discover more, that experience alone was not enough—luck too played a big part in survival.

In the sky above Debden, we, the few older hands, took the new ones under our wing. Incessantly, day after day, we drilled them in the discipline and dodges of air combat. By the end of June, the squadron was operational again. By day, our job was to protect, from dawn to dusk, the coastbound convoys, sailing some ten miles out to sea and continually menaced by the Luftwaffe.

Night flying, for the moment, was not for the new boys; their hands would be more than full during the daytime. Only four or five of us were experienced enough to answer the controller's request for a night patrol; the others were not yet trained in night flying. It was now that I began to accustom myself not to sleep, except in snatches, at night. I lay, clothed and ready to go, on the rough, rude blanket of my camp bed. Our night patrols were fraught with uncertainty. One night our trusty controller, Squadron Leader Reese, and I lost touch with one another. Guided here, there, and everywhere by him for the last half hour in the foggy night, I had not the least idea of my position. If my fuel ran out I would have to jump for it, over land or sea I could not tell. Then, thank God, we were in touch again. Reese apologized that I had been plotted as an enemy aircraft. He brought me home safely in the murk to Duxford, some miles from Debden.

Naturally, the traditional cup of tea was waiting for me. I could have done with a stiff Scotch, but still had to fly back to Debden. No one ever drank alcohol while on the job. A few nights later, and behold, an enemy aircraft, a Heinkel 111, held by the searchlights. But "with everything pushed and pulled," as one said, I was unable to close on it before it eluded the grasp of those long, straight silver fingers.

Our forward base was Martlesham, an uneven field near the coast some eighty miles northeast of London. At dusk one evening in pouring rain, the Luftwaffe, before we could intervene, attacked a convoy not far from the coast. The escorting destroyer, HMS *Wren*, was sunk. It was growing dark as my section was sent off. The most we could do now was to patrol in the rain the desolate scene—pathetic flotsam and jetsam strewn across the oily sea where the brave ship had foundered. With height and visibility fading rapidly, I was called back to Martlesham to land, but there I could see no sign of a flare path, and flying low over the field I understood why. Rain had half-flooded the landing area, which was now generously inundated with small lakes of water. Low in fuel, we had to get down somehow. I came in first with my headlight on, touched down, and ran on between the huge puddles. Talking to my numbers two and three on the R/T, I told them to be patient. I would station myself just short of the touchdown point, headlight on and aligned to give them a clear run. Then I called them in, and with calm and skill they made the difficult landing.

While we had been performing as occasional night fighters, with the aid of these primitive and uncertain techniques, Dr. Jones had been pondering over the scientific evidence he had been able to gather concerning *Knickebein*.

With such clues as he possessed, he went to see his onetime tutor, Professor Lindemann. But "R.V." failed to convince "the Prof" that the Luftwaffe could be using radio beams for long-range navigation and blind bombing. However, Jones was not to be put off. After further work on his theory, he returned to the attack on June 13. This time he won over Lindemann, who, in a letter to Churchill the same day, informed the prime minister that there was reason to suppose that the Germans possessed some radio device with which to locate and bomb their targets in the dark and in cloud. It was imperative to discover its wavelength. "If we knew this, we could devise some means to mislead them . . ." wrote Lindemann.

His astonishing revelation came, admitted Churchill, as "a painful shock." Until now, he had fondly imagined that the fog, mist, and cloud of the British winter would provide enough cover to conceal targets from accurate bombing, especially at night.

Churchill lost not a moment. He ordered an immediate investigation, under Air Marshal Joubert; it went to work the next day. That very day, a Luftwaffe prisoner let yet another big cat out of the bag, telling the RAF interrogation officer that *Knickebein* was a bombing method using two radio beams which intersected over the target and could be picked up by the bomber's Lorenz equipment.

The picture was becoming clearer. Joubert's investigation team now ordered that three Ansons, ancient but reliable reconnaissance planes, should be filled with special radio equipment to detect the invisible beams. The search began at dusk, on June 18, but ended in a blank night. However, another clue had been discovered earlier that day from papers salvaged from a Heinkel 111 shot down in France. They revealed some highly relevant information:

"Long-range radio beacon: VHF [very high frequency]
"1. *Knickebein* (near Bredstedt, northeast of Husum)
"2. *Knickebein* . . . (near Kleve)"

Still one more clue came to hand from yet another crashed Heinkel; its wireless operator had scribbled in his logbook: "*Knickebein*, Kleve 31.5." 31.5 was the waveband (in megacycles) that Professor Lindemann so badly needed to know.

On the night of June 18, a second attempt was made by an Anson to detect the beam. Once again, it drew blank; *Knickebein* was not on the air that night.

Meanwhile a fresh clue, which promised to be vital, was being literally pieced together. In the early hours of June 20, a Luftwaffe wireless operator bailed out of his stricken Heinkel bomber over England, his radio logbook in a pocket of his flying suit. On landing, he set to and tore the pages into thousands of pieces. Unfortunately for him he was caught red-handed in the act of burying them. By 3:00 A.M. on the 21st, RAF intelligence officers had stuck all the little bits together again, and found the vital clue—the exact coordinates of the *Knickebein* transmitters at Stollberg (very close to Bredstedt) and at Kleve.

Later that morning, Churchill, "with anxious mind," as he confessed, presided, in the Cabinet Room at 10 Downing Street, over a meeting of scientists and air force commanders. When Dr. Jones received his summons to attend, he thought it was a practical joke. When eventually he arrived, somewhat flustered and several minutes late, Churchill asked him to open the discussion. For some twenty minutes, the young scientist unfolded the tale of *Knickebein*—"the like of which," Churchill wrote later, "for its convincing fascination, was never surpassed by tales of Sherlock Holmes or Monsieur Lecoq." Churchill, ever sensitive to rhyme and the ridiculous, went on: "As I listened *The Ingoldsby Legends* jingled in my mind:

> "But now one Mr. Jones comes forth and depones
> How, fifteen years since, he had heard certain groans
> On his way to Stonehenge (to examine the stones
> Described in a work of the late Sir John Soane's),
> That he followed the moans, and led by their tones
> Found a raven a-picking a drummer-boy's bones!"

On this occasion, "Mr. Jones" left the assembly of senior scientists and airmen both concerned and incredulous. The German airline Lufthansa and the Luftwaffe had after all been using for years, like the RAF and Imperial Airways, the well-tried methods of dead reckoning and astronavigation. How was it possible that during all this time and in complete secrecy, they could have been working on such a revolutionary and successful method of navigation?

Proof of *Knickebein*'s efficacy was forthcoming that very night, when an Avro Anson, Flight Lieutenant Bufton at the controls with Corporal Mackie, a peacetime ham radio enthusiast, as wireless op, succeeded in picking up the beam. Its direction was roughly east-west, and Bufton and Mackie discovered that it was a beam some four-hundred to five-hundred yards wide, having Morse dots to the left and dashes to the right.

This material evidence concerning *Knickebein* confirmed the worst fears of those present that morning at the meeting in Downing Street. With *Knickebein*, the target, at night or in bad weather, was no longer concealed from the enemy bombers, as they themselves were from the ill-equipped British ground defenses and defending fighters. So far, the Luftwaffe had not yet launched an all-out bomber offensive against Britain. But the Germans were unlikely to tarry much longer now that Hitler was master of most of Europe and Churchill and the British remained defiant.

Indeed, it was on the afternoon of that meeting at Downing Street that Hitler, the victorious Nazi warlord, visited the famous railway carriage at Compiègne, north of Paris, where in 1918 the vanquished Germans had signed the Armistice which put an end to World War I. Among those present during Hitler's visit was one of the greatest of American correspondents, William Shirer (America would not be at war with Germany until a year and a half later). Shirer wrote in his diary of Hitler: "I have seen that face many times . . . . But today! It is afire with scorn, anger, hate, revenge, triumph." In a month or so, Hitler would be venting his feelings on the only country that still defied him —Britain, now half surrounded by German-occupied territory, from the Arctic Circle in Norway to the French Pyrenees.

The Wizard War now became—for the British—a race against time. If our day fighters were heavily outnumbered, they and the elaborate organization behind them were in good heart. Confident in their superb Hurricanes and Spitfires, backed by radar detection and controlled by radio from the ground, they were confident, however hard the fight, of beating back the enemy's onslaught by day. But at night? Our guns, searchlights, and fighters were pitifully lacking in the scientific equipment needed to enable them to come to grips with the enemy under cover of darkness.

Partly filling the gaping breach in their night defenses, the British, for the moment, possessed but one reliable weapon, yet to be improved—the "jamming" of the navigational and blind-bombing radio system upon which the enemy implicitly relied. They had discovered the secrets of *Knickebein*, but others—like *X-Geraet*, which already intrigued them—were in the offing. If the British could contrive effective radio countermeasures in time, the expected enemy night-bomber offensive, though it might not be defeated, could be seriously frustrated. To achieve victory over the enemy night bombers, the British were still wanting, in the summer of 1940, in four types of radar sets each specifically designed for a particular purpose: gun-laying (GL) for the anti-aircraft batteries; searchlight control (SLC) for the searchlights; ground-controlled interception (GCI) for overland ground control; and finally air interception (AI), airborne radar. Working models of these four types of radar were not yet ready; an airborne radar, AI Mark III, was available, but unreliable.

In the meantime, in June 1940, following on Dr. Jones's revelations, it was imperative, without a moment's delay, to organize a means of interfering with *Knickebein*. Churchill gave urgent orders to that effect. Countermeasures—jamming stations and various other devices—were to have absolute priority. A special unit, No. 80 Wing, was forthwith created, with the task of organizing radio countermeasures. The operation was baptized "Headache." It brought a stroke of luck to Wing Commander Edward Addison, who, stuck in an Air Ministry job which he loathed, was now withdrawn from "Air House" to take command of 80 Wing.

Addison faced an immediate problem. Radio jammers specifically designed for the job did not exist. Undeterred, he laid hands on a number of electrodiathermy sets used in hospitals to cauterize wounds. Suitably modified, they could jam the *Knickebein* waveband at short range. The diathermy sets were installed in selected police stations. The policeman on duty stood by, and when 80 Wing telephoned, he switched on. Laughably amateurish as the system was, it was better than nothing.

Addison also commandeered a lot of surplus Lorenz blind-approach transmitters, which he had modified so that they could send out a beam which imitated the dots and dashes and the steady directional note of *Knickebein*. The phony British beam would be laid across the *Knickebein* beam to deceive the enemy bomber and lead it astray. It was a bright idea, but, like the diathermy sets, worked only at short range.

The British "wizards" were working day and night building a type of scientific radio jammer, cover-named "Aspirin," designed to swamp the *Knickebein* signals. The shortcomings of our night air defenses made this job more urgent than any in Britain at the time. It was entrusted to the able hands of Dr. Robert Cockburn at the Telecommunications Research Establishment at Swanage, Dorset. It was to Swanage that my schoolmates and I, in the happy days before the war, would sail in the motorboat *Skylark* from Bournemouth pier. Young as we were, we already believed that England was as impregnable as she had been for nine hundred years against every foe. Now, in 1940, our island stood in imminent danger of invasion.

Cockburn and his team would need some months to turn out Aspirin sets in sufficient numbers. Meanwhile Addison's rudimentary devices would have to do. They were the best that Britain possessed to combat *Knickebein* bombers.

Addison's 80 Wing was fully engaged on another front of the Wizard War—beacons, which, like lighthouses, sent forth a beam, only an invisible one, to which aircraft could tune in and get a fix of their position. BBC broadcasts, transmitted from stations all over Britain, could unwillingly provide the same service; an enemy aircraft had only to tune in to a given program from a known station and so get a bearing. But the BBC outwitted the enemy by transmitting each program simultaneously from all its stations. Unable to identify any particular one of them, the Luftwaffe bomber was left, literally, in the dark.

The Luftwaffe could not do without radio beacons; their system of navigation depended on them. They were installed in German-occupied territory from Norway down to western France. They might even have been planted by German agents in Britain itself. The British soon found a way of confusing the German beacon network by setting up "masking beacons"—"meacons" for short. It was a wicked practical joke; the meacons, scattered judiciously about Britain, picked up the German beacon signals and retransmitted them, thus fooling the German bomber's wireless operator, who, unable to distinguish between his own beacon and the meacon, knew not which way to turn.

By August 18, 1940, nine meacon stations were in place. Two days later Addison's strange jumble of electrodiathermy sets and surplus Lorenz transmitters were ready to cope, within their limits, with *Knickebein.*

7

"WAS NUN?"—"WHAT NOW?"

Exactly two months earlier, on the morrow of France's surrender to the Germans and the flight in an RAF transport plane of General de Gaulle to England, Churchill had declared to the world, "Hitler knows he must break us in this island or lose the war." Heroic, defiant words they were, considering that Britain, the last remaining bastion against Germany's conquering armies and air force, was apparently so lightly armed to withstand the bomber onslaught—the knockout blow —not to speak of a possible invasion. Hitler himself was convinced that Germany had already won the war, and that Britain would see reason, as he put it, and ask for an armistice.

Indeed, neither Hitler nor his generals had ever seriously thought of a plan to subdue Britain by force. After the crushing victories which ended in France's humiliating defeat in June, the army staff asked themselves, *"Was nun?"*—"What now?" Hitler had even ordered the partial demobilization of the Wehrmacht. Churchill's defiance, with the whole of Britain behind him, sorely perplexed the Fuehrer, as it did other important people. Pope Pius XII appealed to both sides to make an honorable peace. Charles Lindbergh, the famous American transatlantic pilot, and one of my boyhood heroes, openly declared that Britain was finished; the RAF could not possibly stand up to the Luftwaffe. An attempt at mediation was made by King Gustav of Sweden, to whom Prime Minister Churchill replied, insisting that there should be guarantees "by deeds, not words . . . which would ensure the free and independent life of Czechoslovakia, Poland, Norway, Denmark, Holland, Belgium and above all France." And that, as far as Churchill was concerned, was that. The question of surrender was never even discussed by him or the cabinet, nor did it occur to the British people.

The frustrated Fuehrer, on the second day of July, had no choice but to decide that an invasion of Britain was "possible," "provided air superiority could be attained." It would be "bloody" and "a horror," he said, but he ordered that preparations should begin immediately. The question of air superiority did not particularly bother the Luftwaffe, least of all its blustering commander-in-chief, Hermann Goering. He was boasting that it would take two to four weeks to beat down (*niederschlagen*) the RAF.

Already, at the beginning of July, the Luftwaffe had begun to unleash its bombers against our coastbound convoys, mainly in the Channel and the Straits of Dover, but the merchant ships sailing in the North Sea to the Thames Estuary and the Port of London were not spared. That sector was guarded by a determined band of fighters, among them 85 Squadron. Fierce combats were fought above the sea; the Luftwaffe was heavily punished—not, of course, without casualties on our side. I was one.

At around six o'clock on the morning of July 11, I took off from Martlesham on a lone patrol, cleaving through the ground mist and climbing up through drifting raincloud. The controller gave me a vector which sent me heading out to sea. "Bandit in the vicinity," he warned me. At 8,000 feet and still climbing through the gray, soggy clouds, I suddenly saw an aircraft above, going the other way. A Dornier 17! I wheeled my Hurricane around and began to stalk it, keeping directly below in the hope that it would not spot me while I closed up to its height. Hardly able to keep it in view through my rain-washed windscreen, I flung back the hood and peered out and above at the German, while the rain lashed my face. A few more seconds and I should be close enough beneath it to fall back astern and fire.

The Dornier, as its upper rear gunner, Unteroffizier Werner Borner, told me nearly thirty years later, was on its way back to base. The crew of four were all singing "Good-bye Johnnie" when suddenly Borner yelled on the intercom: *"Achtung Jäger!"* and began shooting. I waited a few more seconds while closing to point-blank range, then opened fire. Borner would never forget (any more than I) the crisscrossing of our bright red tracers. He could actually see me in the cockpit.

The interior of the Dornier was a shambles. Two of the crew were hit and collapsed. Blood was everywhere. Flying fragments just missed the pilot's head and smashed his windscreen. A bullet knocked Borner's gun out of his hands—but not until he had used it to good effect. I was still firing when a bright-orange explosion in the cockpit momentarily blinded me. My engine was hit, and the last Borner saw of my Hurricane was as it disappeared in the clouds streaming black smoke.

By some miracle I was not hit myself. I called the controller: "I'm bailing out. One, two, three, four, five. Please fix my position," then went over the side. I splashed down into the water some thirty miles from the coast and after half an hour was fished out by a boat lowered from the good ship *Finisterre,* a trawler out of Hull.

A nip of rum from the ship's store was all that was needed to put me back in form. A few hours later the *Finisterre* landed me at Harwick, not far from Martlesham, and I was back on patrol that evening.

The Dornier managed to limp back to Abbeville in France, where it crash-landed. By another miracle, none of the crew were seriously hurt, despite the 220 bullet holes they found in their aircraft.

On July 16, Hitler issued his Directive No. 16: "Since England, in spite of her hopeless military situation, shows no signs of coming to an understanding, I have decided to prepare a landing operation and if necessary carry it out. . . ." The aim of the operation, baptized "Sea Lion," was "to eliminate the English homeland as a base for the prosecution of the war against Germany."

Three days later, on July 19, in a speech in the Reichstag, Hitler, after directing a string of insults at Churchill, appealed directly to the British people. It was useless to continue the war, he said, and he invited the British to be reasonable and give up the struggle. Before the day was out the British people, on their own, had replied. The evening newspapers, as well as the BBC, answered with a massive *no*. Three days later the foreign secretary, Lord Halifax, officially confirmed that popular response.

The day battle grew fiercer. Fuehrer Directive No. 17 of August 1 stated, first, that the Luftwaffe was to overpower the Royal Air Force in the shortest possible time; second, after achieving air superiority, the air war was to be directed against ports and food stores. A sign of things to come—and talking of ports, London was then the biggest in the world.

"On 8 August 1940," wrote General Hap Arnold, chief of the U.S. Air Force, "the RAF Fighter Command took off to save everything and between then and end-September everything was saved." On August 9, as it happened, I had an unexpected encounter. While chasing a Dornier snooping near the convoy Booty, some fifteen miles off the coast, I came around a cloud and bumped, almost literally, into twenty

Messerschmitt 110 fighter-bombers circling just below as they prepared to attack. By coincidence their leader was on the same radio wavelength, and I could hear him singing, in a strong German accent, snatches of the popular song "September in the Rain," interspersed with orders to his formation. How could one wish to harm a nice guy like that? But I had to do something. "Hullo, Hornpipe," I called urgently to ground control, "get the rest of the squadron over Booty, quick." Then, waiting above, I picked out a straggling Me. 110 and went down at him head-on, holding my aim as long as I dared, then zooming skywards—only to be met by one of his friends firing at me from head on. We passed each other within spitting distance as I made for the nearest cloud. Before reaching it I saw a big splash in the sea below and a high-speed launch of the ubiquitous German air-sea rescue service speeding towards it. Was the splash my Messerschmitt? I could not tell. Short of fuel, I headed for base; six Hurricanes of 85 Squadron were by now steering at full speed for the convoy—and the Messerschmitts, two of which they sent down into the sea.

Goering had set the *Grosseinsatz*, the main air assault on Britain, for August 13; the big event had been given in advance the heroic name Adlertag, Eagle Day. On the eve of Adlertag, the Luftwaffe made a determined attack on certain of the RAF's coastal radar stations, intent on depriving Fighter Command of its early-warning system. The vital stations at Rye, Sussex, and Ventnor, Isle of Wight, were put out of action, but the RAF acted astutely, moving into each station a mobile transmitter which deceived the Germans into thinking that the main stations were still working. Three days later Goering told his air commanders that there was no point in continuing the attacks, as the two stations were apparently undamaged. Goering's error, and another he was to make before long, were to lead to the Luftwaffe's undoing.

Eagle Day for the Luftwaffe was something of a flop—order, counter-order, disorder. But it was clear that the Germans were moving inland to attack our airfields. August 15 and 18 were days of furious fighting, with the Luftwaffe losing out heavily. Yet despite their losses the enemy's massed formations kept coming back, ceaselessly pounding the fighter airfields defending our southern ports and, further inland, those which stood guard over London itself.

In mid-August, 85 Squadron was withdrawn from Martlesham, on the east coast, inland to our main base at Debden, where we came under No. 11 Group, commanded by Air Vice Marshal Keith Park. Something new was surely in store for us. Before it came we were involved in a fight which was to prepare us for things to come. It was on the evening of August 18 that the order came through from sector operations room. "Eighty-five, patrol Canterbury, angels twenty [20,000 feet]." This was the first time that 85 Squadron went into battle in squadron strength—twelve aircraft. Guided by the controller ("a hundred-plus bandits," he warned me), I led them southeast, climbing hard, toward Canterbury, in whose beautiful cathedral Bishop Thomas à Becket had been murdered centuries ago. To me and to all who thought about it, England's past, good or bad, was a powerful and unfailing stimulus. It was well worth fighting for.

Long before we reached the cathedral town we found ourselves confronted, over the Thames Estuary, by a massive column of the enemy, about a mile and a half high and stepped up, wave upon wave. It was a formidable sight. At the base were Junkers 87 dive-bombers, above them Heinkel 111s, then Dornier 17s and Junkers 88 bombers; higher still was a layer of Messerschmitt 110 two-seater fighters, and above them, at about 20,000 feet, a swarm of Messerschmitt 109 single-seater fighters. I forced myself to think that we twelve were not the only ones around on the British side, and more, that the horde of enemy could not all attack us at once.

Indeed, as we closed on the bombers, the Ju. 87s and Heinkels veered away seawards. A dozen Me. 110s cut across us. "In we go!" I called over the radio, and a moment later we were milling around with them and the Me. 109s which had leapt on us from above. Now it was a dogfight. Each one for himself and watch your tail. One after the other, three Messerschmitts flew into my sights, turning. But my Hurricane was much too nimble for them. I fired and down they went streaming smoke and white vapor. One of the pilots bailed out and hung there, incongruously, in the midst of all those winged machines.

No. 85 Squadron acquitted itself well that day for the loss of two pilots. One, Paddy Hemingway, bailed out into the sea, but returned home, by boat and train, to Debden. In the evening came a telegram from Chief of the Air Staff Sir Cyril Newall: "Well done 85 in all your hard fighting. . . ." And another ordering 85 Squadron to leave next day for Croydon, on the southern fringe of London—a grass airfield and the capital's airport before the war, but now a fighter base in the Kenley sector defending the area from London southward to the coast between Brighton and Hastings.

After a short lull in the fighting, so fierce did the battle then rage that of the score or so of pilots I led to Croydon, fourteen (myself included) were shot down—two of them twice—within the next two weeks. Croydon airfield, already hit three days before our arrival, was soon to be hit again and yet again.

Hitler had reserved to himself personally the order to attack London. Croydon was in the London area, but the daring leader of that first attack, Hauptmann Rubensdorffer, escaped court-martial. On the way back, he was shot down and he and his gunner killed.

We were now in the very thick of the battle, as the Luftwaffe advanced towards London, smashing our fighter airfields on the way. The airfields ringing the capital were repeatedly bombed, our near neighbors Biggin Hill and Kenley more than most. We at Croydon got off fairly lightly by comparison and were not prevented from making four or five sorties a day.

When we met the massed enemy formations it was as a band of twelve, but this did not worry us. We knew that other bands, each of a dozen Hurricanes or Spitfires, were converging on the enemy's line of advance. Very seldom had we the advantage of height, for the controller held us back until the last moment to avoid being caught out by a feint attack—the Luftwaffe was good at the game. So we had to labor up beneath the oncoming cohorts, keeping if possible up-sun, until we reached their altitude—if we were lucky, before the escorting Messerschmitt fighters descended upon us. Our job was to attack the bombers and ignore the fighters unless they jumped on us, when we had to fight back. I favored a head-on attack on the bomber formations; although it needed more room for maneuver and was a somewhat hair-raising affair, it foxed the enemy fighters and put confusion among the bombers, knocking out the leaders whom the rest were following in serried formation right up to the target. Leaderless, the rest of the formation would sometimes wheel around and head for home.

One fine morning we had a rare chance. Patrolling at 20,000 feet with the squadron in search (open) formation, I spotted a dozen or so Me. 109s well below. Warning the others, I called to them, "Each of you pick his own—down we go!" It was like flushing a convoy of partridges. Most of us got one. I was following a second Me. 109, unaware of another one on my tail. A bullet zipped between my legs and broke up in the cockpit. A violent movement with stick and rudder saved me from more. Never have I got out of anybody's way so quickly.

In between fighting we sat around at the dispersal point, chatting and laughing as the gramophone played. Then the alarm would go, and an hour or so later, back at the dispersal point, one or two of our little band might be missing. We were not afraid as long as there was action; it was the antidote to fear, but like a drug, it made terrible demands on our nerves and bodies. Some of us, myself included, were feeling the strain. Our losses were mounting. Its massed attacks over for the day, the Luftwaffe sent a small number of bombers ranging far and wide in the darkness over Britain, bombing scattered targets. Sometime before leaving Debden I had been rudely disturbed one night by the rending crash, uncomfortably close, of a "stick" of bombs. The din was worse than the damage—a few broken windows and one poor rabbit killed by blast. No. 29 Squadron, based at Debden, was doing its best at night fighting, despite the poor performance of its Blenheim aircraft, with their Mark III AI (radar) and serious problems with the searchlights, whose crews were as ever apparently unable to discriminate between our fighters and the enemy. One night a young pilot of 29 Squadron, while stalking an enemy bomber, was caught by the lights. Again and again he called the controller, "Tell them to douse!" But the silvery-blue fingers had him in their grasp and would not let go. Struggling to free himself from the blinding flood of light, he lost control of his aircraft. He had left his radio on "transmit," and his desperate, terrified cries could be heard until the last moment, when his aircraft struck the ground. Another night a Spitfire pilot from a neighboring squadron, trailing an enemy bomber illuminated by searchlights, unwisely switched on his own headlight and was promptly shot down by the enemy. Much had still to be learned about night-fighting tactics.

In contrast to the Debden raid was the one made by a force of twenty bombers on the Nuffield factory, now tooled up to produce Spitfires, at Castle Bromwich near Birmingham. The bombing was remarkable for its precision, with eleven direct hits.

To oppose the Luftwaffe's night attacks, the RAF's Fighter Command could now put up at best a small and semispecialized night-fighter force. It consisted of six squadrons of Blenheims (29 Squadron included)—converted twin-engined medium bombers fitted with the inefficient Mark III AI radar set and a puny battery of four .303 machine guns mounted in the nose. In addition to the Blenheims were two squadrons of Defiants—single-engined two-seater fighters with a four-gun (.303) turret in the rear cockpit. Designed originally as day fighters, Defiants fought valiantly over Dunkirk and at the outset of the day battle over Britain, but had been decimated. Now they fought at night. Without their own AI radar, the crew, pilot, and gunner had to count on visual sighting. They were called "cat's-eye" night fighters.

To reinforce this small, determined, but ill-equipped night-fighter force, the day-fighter squadrons were called upon, if need be, to perform as well in the night-fighter role. At the close of day when the enemy cohorts retired and the wearying combats were over, the handful of us who were "night-operational" would stand by for night patrol. We, the half-dozen or so tried pilots who led the squadron and its flights and sections, were on duty virtually day and night, finding what time we could to eat and sleep. As long as I could report the squadron at full strength—twelve pilots and aircraft—next morning the others could take turns to slip away to the local pub or movie for a few hours of relaxation, or simply doss down at the dispersal point and sleep off their exhaustion.

Every evening at dusk, gooseneck flares were laid out to mark the flare path, but on Croydon's undulating grass patch they provided an uncertain guide, at least for takeoff. It was safer to aim just to the right of the red light on the hangar roof. That was the last earthly object you saw as you climbed on up into the darkness. The probing searchlights felt tentatively across the sky for the enemy, but rarely succeeded in illuminating him for the benefit of the searching fighters.

Very seldom indeed were the enemy raiders intercepted by our night fighters. A Heinkel, however, did manage to get itself shot down at the end of July, near Newbury—and all credit to the fighter. Their unfortunate adventure led one of the crew, the *Beobachter* (observer), into an even more extraordinary one. A man of considerable resource, he remained at large for nine days, nibbling a chocolate bar and gnawing roots pulled up from the fields at night. By day he hid in the woods among bracken and scrub. While he was dozing beneath a tree, a red handkerchief over his face, two men passed within thirty yards of him but did not see him. When another Englishman, with his spaniel, out pigeon shooting, approached, the German shinnied up the nearest tree, holding his breath as the man and his dog walked by below.

When Sunday came the *Beobachter*, perched high in his tree, observed many a young couple strolling in the wood. He envied them, for his own young wife was expecting a baby. Another night in the woods and he was by then so weak from hunger that he decided to give himself up. He walked to the nearest road. A young couple came bicycling by, but the moment they saw him, they pedaled on furiously. Then came a car, luxurious and shining. It slowed down, passed him, then backed. The rear door opened and the distinguished-looking lady inside opened the rear door and beckoned to the *Beobachter* to enter. "Get in, my good man, and sit down," said Lady Buckland, tapping with her hand the plush seat beside her. Astonished by her gentleness and courtesy, the *Beobachter* obeyed, muttering, half-ashamed, "*Polizei, bitte.*" "To the police station!" her ladyship ordered her chauffeur, and there this unlikely couple took leave of each other.

Between us, the radar fighters seeing but dimly in the dark with their shortsighted and unreliable Mark III AI and we, the cat's-eye fighters, straining our view into the night (helped or more often hindered by the searchlights), we were in no state to fight the Luftwaffe's night bombers, as we were their day bombers. Happily, Headache and the meacons were ready and Aspirin was on the way. Happily, too, the people of London and Britain's provincial cities were braced for the onslaught.

8

CASUALTY

In the early hours of August 24, the whistle and crash of falling bombs rent the darkness at Croydon. They narrowly missed the pilots' quarters, where I was fitfully dozing, and set ablaze two of our Hurricanes. One had just been delivered, sparkling new, with all the latest fittings; we were well rid of the other, described in the vernacular as a "clapped-out old shag-bag." The Croydon raid was yet another infringement of the Fuehrer's personal orders, but not nearly so flagrant as the attack which that same night blasted the very heart of the City of London. The raid on London was unintentional: the Luftwaffe crews involved, ordered to bomb oil tanks at Rochester and Thameshaven, downstream from the City, had overshot their target; they were severely disciplined on their return. Hitler, still believing that the British would be "reasonable" and surrender, did not wish to provoke them. But the Fuehrer's go-softly attitude toward Britain was wrecked by those bombs on the City of London. The following night, on Churchill's order, the RAF retaliated with bombs on Berlin. They dropped leaflets too, saying that "the war which Hitler started will go on . . . as long as Hitler does." But it was the bombs which had the most stunning effect on Berliners. Remembering Goering's crack "If ever a bomb drops on Germany, you can call me Meier," that is what Berliners were now doing.

As defenders of London we could only feel that Berlin, as an impersonal urban entity, was getting what it rightly deserved. My own mind shunned the terrible consequences in terms of humanity, the massacre of defenseless civilians, the butchery among the young and the old, as was happening on our side at the hands of the Luftwaffe. It never occurred to me, however, to blame the young airmen who perpetrated these acts. They were acting under orders, and with few exceptions, doing their best to hit military targets. Their courage in the face of enemy defenses and weather conditions was supreme, and I often doubted, and still do, whether I should ever have found the same courage as they—not only ours, but theirs as well. But there never left my mind the idea that, far more than an inhuman paradox, it was quite unjust and immoral that armed men—young and brave at that—should kill, and worse be ordered to kill, defenseless civilians. If the massacre of the innocents was not strictly intentional, it was admitted, with the basest cynicism, as inevitable.

"Hammer at the enemy day and night to break his nerve," Goering ordered his Luftwaffe. By day the RAF's fighter bases around London were being so battered that, with buildings shattered and telephone wires cut, they had to move out to emergency operations rooms, away from the base. The Kenley ops room was set up anew in a local butcher's shop.

The Luftwaffe's night offensive was mounting too. On the night of August 28 came its first mass night attack. The Germans chose the great docks at Liverpool and Birkenhead as their target. For three more nights they returned to attack the docks; Blenheim night fighters and cat's-eye fighters were dispatched to intercept, but the bombers got through unscathed. Most bomber crews, on their return, reported hits on the target. But German air reconnaissance photos did not confirm all their claims; a mass of bombs had fallen wide of the docks. Was the RAF, the German crews wondered, interfering somehow with their aim?

The answer, which was soon to become abundantly clear, was yes. No. 80 Wing, with its Headache, Aspirin, and meacons, was sowing some confusion among the Luftwaffe bombers where guns and fighters had failed. Many hits, the German air photos showed, fell on what was obviously a decoy fire well south of the docks. The British called them Starfish sites. The ruse had been employed by the Germans themselves; now their own aircrews were being deceived in the same way.

While the Luftwaffe was showering bombs on Liverpool and its environs, RAF Bomber Command was again over Berlin. Ten people were killed, and a cry went up from the German press against the brutality of the British in killing women and children. "Cowardly British attack!" "British air pirates over Berlin!"

The outrage of the Nazi chiefs was exceeded only by their hypocrisy.

It was the German air force which had first bombed London in 1915, proving that civilian noncombatants were henceforth in the front line, potential if not legitimate victims of what Churchill called ''this cursed, hellish invention and development of air power.'' The Luftwaffe had massacred civilians at Guernica, Warsaw, and Rotterdam. Now the Germans were getting a small taste of their own medicine, but before terrible retribution was to overtake them, British cities and above all London had first to submit to the hellfire of Luftwaffe air raids. Already, during August, they had killed over a thousand civilians, nearly half of them women and children.

While the Luftwaffe was attacking more and more strategic targets under cover of darkness, during the daytime it was throwing everything it could into an all-out effort to destroy the RAF day-fighter bases defending London. On August 30 and 31, the day battle reached an unprecedented ferocity. The 31st was our blackest day, when thirty-nine pilots were killed and many more shot down and wounded. Such losses may sound trifling, but there were not all that many of us, and our ranks, particularly among the leaders, were seriously broached.

I was one of the casualties on the 31st. Due to come to readiness (five minutes' notice) at 1:00 P.M., we had just sat down to a quick lunch in the airport building when I was called by the Kenley controller. ''Sorry, old boy, but be on your toes; we may need you in a hurry.'' Feeling rather like a Western sheriff, I called to the hungry pilots, ''Come on, boys, let's get goin'!'' A few minutes later we were in the saddle, that is, in the cockpits of our Hurricanes. I glanced back at my squadron formed up behind me. They looked superb, those Hurricanes, straining at the brakes, their long, eager noses tilted skyward and the sun glinting on their whirling propellers. Every pilot was watching for my hand signal. At last it came. ''Off you go!'' called the Kenley controller, and we were racing forward with the bellow of our combined 12,000 horsepower. It was the last time that I led my squadron into battle by day.

Bombs were already falling toward Croydon. Just off the ground, my engine faltered, then picked up again. Blast had hit it like a punch in the wind. Turning in the cockpit, I saw the rest of the squadron emerging from a vast eruption of smoke and debris. Thank God, they too had survived the blast. I looked up. Thousands of feet above, the 110s were wheeling in the blue, Me. 109s swarming above. A furious chase began.

The low-flying Dorniers which had done the bombing were well away, so I climbed, flogging my Hurricane toward the Me. 110s, calling to the others, "Get the 110s but watch out for the 109s!" I pushed my hood back, better to see the 109s above, and kept straight on toward the 110s. When I was nearly in their midst, down came the 109s. For a minute or so there followed a violent cut-and-thrust combat which I knew must end badly for me. Streams of tracer came past me from behind, then a Me. 109 climbed, turning, in front of me. My favorite shot. Belching black-and-white smoke, he staggered, slowed, and rolled over. No time to see more; a second Me. 109 was in my sights. I fired and it rolled over and disappeared. A third one was just below, so close I could see the pilot; an awkward shot that I never fired. At that instant a Me. 110 was firing at me; I could see in the corner of my eye the flashes of its two 20mm cannons and four machine guns. The salvo blasted my poor Hurricane, holing the central fuel tank, starring the bulletproof windscreen, and hitting me with a thump in the left foot. The engine was dead; a great wood lay below—not a convenient place to crash-land—so over the side I went. Once again my parachute saved me. Hanging on the end of it, I watched my Hurricane dive headlong into the trees and blow up.

The foot was not hurting—yet. So after a few beers with the locals at the Royal Oak, at nearby Hawkhurst, in Kent, I was driven, lying on the floor of a truck, to the Croydon General Hospital. By now I was writhing in pain, but a shot of morphine calmed things down. That night the house surgeon, Brayn Nicholls, extracted a 20mm cannon shell from my foot. As I passed out under the anesthetic I could faintly hear the sirens wailing. The Luftwaffe was closing in on London.

9

ZIELWECHSEL—*TARGET CHANGE*

Fighter Command and, no less, the Luftwaffe were being stretched to the limit of endurance both in men and machines. During those two white-hot days of fighting, never before (or since) did Fighter Command hurl against the enemy, time and time again, so many of its fighters—and never at greater cost. Pilot casualties on our side were now catastrophic, far exceeding the output from the training schools. Worse, as experienced pilots were numerous among the dead and wounded, the gaps they left had to be filled by raw lads with no battle experience.

September 1 was a bad day for Fighter Command, a disastrous one for 85 Squadron. Led by its one remaining flight commander, Patrick Woods-Scawen, it lost four pilots, including Patrick. On September 3 the squadron was withdrawn from the front line and sent to a quiet sector near Leeds, in the northern county of Church Fenton, Yorkshire. This time it was led by Sammy Allard, who, still a noncommissioned officer, was the squadron's best pilot. All this time I lay helpless in my hospital bed at Croydon. Before leaving with the ground crews, Tim Moloney, our faithful adjutant, had come in every day to tell me the news and discuss the running of the squadron in my absence. I was happy to leave it to him. An air gunner at the age of nineteen in World War I, Tim was a wise and experienced man. He did warn me, however, that if I did not manage to rejoin the squadron within three weeks, another commander would be appointed in my stead. I gladly accepted the challenge.

The Luftwaffe's assaults on fighter airfields continued unabated until on September 3, apart from the rubble and ruin on the ground, our daily losses in the air, which hitherto had not exceeded the Luftwaffe's, were now equal, with sixteen down on each side. It looked to Field Marshal "Smiling Albert" Kesselring, commanding Luftflotte 2, that the British fighter force was *kaputt*. Moreover, that same day RAF reconnaissance planes photographed over four thousand invasion craft assembled in French ports. Yet to Hermann Goering, whom Hitler had ordered to "crush" the RAF, it was evident that the RAF was so far uncrushable. Fighter Command, though badly diminished, was still fighting back. Bomber Command was attacking Berlin and lashing out nightly against the German invasion fleet—to the discomfort of the Kriegsmarine, which Hitler was counting on to transport his invasion troops to England's shores.

With a decisive victory over the RAF's fighters still eluding him, Goering believed that his last hope was to launch a mass assault on London, the world's biggest and most prestigious target. In defense of the capital, the *Reichsmarschall* figured, every available British fighter would be forced into the air where the German *Jaeger* would round them up and destroy them. Such a world-shattering success, Goering comforted himself, would incidentally give a badly needed lift to his ego, subdued these recent weeks by the failure of his Luftwaffe.

To Goering's plan, Kesselring gave his enthusiastic support; he had been pressing for some time for an all-out attack on London. But General Sperrle, commanding Luftflotte 3, disagreed, as usual, with Kesselring. "Continue to attack their fighter bases by day," he argued, "and by night, the London docks." His strategy, had it been followed, might well have given the Luftwaffe victory over the RAF fighters. But Goering, who had already made one fatal error in sparing the RAF's radar stations, and Kesselring, an ex-soldier ill versed in air strategy, prevailed. London was to be the Luftwaffe's new target; plans for the *Zielwechsel* (target change) now went urgently ahead. The attack on London was code-named "Loge," after the god who forged Siegfried's sword. It only remained for the Fuehrer to put the new offensive across to the German public.

This he did on September 4, at the opening of the *Winterhilfe* (winter help) campaign, before an audience of women, in the Sportpalast in Berlin. With heavy sarcasm, he turned to the question that everyone was asking—when would England be invaded? "England will collapse," he told the excited ladies, "and if people in England are asking, 'Why doesn't he come?' I reply, 'Don't worry, he is coming.' "

On that vexatious problem of the RAF's night attacks on the capital, the Fuehrer reassured his audience: "We are now answering, night for night . . . we will raze their cities to the ground." He ended with a repetition of his old theme: "The hour will come when one of us will go under and it will not be National Socialist Germany." "Never, never!" came the frenzied response. Next day Hitler confirmed the order for "attacks on the inhabitants and air defenses of British cities, including London."

Though Fighter Command's chief, Air Marshal Dowding, was of course ignorant of the Fuehrer's order, it was to prove the answer to his prayer. On September 6 the plight of his fighter force was desperate. Six out of the seven sector airfields and five advanced landing grounds in 11 Group, which stood guard between London and the Luftwaffe bases across the Channel, were badly damaged. Losses of fighter aircraft largely exceeded production, and reserves were running low. The output of new pilots could not keep pace with battle losses; the little company of fighter pilots, originally about a thousand, had dwindled to about seven hundred. Victory was in the Luftwaffe's grasp, but a miracle was about to happen. The morrow would tell.

The morning and afternoon of September 7 were quiet. Then toward 5:30 P.M., massed bomber formations, heavily escorted by fighters, advanced not as expected on the fighter airfields, but direct on London.

At 1 Helen Street, Woolwich, thirteen-year-old Ray Callow was with his six-year-old nephew Evan, a pink-faced, fair-haired boy, the son of Ray's sister Rose, who was at work in the Arsenal. Mrs. Callow had gone shopping—she always left it till the evening when prices were cheaper. The two boys were alone, busy putting a model airplane together—Ray, the expert, was happy that Evan was already becoming an enthusiast.

As they worked with glue and balsa wood, Ray became aware of a murmur of voices coming from the street and through the window saw crowds gathered outside looking eastward up into the sky. Almost immediately, from the direction of Woolwich Common, came the *whoomf, whoomf* of antiaircraft fire—it frightened Ray at first, for he had never heard the guns so close. All the same, he took little Evan by the hand, and with no thought for the danger of falling shell splinters the two young model-aircraft enthusiasts walked outside to join the crowd. Like everyone else, Ray looked eastward downstream toward the estuary. Never had he seen such a terrifying sight; the sky was dotted with a mass of specks which seemed to be quite motionless. Then as he realized they were approaching, he recognized them as Heinkels and Dorniers, flanked by escorts of Messerschmitt 109s and 110s. The boys could not imagine there could be so many at once. In fact, the Luftwaffe had amassed nearly four hundred bombers and more than six hundred fighters, over a thousand aircraft, for this all-out attack. After crossing the English coast, they had borne down straight on London. This was the curtain raiser of Loge, the knockout blow on the capital. A year had passed since we had waited for it, basking in the sun beside our machines at Tangmere.

Ray stood there mesmerized by the sight of this vast phalanx of aircraft, formation after formation, stepped up one behind the other like a giant staircase mounting in the sky from 16,000 to 30,000 feet. Now they were moving visibly closer to London—and him. But still he stood rooted there, holding Evan's hand, his eyes fixed on the awe-inspiring horde. British fighters were swooping on the bombers, scything through them and jousting with the enemy fighters. Vapor trails were tracing white circles and crisscrossing against the blue background of the sky, smeared here and there by black smoke from smitten aircraft, German and British. Ray watched horrified as a Messerschmitt 109, one wing shorn off, fell twisting crazily to earth. After it came a Spitfire, its pilot apparently aiming to crash-land on Woolwich Common. The Spit did not make it. It hit the road somewhere in front of the long facade of the Gunners' Mess with a huge explosion which sent the pilot's body hurtling through a fence of corrugated iron. (The fence was patched up with a new sheet of iron which for years remained as a local landmark.)

Watching from outside her denture workshop, Ray's sister Melve (an adventurous spirit like him) had seen the wingless Me. 109 crash and ran off, glad to put some distance between herself and the bombing. She found the wreckage of the German fighter lying in the back garden of a row house through which the curious had first to pass. She threw the few pennies she had on her into a bucket outside the front door marked ''For the Spitfire Fund.'' She came to the back garden and the wreckage of the Messerschmitt. In its cockpit there lolled the dead body of the pilot, one of his arms hanging limply outside. Melve was immediately struck by the slender fingers, the manicured nails. Around his neck was wrapped a bright silk scarf, and looking at his young face Melve could not believe that a dead man could look so handsome. He must be from the wealthy class, she thought, this girl from the poorer class, now caught up in ''total war,'' a wholesale slaughter which showed no respect for ''class'' or noncombatants.

The massed bombers were now nearly above where Ray was watching, and the air reverberated with the steady throb of their engines. Then suddenly above the thunder there came the whining crescendo of falling bombs, crashing down into the heart of London's dockland. Ray, gripping Evan's hand, said, "It's time we went inside." Closing the door behind them, the two boys crawled under the dining-room table, as they had always been told to do.

The Dornier 17 *Gustav Marie* of KG 2 was flying in the serried formations of that aerial armada. Its wireless operator, Unteroffizier Werner Borner, looked down through the billowing columns of smoke at the chaos of fire and explosions below. As British fighters cut their way through the escorting Messerschmitts to attack the bombers, it was impossible, said Borner, to tell friend from foe. The Dornier released its bombs, and Borner saw them go down "on the exact spot"—the Royal Victoria and the Royal Albert docks on the north bank of the Thames.

Just opposite, on the south bank, smoke belched from the German-owned Siemens cable works—ironic, for the RAF had hit the Siemens factory in Berlin. Farther downstream, in the streets of Woolwich, the cry went up "The Arsenal's been hit!" A conflagration was raging within the confines of its 120-acre site; bombs had blasted and set fire to workshops and stacks of containers full of nitroglycerine, dumps of small-arms ammunition, and heavy shells which were exploding and careering wildly into the air. Clanging firebells, AA guns, bursting bombs, the diving and zooming and the steady thunder of aircraft overhead increased the din to an unimaginable pitch. Yet, apparently, the Arsenal's Danger Buildings, where Johnny's wife Kathleen worked, had survived, for it was common opinion that if the Danger Buildings went up half of London would go up too.

Ray, as he watched the leaping flames and writhing columns of gray-black smoke mounting skyward, could not believe that somewhere in the midst of that holocaust were his sisters Amy and Rose, and Kathleen, Johnny's wife, and Alf, his brother. His mind went blank at the thought, and he could only pray that they had taken to the shelters or the open ground. He thought of his brother Bert, manning his balloon site up on Woolwich Common; he should be all right. But his father? That morning Ray had, as usual, brought him a lunch of steak-and-kidney pudding and dumplings. In the heavy-gun shop where Mr. Callow worked, the heat was so intense that the men could not simply run out straight into the open air. They had to cool off gradually. For them, no escape to the shelters; they had to stay put while the bombs rained down. Ray refused to think that any harm might have befallen his father. He had always believed him to be indestructible, and still did.

The boy's thoughts turned to his oldest brother, Johnny—the ballroom dancer turned fireman. No doubt he was somewhere in the thick of the firefighting. Johnny, like most of the volunteers in the Auxiliary Fire Service, had so far not seen a big fire. The regulars of the London Fire Brigade would always go in first and the AFS would merely follow to clean up the mess. But neither had the regulars even seen fires such as those that raged that day in east London.

10

LONDON ON FIRE

During the morning Johnny had been sitting around reading and chatting with his comrades in the common room at the substation at Earldom Square, Eltham. Their station was once a school, which had been evacuated. The assembly hall served as a common room for the firemen; the classrooms had been converted into dormitories. Outside waited their ten "pumps," mounted on two wheels and painted gray. Their firefighting apparatus bore no resemblance to the familiar red fire engine with its extensible ladder. The ten pumps of the Earldom substation were each towed by a London taxi. Occasionally private cars, even big, luxurious Buicks and Chryslers, though less maneuverable, would be used as a towing vehicle.

The taxi carried a team of four men. Number one—the leading fireman—was Johnny's role. He sat up front next to number two, the driver. Numbers three and four sat on the backseat.

Around 4:00 P.M. a Yellow warning had come through from Fire Headquarters at Lambeth, via 37 area HQ at Newcross and the main station at Avery Hill (another requisitioned school) down to the Earldom Square substation. The Yellow was soon followed by a Red, which signaled that the raid had crossed the coast. Outside in the streets, air-raid wardens were warning people to go to their Anderson shelters in the garden or to public shelters. Those who could not make it were shepherded into the warden's post, solidly protected by sandbags. By now the atmosphere was tense—everybody was waiting for the bombs to fall.

Tons of them had already gone down into the docks north and south of the river, and a heavy pall of smoke was spreading toward Woolwich. Suddenly the girl on the switchboard at Earldom Square received the order: eight pumps to the Arsenal! She pressed down eight of the ten buttons (one for each pump) and threw a switch which set the alarm bell pealing. Leading Fireman Johnny Callow with the seven other number ones rushed to the control room to get final details, while the remaining members of each team made for their "pump"—the expression included the towing taxi—in which all their equipment was already stowed: long rubber boots, axes, helmets, gas masks, and blue tunics with silvery buttons. Like the others, Johnny's pump was already moving off when he came dashing from the control room, jumped aboard, and took his place next to the driver. Then they were tearing through the streets and, as they went, pulling on their long boots and uniform coats, adjusting their tin hats—all except number two, the driver. He would have to wait till they arrived at the fire.

On the way there the men were silent. Johnny felt his stomach turning and he knew the others felt the same. Then Johnny spoke: "Well, mates, we've all got the wind up properly, haven't we? So grit your teeth—this is the job we're paid for, even if it's only three quid a week."

Johnny's pump reached Beresford Square, next to the Arsenal main gates, just as the first bombs were falling. Pumps from other stations were lining up to get in, and when Johnny's pump entered, the place was a tempest of fire, shooting sparks, and exploding bombs. In the suffocating smoke they could hardly breathe, let alone see.

This time it was the real thing, the test of all their months of training. Each man knew exactly what to do. The taxi came to a halt near a hydrant, and the four men jumped out. Johnny, number one, strode forward toward the fire to get orders from the control officer; he moved with the ballroom dancer's step, heel and toe. It was second nature to him, and all his comrades' teasing would never change it. Back he strode to his pump, where number two had already started up the motor; numbers three and four had run out the connecting hose and standpipe and joined them up to the hydrant. They were back at the pump, unloading the eight reels of hose and connecting them together. Johnny directing, the two men ran the hose out toward a blazing stack of nitroglycerine containers; they advanced, both of them holding the "branch," the brass nozzle which was adjusted to throw a fan jet to protect them as they closed in. Then Johnny gave the order "Let it go!" and the men, taking a firmer grip on the branch, adjusted it to give a power jet. They felt as if they were fighting with a rearing horse. Holding down the branch with all their strength, they aimed the jet so that its deluge of water fell full upon the flames, damping them down into clouds of steam and acrid smoke.

Johnny and his number two took five minutes off for a cup of tea and a sandwich. They had not far to go; the Salvation Army's mobile canteens were on the spot, and young men and women, in their blue uniforms and tin hats, were handing out refreshments: " 'Ere, guv'nor, a cupper and a sandwich." Johnny admired them; they had ventured as close as they dared to the fire and were indefatigable as they served the firefighters. He and his mate swallowed down their tea and sandwich, then went to take over from the men on the branch; it was now their turn for a break.

The fading daylight brought no reprieve to the firemen. Night bombers were streaming up the estuary toward London. Hauptmann Hajo Hermann, piloting a Junkers 88 bomber, remarked: "A very clear night. Everything was lit up by fires, like a huge torch in the night." Until that night, Luftwaffe aircrews had obeyed strict orders against indiscriminate bombing. Now they simply tipped their bombs into the sea of flame and smoke below.

Since the beginning of the attack at 5:30 that evening, more than fifty pumps had come to the Arsenal's rescue. They had been fighting, regardless of the ceaseless bombardment, for four hours. Now it was getting on for 10:00, and more pumps came in to relieve them. Johnny's team was ordered to knock off, "make up," and return to the substation.

The Callow family, most of them shaken, but all unhurt, had gathered at 1 Helen Street that evening. The old man was still missing, and Renée, the youngest daughter, was on duty ushering at the Granada Cinema. In the middle of the evening performance a near miss blasted open the Granada's doors. People started to hurry out into the street, only to find it blocked by broken glass and rubble. Back they trooped inside, shepherded by the manager and ushers, who soon had them going in a rollicking sing-song.

At that moment Renée's sister Melve, escorted by her brother Alf, was approaching the Granada. Alf, not yet seventeen, had nevertheless wangled his way into the Home Guard and proudly wore the khaki uniform and forage cap. He had insisted on accompanying Melve on her risky errand. When the bombs struck, the two were knocked flat and covered with dust. Alf, the gallant but untried soldier, passed clean out under the shock, and rescue men searching for the dead and wounded loaded his recumbent body into an ambulance. Melve, now on her feet again and brushing the dust from her hair and clothes, suddenly noticed what was going on. "Hey!" she shouted. "That bloke's me bloomin' brother. There's nothing wrong with him!" Alf was pulled unceremoniously out of the ambulance and dumped on the ground. A minute later he and Melve were threading their way through the debris to deliver Renée's supper.

It was around 8:00 that night that a tall, heavily built man presented himself at the door of the Callows' home. Ray opened the door. Before him stood an apparition, the hair singed off its head; its body, half-naked in the tattered remains of a boiler suit, was black from head to foot. "It's Dad," said Mr. Callow. "Not many of us got out alive when the big-gun shop was hit. I've walked back, but I feel a bit groggy."

Mr. Callow was badly shell-shocked. Ray helped him upstairs to the bathtub. "You can leave me, mate," Mr. Callow told his son, then turned on the cold tap—there was no hot water. Within half an hour he had washed himself down and changed into clean clothes. He told Ray, "Now I'm slipping down to the Bull for one or two."

By the time he was back, Ray had left for the Town Hall to report for duty. Clad in Boy Scout uniform, pepper-colored sneakers, and tin hat with the initials ARP on it, he felt very proud of being able to help in the defense of his country. The waxing moon had risen, its feeble light only occasionally visible through the pall of smoke that hung over Woolwich. In one hand Ray held a dimmed-out pocket torch, though he rarely used it, knowing the streets as he did like the back of his hand. There was a sharp nip in the air, and he walked on briskly, noticing that although the row houses were apparently not hit, the windows of all of them, like those of his own home, had been blown in. The occupants of those houses would be shivering that night.

It was getting on for 9:00 when Ray reached Beresford Square, still choked with fire pumps and ambulances, the former pressing forward toward the fires, the latter going in and coming away with the injured. Yet despite the confusion and the ceaseless rain of bombs, the square-heads' food stalls were still open, with customers queuing to make their last purchases and reasoning that as long as the costermongers stood their ground, they had better do so too, or lose their place in the queue. "Business as usual" was the watchword of these extraordinary, resistant people. Ray, as he threaded his way among them, was amazed, not least at himself. They had all known for months that they were going to get it in the neck sooner or later. Yet now, though slightly dazed by the weight and horror of the bombardment, they still did not seem to realize fully the disaster that had befallen them.

Ray, himself unperturbed by the drone of bombers overhead and the din of bombs below, walked on and came to the Town Hall, where, at the ARP headquarters in the basement below, he reported for duty. For the next three hours he dashed here and there carrying tea and sandwiches, and the occasional message, to the men and women of the civil defense and the heavy rescue squads as they hacked and picked and shoveled away in the debris, searching for survivors. Ray felt there was nothing more worthwhile, and exciting too, than to be able to help these brave men who, faces and arms covered with dust and sweat and sometimes blood, toiled away in their filthy blue overalls, hailing each other as "mate" and "guv'nor" and despite the macabre scene cracking an occasional joke. Though relieved by a new shift in the early hours of the 8th, they refused to leave, so the work went ahead at double the pace.

It was not until well after midnight that young Ray reported back to HQ at the Town Hall. The duty warden thanked him and said, "Off you go, mate, and get some sleep." Half an hour later the boy flopped onto his bed at 1 Helen Street. The Callow family had had a basketful that day—and Johnny was still fighting the fires.

After receiving the order to knock off from their four-hour battle with the fires at the Arsenal, Johnny and his team got back to the substation, their clothes soaked through, their faces and hands begrimed. They straightaway washed down and changed into dry clothing. Before they had time for a cup of tea and a sandwich, the alarm bell pealed again. "All pumps to the Surrey Commercial Docks!"

As they raced through the streets, here and there they saw a burning house and were tempted to stop and extinguish the fire. But the orders were to go to the Surrey Commercial Docks, where, at the Canadian dock, a conflagration was devouring some one million tons of pinewood, sending flames and sparks flying hundreds of feet into the sky. When a wooden partition stood in the firemen's way, a burly Canadian lumberjack appeared from nowhere and with his long ax laid in furiously at the obstacle and hacked it down. The firemen advanced some way under the protection of their "fan jet." Then they readjusted the branch, and the power jet, under hundreds of pounds per square inch of pressure, tore into the flames. This was going to be a long and exhausting fight.

But the Salvation Army and other volunteers, like the Women's Voluntary Service (WVS), were also at the rendezvous. Johnny swore that without their aid the firemen could never have held on, as they did, with an occasional cup of tea and a sandwich, until 6:00 next morning.

It was only then that the last of the Luftwaffe night bombers was on its way back to base. London had endured a ceaseless bombardment lasting twelve hours, the like of which no other city on earth had yet suffered—neither Guernica nor Warsaw nor Rotterdam. The day battle was not yet over, but the night battle had begun. Among the smoke and ruins of London that morning of Sunday, the 8th, 430 Londoners lay dead—nearly as many as the fighter pilots killed during all the four months of the day battle—the "Battle of Britain." This was only the first night of London's agony; the capital was yet to endure, night after night, without respite, another two months of mass attacks.

All that night I lay in my hospital bed at Croydon, alone in a spacious ward, save for Pyers Worrall, a freshman in 85 Squadron, and a chubby young Australian from a Spitfire squadron at nearby Biggin Hill. Passively, we listened to the incessant din of bombardment, trembling with the vibrations of exploding bombs which fell close by, shattering the windows of our ward and strewing the floor with glass and steel splinters. At each approaching scream of a falling bomb I said to myself, "This one may have my name on it," and I lay there filled with fear, yet philosophical, waiting to be blown to pieces. The nurses seemed heedless of the danger. They may have been as frightened as we, but never showed it; they just pulled our beds away from the windows, joking among themselves and with us. "Heads down!" they would cry as the scream of the next bomb rose to a piercing crescendo. Then came the rending explosion and the mighty blast which blew in the windows, the showers of glass and splinters. "Gosh, that was a near one," the girls would chorus, forcing us to laugh too while silently thanking God that we were still alive.

Those marvelous girls were professionals, all save one, a volunteer from the British Red Cross. She could not have been more than eighteen, a shy, pretty girl with clear, smooth skin and fair hair. She attracted me but without inciting any particular longing for her; she was too reserved, I too much the hardened warrior to succumb to sentimental feelings. I greatly admired her courage, though, and told her so. Being so junior, she had to cope with most of the dirty jobs; as a volunteer she received not the merest pittance. "You deserve to be paid," I said to her. "No," she replied, "more important to me than pay is gratitude.'' A beautiful answer from this brave and tender-hearted maiden. I could only pray that my own gratitude brought her some recompense.

During the fortnight spent in Croydon hospital I was cut off from my squadron. Tim called a few times, but being stuck in bed, my footing under a protective casing, I could not move to answer the telephone. I lived in a separate world, far from the carnage, yet so close, listening to the whistling and crash of nearby bombs, the thunder and whine of aircraft in combat and the clatter of machine-gun fire. One day a young mother and her child were brought into our ward for emergency treatment. They had been crouching in their Anderson shelter when a Spitfire crashed a few yards away. Fuel from its tanks, all aflame, came flooding into the shelter. The two innocents were horribly burned and died a few hours later.

One day the senior sister appeared at the end of my bed, forceps in hand. Looking at me over her horn-rimmed glasses, she smiled encouragingly as she told me, ''I am going to remove the dressing from your wound. It may hurt a little.'' A little! As she drew out about six inches of gauze from the hole in my foot, it was all I could do to stop myself yelling out in pain. Then the worst was over; it would take a long time, sister said, for the wound to heal.

Between us, Pyers, Bill, and I used all the charm we could summon to break down the official severity of the matron, clearly a good and competent lady, but distant and unbending. We succeeded: we threw a sherry party for the ward nurses, and Matron, sitting on my bed, was soon chatting away, proving to us all the real warmth of her heart.

Such charming distractions helped to while away the time, but did not allay my impatience to rejoin 85 Squadron by September 21, the end of my three-week respite. That first massive raid on London on the evening and night of September 7–8 marked the end of my first week in the hospital. It was now Sunday morning, the 8th.

11

INVASION POSTPONED

That morning, while the flames had been subdued, clouds of smoke still drifted over Woolwich. Mr. Callow, though still feeling far from himself, was up betimes, as usual, making tea for the family. He brought Ray a cup. "Listen, me lad," he told his son, "I'll not be around for a week. Doctor's orders." Ray smiled but said nothing. He had never admired his father more. He would miss him, but it would not be long before he was back.

Young Ray had made daring plans for the day. He swallowed down his tea, dressed, and left the house, making for the Woolwich free ferry; its skipper, Captain Hudson, had been plying back and forth across the Thames during the previous night, steering between flaming barges, bringing refugees, clinging to their belongings, which included cats, dogs, white mice, and parrots, from Canning Town and Silvertown on the north bank. Rumor had it that those two places had been burned to the ground, and Ray, as if he had not already seen enough at Woolwich, was curious to find out how things looked on the other side of the river.

He stepped off the ferry at North Woolwich, on the opposite bank, and made his way through the smoking ruins of Silvertown, past the royal group of docks—Victoria, Albert, where Borner's bombs had struck, and the George V Docks. When he came to Canning Town, fires were still burning. In the shambles of burned wood and shattered masonry he suddenly came upon scores of one-pound notes scattered in the street. Ray stopped dead. He had but one thought: don't touch! Run for it. He ran all the way back to the ferry, crossed to the south bank, and kept running until he reached home. Breathlessly he told his mother about the pound notes. "You didn't touch anything, did you?" "No, Mum, honest I didn't," answered Ray. She believed him; he was a good boy, better than others she had heard of who would have made off with such easy loot.

Following its gigantic effort, the Luftwaffe laid off during the day. Goering, in his special train, *Asia*, with its cooks and servants and its stocks of wine and food, was now in personal command, as the German radio solemnly announced. Pleased with the destruction wrought by his Luftwaffe, he warmed to his task of destroying London. He was convinced that sustained attacks would lead to a crack in the morale of Londoners. Hitler, fed by Goering's rosy reports, thought the same; he had been obsessed by the British refusal to surrender. But now he had lifted his ban on attacking London, "a stroke at the enemy's heart," he was sure, he informed his generals, that this would create mass hysteria and revolution, with the people pleading for an armistice. He was only as wrong as the Luftwaffe's chief.

Goering that day divided London into two zones: A, east London, and B, west London. Zone B with its railway termini and power stations was to be as fair game as Zone A and its docks and warehouses. With a laughably naive act of generalship, Goering ordered that the main effort that night was to be concentrated on Kensington, Buckingham Palace, and West Ham. London again suffered cruelly; 412 civilians died, half of them women and children. Next morning's *Völkischer Beobachter* reported, with cynical falsehood, "attacks against military and economic targets by strong forces and the heaviest bombs." The heaviest of them all was the "Satan," whose blast was effective five hundred yards away.

When, in the late afternoon of the 9th, the Luftwaffe planes returned to the assault on London, they were in for a surprise. London's brave action in drawing the enemy's fire from the fighter airfields had enabled the RAF fighters to make a remarkable recovery. The German fighter leader, Hauptmann Hannes Trautloft, at the head of Jagdgeschwader 54, reported: "The sky was full of the RAF's red, white, and blue roundels; for the first time we had the feeling we were outnumbered." The raiders were repulsed, the German high command nonplussed by the unflagging resistance of the British fighters.

But after nightfall the bombers were back in force; 370 Londoners were slain, 1,400 badly injured. The *Völkischer Beobachter* rejoiced next day: "London witnesses a morning of terror after nine and a half hours of air raid." Valiant London. During the daytime the British fighters still fought to protect her. But by night the capital lay wide open to attack. The night fighters, with unreliable radar, or none at all, searched vainly in the dark for the assailants. Nor were the AA guns and searchlights, themselves without radar, able to stem the incoming tide of bombers.

The day did not go so well on the 11th for the RAF's day fighters, who had to fight through the enemy's screen of escorting Messerschmitts before closing with the bombers. One of these, a Heinkel of KG 26, provided some comic relief to the murderous combats. Hit by Spitfires, it dropped out of formation. The pilot shouted orders to the crew to bail out, and dived out himself through the front hatch. The other three of the crew were made of sterner stuff; they stuck to their ship. The observer, grabbing the abandoned controls, yelled, "Jettison everything!" Some minutes later, watchers in the Tunbridge Wells area were intrigued to see an unusual object descending toward them. It fell at their feet—a full-dress Luftwaffe uniform, complete with Iron Cross, ceremonial dagger, and, in one pocket, shaving gear and toilet requisites, which had floated down on a coat hanger from the heavens. The owner, Unteroffizier Schilling, wireless operator, with his two companions, managed to limp back to base in their badly damaged Heinkel.

After the day's fighting, hopes rose again in Berlin. To the German High Command it looked as if the British fighters were at last on the verge of defeat. This brought little joy to the Kriegsmarine; that night, after attacks by Royal Navy light craft and RAF bombers, the invasion ports of Ostend, Dunkirk, Calais, and Boulogne were declared "completely unsafe."

The same could be said of certain districts in London, once again the target that night of a mass attack. Luftwaffe bombers, mingling with the stream of returning RAF bombers, greatly confused the British coastal radar. Not that it made any difference to our night fighters or AA guns, which, with or without coastal radar, and without any of their own, were helpless to protect the capital.

To Londoners the guns did, however, sound more aggressive than usual. Indeed their meager numbers had been doubled by reinforcements from the provincial cities. The ceaseless din of gunfire gave heart to Londoners. Now we're giving it back to them, they thought, and felt all the better. Young Ray imagined that in that appalling din enemy bombers were plunging earthward, victims of both guns and night fighters. But that night the 13,500 shells fired by the guns did nothing, any more than did the night fighters, to cause the imagined slaughter among the enemy, who admired the fireworks from a safe height. And not everyone in London appreciated this increased tumult of noise. It terrified children and their mothers and, more than the bombs, disturbed the sleep of those innocents.

Gray nimbus clouds and blessed rain during the day of September 12 brought relief to London. Among those who welcomed the lull was Unteroffizier Karl Missy, whose Heinkel I had shot down near Whitby seven months before. He had been transferred to the Royal Albert Hospital at Woolwich, reserved for wounded German airmen. Poor Karl—for him and his comrades it was out of the frying pan and into the fire. In his hospital bed he lay, a helpless target for the bombs of his *lieber Kameraden*. When the sirens started wailing, three cigarettes were handed to each prisoner. But now they were wailing so often that cigarettes were in short supply.

More and more Luftwaffe prisoners kept arriving at the hospital. Invasion, they told their comrades, was for any day now. Hitler would soon be in London. Encouraging news for Karl, lying in bed with the risk of being killed by German bombs.

When the air-raid warning sounded, soldiers would enter the ward and stand guard, one at the end of each bed. As the bombs came crashing closer, the guards would dive under the beds, whose occupants would lean over and inquire, "How are you there below?" only to be answered by a string of oaths. The nurses alone remained faithful to their duty.

It was the same with the nurses at Croydon General Hospital, twelve miles away from Karl Missy, where I myself was still confined to bed, unable to walk. There the bombardment was not so fierce, but we were still getting our share of smashed windows and bomb splinters. Serene and smiling as ever, the nurses would come and hold our hands, telling us, the supposed heroes of the battle, not to be afraid.

The lull on the 12th was short-lived. During the hours of darkness, while single enemy bombers ranged as far as Merseyside, a large force again concentrated on London.

All day long on September 13, German radio stations kept blaring bellicose tunes like *"Wir fliegen gegen England"* and *"Bomben auf Eng-el-and,"* working the public up into a fever of expectancy. The Wehrmacht and the Kriegsmarine were ready to sail. Goering had fixed a date for victory next day. Yet Hitler was in a quandary: to invade or not to invade? That was the question tormenting him. But Goering was reassuring: leave everything to me and my Luftwaffe; the attacks on

London had produced a terrific effect. Even Buckingham Palace had been hit; though Goering did not know it, the king and queen had escaped death by only a few yards. Queen Elizabeth was now able to say, "We feel we can look the East End of London straight in the face." These were hard days—and nights—for Londoners of all sorts and conditions.

Goering felt confident. "British nerves," he told his Fuehrer, "are at cracking point. The RAF has only fifty Spitfires left." (He made no mention of Hurricanes, which had done even greater execution.) Hitler cheered up. The air battle, according to Goering, was going so well that there was now no need for invasion. That night he sent another mass raid to London—one more red-hot nail, he imagined, in the British coffin.

On the 14th, Admiral Raeder, chief of the Kriegsmarine, submitted his own views, far more objective than Goering's, to the Fuehrer: "The present air situation does not allow the undertaking of Sea Lion"—the cover name for invasion. Hitler, not altogether freed from Goering's spell, reacted: "Four or five more days of fine weather and we have a good chance of forcing England to her knees." But there still remained one snag which exasperated the Fuehrer. "The enemy keeps on coming back," he observed. But still, even if it would need as many as ten or twelve days to liquidate the British fighters, the chances were, he predicted, that the British public might meanwhile succumb to mass hysteria.

Thus the German Fuehrer. The British prime minister saw things otherwise. "The attacks on London were for us a breathing space of which we had the utmost need."

However, Fighter Command's defense had been scrappy that day: fourteen aircraft down on each side. In Berlin, hopes of eliminating the RAF fighters were still high. "Four or five more days . . ." The Fuehrer agreed that preparations for Sea Lion should continue. "A new order will follow on the 17th," he promised. Meanwhile, the Luftwaffe was all set for a supreme effort on the morrow. It was to deliver the *coup de grâce* to Fighter Command.

Not long after sunset, the night bombers were back as usual, with impunity, to give London another pounding. Just before it started, the Callows received an unexpected visitor, an official of the Home Office, formally clad in black jacket, striped trousers, and bowler hat. Having spent the day with the Woolwich civil-defense authorities, it was now too late for him to get back to London. The Town Hall had sent him to the Callows, who received him hospitably and showed him up to a spare room on the third floor. Before the night was far gone, the Callows and their guest were to have a narrow escape which, at least for that indestructible London family, ended in a good laugh.

Despite the bombs and the admonitions of the ARP wardens, the Callows, like thousands of others, never went to the shelters at night. They preferred to sleep at home in their own beds, come what may. And so it was that Melve was awakened in the night by a weird flapping noise. It sounded as if scores of wet sheets were being shaken out. The noise came closer, then ended abruptly with a vague bump and a clatter, maybe of tiles. Melve turned over and dropped off to sleep again.

Early next morning she left the house to get the Sunday paper. She did notice that the roof of the tall house (once notorious as a gambling den) on the other side of the narrow street looked a bit odd, but thought no more of it. On her way back, dawdling as she read the headlines, she looked up again at the house opposite. Only then did she realize that there was a big hole in the roof, while the chimney looked distinctly cockeyed. Opening the front door of her home, she called out, "Hey, everyone, come and have a look." Her mother, Alf, Renée, and Ray came to the door. "Looks a bit suspicious," they all agreed. "Better call the police."

Some moments later a red-haired policeman rode up on a bicycle; the Callows had already placed a wooden and rather whippy ladder against the wall opposite. Cautiously the policeman began to climb, rung by rung, while Ray and Melve held the ladder. He kept climbing while the ladder swayed and once nearly fell backwards on top of Ray and Melve, who were struggling to hold it in place. At last the policeman reached the top rung. Gripping it firmly, he leaned forward, balancing precariously, and looked down through the hole in the roof. What he saw so terrified him that he nearly toppled off the ladder. While Ray and Melve below still fought bravely to keep it in place, he managed to draw his whistle and blow a long blast. Then, the whistle clenched between his teeth, he began a hurried, ungainly descent, whistling all the time as strenuously as his lungs would allow. As he neared the ground the Callows demanded, "What's up, Officer?" "A land mine, a land mine!" gasped the breathless bobby. Inside the house a two-ton land mine was hanging on the end of its gray-green parachute, which had been caught on a broken beam.

At that moment the Callows' guest—awakened by the shrill blasts of the police whistle and cries of "Land mine!"—appeared clad only in underpants and vest and carrying in his arms the rest of his clothes and his shoes, bowler hat, and attaché case. In this disorderly negligee he bolted down Helen Street, swerved around the corner, and was never seen again.

Meanwhile wardens and police came running. Five pumps arrived—and so did Mr. Callow, back from his week's sick leave. A policeman stopped him in front of No. 1. "Sorry, guv'nor, no one's allowed to pass; we're evacuating the area." "Yes, but that's my bloomin' home!" remonstrated Mr. Callow, without the slightest effect. His wife and children and scores of others living within five hundred yards or so were already being hustled away, carrying a few belongings, by wardens and police. The Callow family, Mr. Callow included, camped that night in the Town Hall.

September 15 dawned misty over southern England, but soon cleared. On the other side of the Channel, Goering's bombers and fighters were arrayed for his triumphal day. It would be a walkover, with only fifty Spitfires left. So, let the battle commence!

It did, around 11:00 A.M. German tactics were a repeat of those on the 7th; hordes of bombers in massed formation and escorted by fighters bore down on London. The RAF fighters, with ample radar warning and perfect visibility, were able to face them squarely. All day long the German airmen, with dogged courage, came back and back again. But the British fighters, Spitfires and Hurricanes by hundreds, and antiaircraft were too strong for them. At 6:00 that evening, Goering, at Cap Gris Nez, was being told by Kesselring, "We cannot keep it up like this; our losses are rising above the danger line." The assault was called off. The "invincible" Luftwaffe had been routed by the RAF fighters that Kesselring had believed *kaputt*. They had downed fifty-six of the Luftwaffe for a loss of twenty-six of their own, with thirteen pilots saved. In Churchill's words, September 15 was the "culminating date" of the day battle. Henceforth it began to turn in favor of Fighter Command.

Not so the night battle—if battle it could be called, at least for the night fighters and guns, which were yet unable to oppose any serious resistance to the Luftwaffe's unrelenting mass attacks by night on London. Even the indomitable Churchill admitted, ". . . we viewed with stern and tranquil gaze the idea of going down fighting amid the ruins of Whitehall." The king himself, one of the best shots in the land, kept in practice at his makeshift shooting range in the gardens of Buckingham Palace.

It was on the RAF's victorious day, September 15, as the sirens shrieked a warning for the second time of another enemy attack, that I left Croydon Hospital. Having graduated from crutches to a cane and one leg, I set off to say hello to my mother in Sussex; it was months since I had seen her and months more since she had seen her two other sons—Michael, a destroyer captain, and Philip, commanding a battalion of Gurkhas in Burma. The courage of mothers, wives, and sweethearts, of a different sort from their loved ones', was every bit as fine and may well have demanded more of them.

My mother was glad to see me. We dined simply, exchanging our news. Michael's ship, she told me, was at Southampton. Next evening I hobbled up the gangway of the destroyer *Viscount*. After dark, we cast off, and all night long, with the ships of his flotilla, we scoured the Channel for signs of the invaders.

We need not have worried. Hitler's order, promised for the 17th, was received by his Supreme Headquarters in the early hours of that day while we were still at sea: "*Wird bis auf weiteres verschoben.*" Five words which confirmed the postponement of invasion until further notice.

12

TERROR IN THE NIGHT

D espite his gloomy forebodings about the ultimate fate of London, Churchill was more immediately preoccupied with the diverse ways of avoiding such a catastrophe—for if London gave in it would spell the end of British resistance. He kept a close eye on the production of scientific devices, notably special radar for fighters, guns, and searchlights. A small number would soon be ready, as would the first of a purpose-built night fighter, the Beaufighter. He encouraged the development of other devices, strange figments of the inventive boffins' imagination which, he thought, were worth a try in the hope of stiffening the feeble night defenses. He protested at the hours of work squandered by men and women in factories and offices, obliged by the regulations to take to the shelters. He directed that they should remain steadfastly at their posts until warned by the roof watchers—nicknamed ''Jim Crows''—that the enemy was overhead. The new system saved millions of working hours and gave workers and officials a proud place in the front line alongside the civil defense.

Churchill worried incessantly about other, more insidious problems which could bring about the downfall of London. He personally investigated them, suggesting his own remedies. One was drains and sewers which had been smashed by the bombing and threatened the city's water supply. Another was public health. Night after long night, cramped in the cold and damp of their corrugated-iron Anderson shelters in the garden, millions of Londoners were exposed to the risk of colds, flu, and other more serious epidemics. One of the Luftwaffe's vain boasts was that they would smash, with the blast of their bombs, every window in London. They reasoned, with some naiveté, that buildings would thus be rendered uninhabitable and consequently fall into rot and decay. They had made some progress; there was now a glass famine in Britain.

But in the end, as Churchill said, everything was mastered. Drains and sewers were disinfected and repaired and the city's water supply saved. Londoners, gradually inured to the hardships and privations of the blitz, grew resistant to disease and exposure. Gaping windows were made airtight with sheets of reinforced plastic. If the bombing destroyed many, if not all, of the possessions of thousands of Londoners it never diminished their heart or their will to resist, not did it damp their ir-repressible sense of humor. Heart, will, and humor; these were the arms with which Londoners would defeat the Luftwaffe. And this with but scant refuge from the bombardment; only a very few bombproof shelters existed, and sleeping space on the platforms of the Underground stations was limited. The great majority of Londoners slept, like the Callows, in their house or in the garden, beneath their Anderson shelter, which was blastproof—that was all.

Delayed-action (DA) and unexploded bombs (UXB) increasingly menaced London's life. They would paralyze a city district, block the entry to a factory or railway terminus, arrest the traffic on roads and railway lines—until they were dug out and defused. The men of the Bomb Disposal Units, with supreme courage and consummate skill, took charge of this highly dangerous and delicate job. Yet there was no lack of volunteers. One of them, as Churchill recalls, was the Earl of Suffolk, who enlisted his lady secretary and elderly chauffeur to create his private unit. They became known as the Holy Trinity. "With urbane and smiling efficiency," remarked Churchill, they defused thirty-four bombs. The thirty-fifth sent the Holy Trinity heavenwards, where, Churchill continues, he felt sure "that all the trumpets sounded for them on the other side." It was not long before the heroic Bomb Disposal Units mastered the DAs and UXBs.

Unexploded "land mines" (sea mines attached to a parachute) were tackled by them with equal valor and skill. Land mines, like the one which, had it exploded, would have blown the Callows and their guest into eternity, were the ultimate in indiscriminate terrorism against the civilian population. Bombs could be aimed, and usually were, with a precision bombsight against military targets. Though they often missed, the will to hit the target was there. But "this hellish invention," as Churchill had called it years ago, of aerial bombardment was rapidly degrading men, young men, decent and brave and good in themselves, into callous murderers of innocent people. The land mine as a weapon represented the first step in the willful, wholesale massacre of civilians. It is impossible to aim a land mine. It drifts down, carried here and there by the wind currents, striking where chance may decide.

Churchill's first impulse was to retaliate, quite simply, land mine for land mine, on selected German cities. He bowed, however, to the remonstrations, on moral grounds, of his advisers. Two or three years more and moral objections were to be swept to the winds until, after Hiroshima and Nagasaki, decent men and women would rise up in anger against the massacre of innocents.

For the time being Churchill and his air chiefs contented themselves with avenging, within the limits of morality—that is, by aerial strikes on German military targets—the bombed and beleaguered British and, in every way possible, assuring their ultimate survival. To this end, incidentally, he began to pay attention to the survival of the War Cabinet, himself included. An impregnable administrative citadel had been prepared out at Hampstead Heath, in north London. After their first meeting there, followed by what the prime minister described as a "vivacious" luncheon, the cabinet members decided they would rather be back in Whitehall, in the thick of the action, even if some of the government buildings, including the prime minister's residence at 10 Downing Street, were of ancient and somewhat rickety construction. In time the cabinet offices were to be moved to the "Annexe," at Storey's Gate, not far from 10 Downing Street, and proof against direct hits.

Churchill's anxieties were not confined to the blitz on London. His thoughts went out far beyond our coasts and the continents beyond. He feared for the safety of Malta, the island fortress in the Mediterranean, within easy reach of attack from Italy. He pressed for the reinforcement, by units in Palestine, Kenya, and South Africa, of the thirty thousand British army troops guarding their stronghold in Egypt, against which an Italian army, some quarter of a million strong, was already advancing. Churchill was particularly concerned for a Free French force, with General de Gaulle in command, which was at sea heading for Dakar, the Senegalese capital, with the intention of seizing it from the Vichy French, Hitler's allies. Fears for the secrecy of de Gaulle's expedition were already felt. The brave Free French, indiscreetly clad in tropical uniform as they awaited embarkment at Liverpool, were enthusiastically toasting, "*Bon voyage à Dakar*," ignoring those charming little posters in every railway carriage and public place: "Careless talk costs lives." Vichy was thus forewarned.

Of all Churchill's many worries, the greatest, inevitably, was for Britain's Atlantic lifeline. Britain's lone stand would be in vain could she not maintain her line of supply, hundreds of ships, sailing in convoy from the ports of her ally Canada and of her good friend America— not yet an ally by the rules of the war—and bringing food, equipment, and munitions to Bristol, Cardiff, Swansea, Liverpool, and Glasgow, all of them, now that London was ceaselessly under fire, Britain's most vital ports.

The defeat of Britain's ally, France, had left that ill-fated country's airfields at the free disposal of the Luftwaffe for the close-range bombing of Britain. France's ports provided convenient bases for the Kriegsmarine's U-boats to prey with greater ease on Britain's Atlantic convoys. The U-boats were now inflicting devastating losses on British shipping.

The Royal Navy was short of destroyers. Churchill had been promised fifty more by President Roosevelt in return for the lease of British bases in the West Indies. But despite his repeated pleas to the American president, the delivery of destroyers was lagging, and when they did arrive, they needed a lengthy refit.

In all this broad panorama of anxiety, doubt, and disaster, one central fact was certain. Hitler, in July, had decreed the elimination of Britain as a base for continuing the war against Germany. For this very reason Britain had to survive.

13

NIGHT FIGHTERS

It was with joy that, on September 22, I rejoined my squadron at Church Fenton, a grass airfield in Yorkshire. Though still on one leg and a stick, I did not need a walking stick to fly. Willing hands bundled me into the cockpit of a Hurricane. I rested my left foot, between instep and heel, on the rudder bar, and it felt comfortable enough. It was only the end of the foot, where the wound was still open, that hurt (and still does if it hits anything). I took off and performed a few aerobatics over the airfield. When I reported fit for flying to the medical officer, several witnesses were ready to support me. They were not needed; the doctor understood.

Three months of fighting had thinned out the ranks of the battered squadron I had been sent to command in June. Since then we had been battered even harder; a score of pilots had left for one reason or another—killed, wounded, burned, and occasionally posted to fill a gap in another squadron. Seven pilots, myself included, remained, and we found ourselves doing the same job as we had done in June: teaching pilots fresh from the training schools to be war pilots. British, Poles, Czechs, and French came to us. We kept some, to make up our numbers; the others went on to squadrons in the south. François de Labouchère and Emile-François Fayolle—we called him Emile to avoid confusion —stayed. Why, I do not know, in view of what was to befall us. Their English was barely sufficient to understand the clearest instructions on the R/T. But both were, in the French sense of the word, extremely *sympathique*. We were happy to have them, and they, as it turned out, were glad to be in our midst.

For a month, as teacher or pupil, we all worked conscientiously at our task of war training—formation flying, aerobatics, mock combats, and practice shooting—a regular day-fighter routine. We even flew low over Leeds in close squadron formation to inspire people to give to the Spitfire Fund—rather galling for pilots of a Hurricane squadron, but worthwhile, like everything else we were doing. "Worthwhile," however, was not enough. There was not one of us who did not feel it his duty to be back in the fray, down south where our comrades were still fighting and dying in their fierce and victorious battles against the Luftwaffe's day offensive.

Gradually, the Luftwaffe was wilting. On September 27 it took another terrible hiding from the British day fighters, losing fifty-five of its aircraft. Such losses, as Kesselring had warned Goering two weeks before, were more than the Luftwaffe could stand. Now they were bleeding it white. The following day a dramatic change appeared in the German tactics. Only thirty of their fastest bombers, Ju. 88s, escorted by nearly three hundred fighters, advanced cautiously on London, but were repelled. Goering had to admit that his much-vaunted "knockout blow" had failed.

The Luftwaffe chief, chastened and depressed, had departed from the battlefield for his hunting retreat, the Reichjaegerhof, a log cabin near Rominten in East Prussia. He discarded his garish uniform of Luftwaffe *Reichsmarschall* for the more folkloric apparel of a Reichjaegermeister: green suede hunting jacket over a silk blouse with long puffed sleeves, hunting top-boots and a hunting knife slung from his belt. There, at the Reichjaegerhof, while trying to console himself in his humiliation at having betrayed his Fuehrer with empty promises, he was still dreaming up new and more horrible schemes to crush the British.

On October 7 he declared his new aims for the Luftwaffe: progressive and complete annihilation of London; the paralyzing of Britain's war potential and civil life; and, through terror and privation, the demoralization of London and the provinces. These congenial tasks he assigned to his night bombers. On October 18, in a pep talk to bomber crews, he said, "You have caused the British world enemy disastrous losses. . . . Your courageous attacks on the heart of the British Empire, London, have reduced British plutocracy to fear and terror." That last remark, had they heard it, would have given a good laugh to Londoners like the Callows!

On October 20, Goering called a halt to his day-bomber offensive. While costing his Luftwaffe very dearly, it had not fulfilled his dream of conquest. Now that the night offensive was well under way, Goering began to feel better.

On October 21, Trafalgar Day, I received a signal from Fighter Command that "85 Squadron has been selected to specialize in night fighting forthwith. . . ." Some people have used the expression "relegated to night fighting." They would hardly have done so had they first tried for themselves this difficult and hazardous occupation. Searching for the enemy in the darkness of the blackout, unaided by radar, unable to depend entirely on our radio, flying alone in an unheated cockpit through cloud and rain, snow and ice, was in future to be our lot. It promised to be a test for the bravest.

14

GROPING IN THE DARK

I was at first dumbfounded by this unexpected news. While it is always flattering to be "selected" to do some special job, it had never occurred to me that I should be asked to transform 85 from a seasoned and successful day-fighter squadron into a "specialized" night-fighter squadron. Not a word was mentioned about any specialized equipment which might aid the process. About the Hurricane there was practically nothing that could remotely qualify it as a specialized night fighter. It did, admittedly, possess a headlight mounted in the wing, but this little luxury was more useful on the ground than in the air. The dashboard instruments were luminous, but could not possibly be a pretext for assuming that the Hurricane was fit for a specialized night-fighting role, any more than could the two small adjustable lamps which diffused a somber orange glow in the cockpit; they helped just a little in reading the compass, already half-hidden beneath the dashboard, and might have helped to read a map. But what good was a map when flying in the pitch darkness of the blackout? The optical gunsight could be illuminated by the throw of a switch, and always was before going into combat, by day or by night, so there again there were no grounds for claiming it was specially adapted for night fighting. And on the right-hand side of the cockpit was a Morse key which operated a light beneath the cockpit, practically as invisible to ground observers by night as it was by day.

While the Hurricane was a formidable day fighter, had operated at night, and would in future do so, it was not designed as a specialized night fighter and would never properly perform as one. What the Hurricane did *not* possess told even more heavily against its suitability as a night fighter. First, it was not fitted with a radar set. Had it been possible to install one, there would be need as well for a radar operator. But the Hurricane was a single-seater. Single-engined too, which put it at a high risk in case of engine failure at night. If the "elastic" broke, there was little for it but to bail out. Moreover, its lusty Merlin engine spouted tongues of flame through "kidney"-type exhaust ports which, to prevent the pilot being blinded, were ingeniously screened from his sight. They were, however, visible to the enemy from afar.

And again: flying by night throughout the coming winter would expose both pilot and machine to subarctic temperatures. The Hurricane's cockpit, so uncomfortably hot low down in summer that I nearly always flew in shirt sleeves, became excruciatingly cold high up during the autumn nights. The nights of midwinter were sure to be torture, for the Hurricane's cockpit was too cramped and its instruments and levers too closely grouped to allow the wearing of bulky flying suits, boots, and thick gloves.

I pondered on all these forbidding thoughts, but it was not long before I felt resolved. Another passing thought for Nelson: it was Trafalgar Day and "England expects . . ." My mind dwelt no longer on the terrors of the night. We were, after all, fighters whose duty it was to defend Britain by night as well as by day. The day battle had been won, but London was still being cruelly and ceaselessly assaulted night after night, and that for the last six weeks. Nor were provincial cities spared. No one, not even Churchill, could possibly tell if, or when, the attacks would cease. He pondered gloomily at the time on the prospect of London's being gradually reduced to a rubble heap. Yet Londoners continued to treat the bombardment with disdain. They went about their business as usual, their pleasures too. Pubs, restaurants, and theaters were full, and it was always possible to jump on a tram or a bus, or hail a taxi to get you home. Churchill, who during the grim days of the Battle of France had frequently flown to Paris for talks with the government, was happy to see how the spirit of Londoners compared with "the frightful squawk" which had gone up from defeatist elements when the first few bombs fell upon the French capital.

London was "taking it," and at heavy cost. But we, its appointed guardians, were incapable of defending its seven million citizens at night. It was high time we came to their rescue. The bewildering contradictions of leading a specialized night-fighter squadron that might help, as we had by day in the defense of London and the provincial cities, no longer worried me. I now viewed the prospect as a formidable challenge, one which, in any case, could not be refused. But what tribulations lay ahead! On October 23, the squadron moved to Kirton-in-Lindsey, a grass field (yet another) in Lincolnshire. Ten miles away, at Caistor, we were allotted a spacious meadow as a "satellite" airfield. Half a dozen of us were well tried in night-flying, though hardly of the "specialized" type. The rest had yet to be converted and disciplined in this exacting and frustrating sort of warfare.

15

INVISIBLE BEAMS

While all through the long summer days the air battles had raged, the Germans and British were engaged, silently and obscurely, in the Wizard War. After the Dunkirk evacuation, in early June, the Germans set to, without delay, to erect a chain of *Knickebein* transmitters in northern France; word reached Dr. Jones through the underground that a Wotan transmitter—he had not yet any idea what that might be—was going up on the tip of the Cherbourg peninsula. The *Knickebein* chain was extended through Belgium and Holland as far north as Norway, but it was above all the collaborationist French Vichy government that, in handing on a platter to their friend Hitler airfields, ports, and beam-transmitter sites, gave the German conqueror all the additional means he could desire for subduing Britain, France's ally of yesterday. It was hardly thinkable that Hitler, with all these winning cards in hand, could possibly fail to "bring the British to their knees" (one of his favorite and oft-repeated expressions). Yet, while admiring the British people, he had still to discover their peculiar tenacity, never greater than when faced with an invader.

Like the airfields in France, the beam-transmitter sites, were they destined for *Knickebein* or, like Wotan, for some other electronic device, put the Luftwaffe within point-blank range of Britain. It was thus that during August, their bombers, with their easy-to-use *Knickebein*, were able to range at night across the length and breadth of the country, attacking small targets at will. Apparently it did not occur to them that they were prematurely showing their hand. When the British had once sorted out their own they would find that with their Headache, Aspirin, and meacons, it was they who held the winning cards.

On August 11 a Luftwaffe bomber unit, Kampfgruppe 100, moved, with its thirty or so Heinkel 111s, from its base in Germany to Meucon, near Vannes in Brittany. The field possessed only one small hangar and no runways; it had been used before the war by a private flying club. The men of KGr 100, after fighting hard in the Norwegian campaign (where a number of them were taken prisoner), returned to Germany to reform and train. After the rigors of Norway those were pleasant days; the sun shone and the water in the nearby lakes was warm. Often they would fly dressed only in swimming shorts and flying suits. Their move to Vannes excited no particular attention except among the locals, who remained distant, but polite, toward the first uniformed Germans they had yet encountered—an attitude which was not to last forever.

KGr 100's Heinkels were now painted black, with a matte distemper, which made them less visible at night, especially to searchlight crews. Apart from that they looked like any other Heinkel, except for the three short radio masts projecting from the top of the fuselage and, of course, the unit's own badge, a Viking ship, painted on the fore end of the fuselage. On August 13, as darkness fell at the end of Eagle Day, KGr 100's Heinkels took off on their first raid on England. It was they who scored those remarkable eleven direct hits on the Nuffield factory at Castle Bromwich, near Birmingham.

The expression *X-Geraet* (X-apparatus) was not unknown to RAF Intelligence. As early as March 1940 it had been pronounced by a Luftwaffe prisoner of war, who told his interrogator that *Knickebein* was "something like *X-Geraet*." The Y-service, too, had intercepted German Enigma high-grade cipher signals which when broken down by the cryptographers were found to mention *X-Geraet*. But still the intelligence men remained none the wiser—until mid-August, just at the time when KGr 100 began to bomb Britain. It was then that the Y-service picked up some unusual beam signals which at first mystified the experts. Dr. Jones had them code-named "Ruffians."

During the rest of August the Y-service, listening day and night, heard further references to *X-Geraet*. What was more, RAF direction-finding (D/F) stations succeeded in pinpointing the sources of the mysterious signals, one on the Cherbourg peninsula, others in the Pas de Calais. One night early in September, specially equipped RAF aircraft went up to sniff out the beams. The Cherbourg beam was found; it was in some ways comparable to *Knickebein*, which made it suspect of being a navigational aid. But as far as RAF Intelligence knew, the Luftwaffe possessed no radio receiver capable of being tuned to the extra-high frequency of the beam in question. So they assumed for the moment that the baffling signals must be used by the Kriegsmarine for guiding their ships into harbor.

In the Luftwaffe it was fairly common knowledge among aircrews that there did exist a hush-hush unit, which no one could name or number, a unit specialized in blind bombing. RAF Intelligence itself, vaguely aware of the same rumor, was certain sooner or later to discover the truth. This it eventually did during the interrogation of a KG 53 crew, shot down late in August. The German airmen named the specialized unit as KG 100—most precious information, though erroneous in one respect. Instead of KG—*Kampfgeschwader*, with a strength of about one hundred aircraft—they should have said KGr—*Kampfgruppe*, a unit some thirty-five aircraft strong. Small matter (though the error was to persist for some time in British secret documents). With the Luftwaffe unit's number—100—Air Intelligence were now hot on the scent, helped by the Y-service. Further indiscretions by captured Luftwaffe aircrews during interrogation or as they chatted to one another, unaware that the British were eavesdropping with hidden microphones, gave away more secrets.

By the end of September, Dr. Jones had fitted together enough pieces of the puzzle for Professor Lindemann to inform the prime minister that "the Germans are making great efforts to improve the accuracy of their night bombing." He mentioned that the new beams had been detected and went on: "One *Kampfgeschwader*, KG 100, consisting of about forty machines, has been equipped with special new apparatus to exploit the beams," which, he believed, would enable them to put down their bombs within twenty yards of the target. Here he exaggerated somewhat. Their accuracy, in practice, was more like 120 yards, but such marksmanship was deadly enough.

"The Prof" also confirmed: "We know the exact location of the sources of the beams in question." This being so, he suggested three possible means of defense against the new bombing menace. Either the enemy bombers might be destroyed on the ground by the RAF bombing Vannes, or the beam transmitters might be knocked out by aerial bombing or commando attack, or, finally, the beams themselves could be neutralized by radio jamming.

The last method, in which the RAF was becoming expert, was the one chosen. Dr. Cockburn, of the Telecommunications Research Establishment at Swanage, was immediately summoned to produce a suitable jammer. But, as in the case of *Knickebein*, no such ready-made apparatus existed, so the ingenious doctor borrowed an army radio set and modified it, giving it the code name "Bromide." Like Aspirin, the special *Knickebein* jammers, Bromide could not be manufactured overnight in sufficient numbers. Many, many nights of Luftwaffe raids were to pass while Cockburn and his team toiled away to meet the demand. In the interval, "KG 100," the suspected villains, continued with impunity and precision to "mark," with medium-weight explosive bombs, the selected target, from which the upward-leaping flames formed a beacon for the rest of the attacking bombers, navigating with less accurate *Knickebein*. Sometimes KGr 100, instead of marking targets for mass raids, attacked on its own some isolated target, unaware that, on each occasion, it was imprinting its own particular trade mark on the target. Dr. Jones's intelligence sleuths, true to the Sherlock Holmes tradition, were quick to discover that the line of craters left by the "stick" of German bombs, when extended southwards on a map, invariably led back to the *X-Geraet* directional-beam transmitter on the Cherbourg peninsula. Elementary, my dear Jones!

Knickebein was beginning to run into trouble. At first the Luftwaffe crews had been excited by their new and simple navigational aid. But captured airmen confirmed that they very soon had the uncomfortable feeling that the British were fiddling with it. To begin with, when only Headache, the collection of modified diathermy and Lorenz sets, was at work, the jamming, though fairly weak, was enough to give disconcerting proof to the Germans that the enemy had rumbled their *Knickebein*; that he knew exactly the target for which the bombers were heading, and could warn the defending night fighters and AA guns accordingly. Considering the shortcomings of our night defenses, the effect of Headache was rather more psychological than practical. But it was a good start to the jamming offensive, soon to be reinforced by Aspirin.

Aspirin was ready to join the invisible defense just as the night blitz against London began in early September. Its dots and dashes, disagreeing with *Knickebein*, put confusion among the German bombers, sending some of them literally flying in circles or ending up lost in the pitch dark. The meacons, false radio beacons planted by the British, added to the havoc played with the enemy's radio navigation system. Even KGr 100's planes, so far immune to jamming as they approached the target, were not spared as they tuned in to their radio beacons on their way back to base. One of their Heinkels returning to Vannes after a raid on Birmingham in late August was caught out by one of the phony beacons, situated at Templecombe in Somerset. The *Beobachter* (observer), Feldwebel Hilmar Schmidt, was certain they were homing on the beacon at Brest, south of Vannes, when he became muddled by a series of bearings so misleading that he yelled over the intercom, "Christ, we're not flying backwards, are we?" When searchlights held their Heinkel, Schmidt called to the *Fleugfuehrer* (pilot), Knier, "I think we're over England!" Knier then turned onto a southeasterly course which, he hoped, would lead them to hit the French coast somewhere. When at last they landed, bewildered and exhausted, it was at Berck, near Boulogne, about 250 miles from their base at Vannes!

By the end of September, KGr 100 had made some forty raids on Britain, half of them on London, the rest on industrial targets; if "near misses" were more frequent than direct hits, the exceptional precision of its bombing, compared with that of other units, was evident. In October the usual load of high-explosive bombs carried in KGr 100's Heinkels was replaced by a full load of incendiaries, packed into containers which opened automatically as they fell, scattering their fire-setting devices. Considering KGr 100's prowess in precision bombing, it was surprising that the unit should switch to such a nonprecision weapon. But the precision, however diminished, would prove adequate, and the reason for the incendiaries was soon made clear. In the meantime, RAF Intelligence had enough evidence, both hearsay and that culled from the air by the Y-service, to link "KG 100" (as the British still called the unit) directly with *X-Geraet*. Tangible evidence, which would reveal the whole system and its possibilities, was still lacking. The British would have to wait a little longer.

16

BOMBERS' MOON

Autumn was fading into winter. Since the first week in September, when the blitz started, the city had been raided every single night by an average of over 150 bombers, and often there had been day raids too. People were now beginning to find the deadly routine almost monotonous. The sirens would begin wailing just as, in the failing light, workers left the office or shop to queue patiently, perhaps a little fearfully, in the damp cold for the next bus or tube train. Home at last and weary, they would sit down to a dull and meager supper, then automatically go off to the shelter—if minded that way—or like the majority go straight to bed. Sleeping fitfully through the night bombardment, they could rely on the "all clear" to wake them around 6:00 next morning. Then, after a quick breakfast of tasteless "national" bread, sparingly spread with butter or, failing that, margarine and washed down with a cup or two of tea, they would be off soon after 7:00 for another day's grind. Yet Londoners seldom failed to find something to laugh about in their dreary, daily round.

At 1 Helen Street, Woolwich, all the Callow family went off cheerfully every day to work. The old man was back at his job in the big-gun shop, now temporarily repaired. The day over, he would pay his customary visit to the Little Bull, where he would stand chatting with his mates and sinking pint after pint until closing time. Nothing on earth, and least of all in the dark heavens, could intimidate either publicans or their patrons; opening and closing times were faithfully respected. Mrs. Callow, "the old girl," as her husband called her, seldom went out, but did sometimes accompany her husband on Saturday nights to the local. For this good lady a visit to the Little Bull was as good as going to Buckingham Palace, and she dressed up in her finery for the occasion. One port and lemon, or at the very most two, would last her the whole evening.

It was during a heavy raid one night in mid-October, when the moon was full, that the door of the Little Bull was flung open and there stood a man, panting and shouting: "Heard the terrible news?" While he caught his breath, the startled patrons were expecting at least to hear that the Germans had landed or the prime minister was dead; then the man spluttered, "The Eagle's been hit!" A groan went up from the patrons of the Little Bull; the Eagle was another of their favorite pubs. The news was bad enough, but sadly worse was to come—many of the Eagle's patrons had that night drunk their last pint on this earth.

Cinemas, too, never closed. Renée, Ray's youngest sister, was on duty ushering at the Granada every day. When the sirens went, a polite warning was flashed on the screen. "If patrons wish to leave, they are invited to do so." Few did. At the Arsenal, vital target as it was for the Luftwaffe, the workers, Ray's sisters, Amy and Rose, and Kathleen, Johnny's wife, among them, were now so used to the sirens, the "moaning minnies," that they left their work for the shelters only if the raid was signaled overhead. Mercifully, of the scores of bombs which fell on the Arsenal, none scored a bull's-eye on the Danger Buildings, where Kathleen was sewing up bags of cordite. Kathleen was on the job at 8:00 every morning. Back home at 7:00 P.M., her day was not yet finished. Kathy spent two out of three nights alone, while Johnny was on duty at the fire station. Throughout the night, as an air-raid warden, she stood by, sleeping fully clothed, waiting for a possible telephone call. When it came she reported, a few minutes later, to the air-raid post. Next morning, around 7:00, she was off again to work in the Arsenal.

Young Ray, too, was busy day and night, though at his school, Burrage Grove, where the ground floor had been taken over by the AFS as a substation, a shortage of teachers meant less work and more play —fun while it lasted, but Ray would later have to make good his neglected education. His day began with football, but when, after their night's battle with the flames, the firemen returned, their equipment was washed down on the playground. That put an end to football and there began a long session in the classroom, where, at least for Ray bent over his aircraft models, the hours passed quickly. Back home at the end of the afternoon, the serious work began. As the family shopper, he ran, literally, errands for his mother, buying the few household necessaries she could afford and food, in return for ration coupons. At the same time he scrounged firewood to keep the single home fire burning. Ray ran everywhere; it was the best way of keeping warm, now that winter was round the corner. He and the gang had invented their patent hand-warmer—a fifty-cigarette tin pierced with a few holes and filled with smoking embers. They whirled it round on the end of a length of string. The embers glowed, heating the tin, which they clasped with their frozen hands.

Every evening, in scout's uniform and tin hat, Ray ran down to the Town Hall to report for duty to his troop leader. From the basement, which could shelter two hundred, the incessant demand for tea kept him busy. But working outside appealed far more to his adventurous spirit. No matter if the bombs kept raining down, Ray kept running, alone, taking messages from the shelter marshals, carrying bags full of fish and chips to the hungry wardens. Around midnight he ran back home, and then, as he would say in his Londoner's rhyming slang, it was up the "apples and pears"—the stairs—through the "Rory O'More"—the door—and into "Uncle Ned"—bed, tired and happy at having done his bit for his country.

On Sundays he would put on his "whistle and flute"—his suit—and go for a "ball of chalk"—a walk—which nearly always took him up to his brother Bert's balloon site on Woolwich Common. He was never without a bucket as he walked, for Ray and his gang vied with each other in collecting shrapnel—shell and bomb splinters. The nosecap of an AA shell was their most coveted find.

Early in October, one of Bert's balloons came under enemy fire when a German plane dived down out of the night, its guns blazing. Holed by bullets, the unwieldy gray monster began to deflate and sink earthwards. It flopped down in the middle of Woolwich, its wire cable, nearly a mile long, wrapping itself round houses and a tramcar. Firemen took many hours to unravel the tangle.

The embarrassment caused by Bert's balloon was, at least for the firemen, a minor incident compared with the perils of firefighting. During these ceaseless nights of bombardment, Johnny and his comrades, armed only with hoses, yielded not an inch of ground in their private war against the Luftwaffe. One of their fiercest battles was fought at the Rotherhithe oil refinery, on the U-bend of the Thames. Johnny's number two, Fred Cosh, was at the wheel as they sped down Evelyne Street, where his parents kept a café. Fred's first thoughts were for them. "Hope the bleedin' café's not burning,'' he murmured feelingly. It was not, but houses nearby were going up in flames. These were personal tragedies, destroying the cherished belongings and often the lives of the occupants.

The Rotherhithe oil refinery was another affair, a monstrous impersonal conflagration. One of the huge, shiny cylindrical oil tanks had become a volcano of belching fire and dense black smoke. Pierced by bomb splinters, it spewed forth hot crude oil, greenish in color, which fed the encircling flames and seeped further afield, forming a slimy, evil-smelling lake. Into it the firemen waded in order to play their cooling jets of water onto another tank and prevent it exploding. As they advanced nearly waist-high in oil they could feel it oozing over the top of their high boots, filling them from the feet upwards, then creeping up their thighs till it soaked through to their underpants. At least, at that depth, the surrounding oil helped to support them. As it dispersed and the level fell, the firemen began to slither and flounder in the foul green sludge. Occasionally one of them slipped and fell flat, and his mates, laughing, helped him up again, daubed from head to foot in the smeary, viscous mess. Thus Johnny and his team, with dozens of other firemen, fought on for twelve hours through the night until dawn, when relief came at last. It was not before that evening that the blaze was extinguished, the battle won.

Toward mid-October the moon, to the Luftwaffe's relief, was waxing. For them, bombing in the pitch dark held no appeal. They had been trained to perfection to bomb by day, and this they did during the Battle of France, though frequently attacking towns without the slightest discrimination for the civilian population. The devastation and terror they caused earned them the name "the invincible Luftwaffe." The Battle of Britain robbed them of that envious title. Their losses were far heavier than the RAF's—every aircrew knew it, and realized too that such losses could no longer be sustained. The Luftwaffe bombers were thus driven to attack under cover of darkness—a lesson that RAF Bomber Command, following its own appalling losses during daylight raids, had more quickly understood. With their traditional practice of D/R—dead reckoning—navigation, the RAF crews more often than not managed to pinpoint their targets at night, though they did not always hit them.

The bombers of the Luftwaffe, when attacking British targets by day, had generally obeyed strict orders not to bomb unless the target was clearly visible; when it was not they returned to base with their bomb load. Identifying a target in daylight was one thing; at night it posed a far more serious problem, and the Luftwaffe's system of radio-beam navigation and the automatic release of their bombs did not require any precise pinpointing of the target. Certainly, there were conscientious aircrews who tried, but in the darkness they all too often failed.

With such inhibitions, the Luftwaffe soon began to feel that there was little profit in night bombing, though this did not deter them in the least from scattering high explosive and incendiary bombs all over London. Those crews who fell into British hands tried to justify themselves by claiming that they had aimed at searchlight and AA sites. Crews who were known to have dropped land mines—which, impossible to aim accurately, were the ultimate in indiscriminate attack on the civil population—would not admit to it, though they agreed that these weapons were being used. One Luftwaffe man remarked that land mines were, after all, just the thing for blasting small houses into ruins. Others like him betrayed the same streak of sadism—as indeed did some of our own bomber aircrews, like the distinguished pilot, a man of dauntless courage, who harangued me one day with the need to "give it 'em back": "We must bomb the lot, men, women, and children." Not all bomber crews were so inhuman. Their chief concern was to hit the target. A Luftwaffe bomb aimer, when told that his bombs had fallen on workers' houses and killed women and children, broke down and sobbed, "I'm sorry, it's terrible."

Londoners also cried out to be avenged. When Churchill came among them in the ruins of their homes, they cheered him and shouted, "Give it 'em back!" Londoners were "taking it," and it was hardly surprising that they called out for vengeance against equally innocent and defenseless German civilians. This was total war, fought not by armed men alone but by civilians too. They were in the front line and as brave as any.

The Luftwaffe was well in its stride in the offensive aimed, in Goering's words, at "the progressive annihilation of London." Its bombers were provided with improved equipment: dinghies fitted with automatic SOS radio transmitters and, on some of the Dornier 17s, inflatable bags to keep the aircraft afloat. For the comfort of the crew there was an extra supply of first-aid kits, tins of chocolate dosed with caffeine, and special "Pervertine" pills to sustain them against the rigors following a "ditching" in the sea—and, an innovation, special steel helmets for wireless operators, apparently more vulnerable than their crewmates.

The clean lines of many Dorniers and Heinkels were disfigured by a clumsy-looking but effective antiballoon device—a metal bar extending from each side of the aircraft's nose to the wingtip, with a cutting edge to sever the cable. However, all this additional paraphernalia, which also included side machine guns, armor plating, and, eventually, a fifth crewman, had to be paid for by reducing the bomb load; otherwise, with the limited takeoff run on most Continental airfields, the bomber could not get safely airborne.

The bombs with which the Luftwaffe assailed London were of several types, each with a resounding name: *Splittenbomben* (metal fragmentation), *Betonbomben* (concrete fragmentation), *Sprengbomben* (high explosive), *Minenbomben* (mines), and *Panzersprengenbomben* (armor-piercing). They came in a variety of sizes and, again, under a bizarre assortment of names: Satan, the super-heavy (*uberschwere*) of 1,800 kilograms; Kampfgeschwader 55 was the "Satan" specialist, bombing with the high-precision Lofte sight from about 20,000 feet. Next came another super-heavy, Fritz, weighing 1,400 kilograms. The "heaviest" (*schwerste*) category included two high-explosive bombs of 1,000 kilograms, Esau and Hermann (a doubtful compliment to Goering). Bombs of 500 kilograms were labeled "heavy" (*schwere*); then followed the lighter weights, 250 and 50 kilograms. Every one of them hellish weapons in their particular way, they brought death and lasting injury to tens of thousands of British civilians. Yet those which, in the end, were to prove more devastating were the *Flammenbomben* (literally "flame bombs") and *Brandbomben* (firebombs or incendiaries). The Flam 500 and Flam 250, filled with oil (the British called them oil bombs), sent up a huge mushroom flame on impact. The *Brandbomben*, each weighing a kilogram, were packed, thirty-six at a time, in containers which, as they fell, opened automatically, scattering their fire-raising contents.

Such, then, were the arms and the men pitted against the people of London, and later her sister cities in the provinces, in the implacable war in the dark.

Another arm had for some time been the subject of talk among the Luftwaffe—gas. Rumors had been circulating for some time that the British had used gas shells at Dunkirk and that a Whitley bomber, forced down at Oldenfield, in Germany, was loaded with canisters containing "microbes." Although these rumors were entirely groundless, it was true that the British were well prepared against gas warfare. As young Ray had experienced, the risk of gas had been ceaselessly drummed into the public, young and old. Wardens lectured Ray and his fellow pupils at Burrage Grove School on the subject. Every British citizen possessed a gas mask. Johnny and his friends invariably carried theirs wherever they went. We, too, in the armed forces. I myself had been on a gas course and learned how to identify, by smell or otherwise, the various types of gas. I had been made to wear gasproof clothing—"goon skins"—and had stood with a group on Salisbury Plain while an aircraft flew overhead and sprayed us with a reddish liquid which, had it been the real thing, and but for our goon skins and masks, would have blistered our skin, congested our lungs, and finally left us dying in agony.

Although the frightful eventuality of gas warfare had not yet materialized, it was never far from the minds of Luftwaffe aircrews. They were firmly convinced, however, that Germany would not be the first to use gas. The Fuehrer, they recalled, was an old infantryman, he was "kind and human," and so, they thought, would never employ such a fiendish weapon. But if the British were to employ it first, Germany would retaliate with both gas and bacteria warfare. And Britain, the theory went, being small and overcrowded, would be at a disadvantage.

As the war, to Hitler's dismay, dragged on into October, attitudes began to change. If things came to a stalemate it was possible that Germany might attempt to force a decision by using gas, the lethal kind or, perhaps, *Nervengas*, which had a stupefying effect lasting six hours or so. If, on the other hand, the British became desperate, it was they who might be the first to resort to gas warfare, in which case Hitler (kind and human as he was thought to be) would order immediate reprisals. In any case, the German public, whose gas-mask filters had not been renewed since the outbreak of war, were now being prepared for the worst. The Luftwaffe, too, was ready, with 50-kilogram gas bombs, and trials had been held at Neustadt with low-flying Dornier 17s spraying gas.

There were not a few Luftwaffe men who during the months-long air offensive to subdue Britain had "outflown" themselves, were worn down to nervous wrecks or suffering from "tummy trouble" and various other disorders. They were sent off to sanatoria in Germany for treatment. But the men now flying against London were in good shape, despite their doubts about night bombing. The euphoria generated by the promise of invasion and a quick victory had passed. Now they were more philosophical. The war against Britain was not going to be easy, but their confidence in the Fuehrer remained undiminished. Invasion, if not for now, would certainly be for spring 1941. In the meantime the war of attrition they were themselves waging against Britain would wear down "that contemptible little island," as some of them called it, and make it easy for the Wehrmacht, when it invaded, to overrun it in a few weeks.

Luftwaffe airmen showed surprise at the prolonged resistance of Londoners, and wondered whether Berliners, if put to the same ordeal, would ever hold out so long. But they still felt little fear for our night defenses, although they seemed to be improving. Balloons were a nuisance and had on occasions proved fatal to German bombers who had ventured too low. British searchlights appeared to be more numerous and powerful than their own, and our AA guns, which, unknown to the Germans, were now being fitted with radar GL (gun-laying), were unquestionably shooting with greater accuracy. Both searchlights and guns, however, sited as they were in and around London and other great cities, were a help to the Luftwaffe pilots in identifying, if not their precise target, the city where it lay.

Identification of the target was always the bugbear. The Luftwaffe men longed for the bombers' moon, when, given good weather, they could find their way around London with ease. In clear moonlight it was simple to follow the Thames—the river itself or the fog hanging over it. Large parks, where there were lakes or ponds, were familiar and favorite landmarks, as was St. Paul's, especially at sunrise and sunset or under the moon when London's great cathedral cast long, sharply defined shadows. Railway lines, too, converging on the main termini, glistened in the moonlight, which revealed as if in the daytime such unmistakable landmarks as Buckingham Palace, Trafalgar Square, Hyde Park, and the Houses of Parliament.

Now, in this month of October, under the waxing moon, London lay wide open to the Luftwaffe, whose aircrews rejoiced. Toward the middle of the month, Londoners began talking of the "bombers' moon" and told each other, "We're going to get it heavy tonight." The enemy bombers made the most of the moonlight period to batter the capital with repeated, well-directed blows. The heaviest raid of all hit London on the 15th, under the full moon. More than 400 aircraft attacked; 430 civilians were killed and 900 more were maimed and mutilated while all night long the moon shed its gentle light on the massacre. Five main railway termini—Waterloo, Victoria, St. Pancras, Marylebone, and Broad Street—were so badly knocked about that traffic had to be diverted for some days. Yet the following morning commuters from the suburbs somehow managed to get into the city for another day's work—late perhaps, after picking their way through streets strewn with shattered masonry and the tangle of firemen's hoses. No matter how awful the shambles, the tradition was "business as usual."

The Callow family had some narrow escapes, but their luck held. Incendiaries fell on the house next door to Johnny's. Luckily he was at home, off duty, that night. He rushed in through his neighbor's front door (unlocked, as custom decreed) and up the stairs, where an incendiary bomb was sputtering on the floor of a bedroom. He threw a bucket of water at it, but missed. So with his bare hand he picked up the incendiary and hurled it out through the hole it had already made in the roof—a brave act, for a proportion of the Luftwaffe's *Brandbomben* were fitted with an explosive charge. As it was, Johnny got away with burns on his hand. "All right, old Callow," his chief, Fire Commander Thompson, told him, "you needn't report for duty tomorrow." But Leading Fireman Callow turned up all the same.

Fate played curious tricks, some tragic, others, fortunately, comic. A few nights later, Thompson, a fearless and respected leader, was dozing when the alarm went. With a sudden effort he rolled off his bunk and bent over to pull on his boots. The movement dislodged his two false teeth, which he promptly swallowed. Johnny hurried him off to the hospital, where, next day, the denture reappeared from the other end of his digestive tract. Johnny, on hearing the news, called on his chief. "Congratulations," he told him with a smile, "I hear you've had twins."

In Mr. and Mrs. Callow's bedroom at 1 Helen Street were two beds, a wide one in which the old man slept when off for the night, and a truckle bed beside it, in which the old girl lay beside him. When he was away on night shift, she slept in the big bed. And so it happened that one night, while he was away at work, a heavy jagged splinter fell on the house, smashing clean through the roof and tearing a hole in the bedclothes and mattress of the bed where Mrs. Callow usually slept.

Some nights later, Mrs. Callow's daughter Rose was rudely awakened when a dud AA shell came clattering down the chimney and plopped onto the floor of her bedroom. A lady in a neighboring street, on the other hand, while sitting out a raid before her empty fireplace, was blown up the chimney by the blast of a nearby landmine. She emerged, bruised but unhurt, and as black as a sweep.

Young Ray, too, was in luck one night. As he closed the main door of the Town Hall behind him and ran into Wellington Street, there came the whistle of a bomb, uncomfortably close. He made to throw himself flat, but the bomb beat him to it, as it exploded not many yards away.

The blast bowled him over, landing him in a small heap on the pavement and paralyzing the right side of his cheerful young face. Ray, forty-five years later, still suffers.

As the moon waned, there came no letup in the savage, unrelenting monotony of the bombardment—save for a single night, November 3, when poor weather and pitch dark deterred the Luftwaffe. Then the November moon began to wax, and Londoners once more told each other, "We're going to get it heavy." No one could tell how much longer London would have to endure. Churchill himself expected the city to be reduced to "a heap of rubble." Luftwaffe aircrews themselves felt the "London run" was becoming a dreary routine. While Unteroffizier Horst Goetz, a pilot in KGr 100, admired the "great show" provided by the London AA guns, they seldom scathed any of the unit's aircraft. His own was never touched. Occasionally he caught sight of a night fighter which apparently never saw his Heinkel. He summed up those ten weeks of ceaseless nightly raids on London as being like running a bus service. A bus service which accounted for the lives of nearly thirteen thousand Londoners—innocents like the family of seven, parents and five young children, who were all killed by a single bomb in Woolwich one night. But secret signs were coming through to British Intelligence that the Germans had by now realized that just as they had failed to crush the British fighters, they would never succeed in subduing London. The signs portended a change in Luftwaffe strategy.

•

17

NIGHT LIFE, NIGHT DEATH

While London fought the Luftwaffe and the other great cities stood firm under occasional attack, Britain's night defenses, as Unteroffizier Goetz had noticed, were having but a negligible effect against the Luftwaffe's offensive. During those long nights of London's martyrdom, we in 85 Squadron, destined as we were to be a specialized night-fighter unit, could not raise a little finger to help. Our pilots, unaccustomed to flying in the dark, had been zealously training, night after night, to attain the necessary skill and confidence, while the few of us who were already initiated flew regular but futile night patrols.

Since our move to Kirton-in-Lindsey on October 23, our night life had been full with training and patrols, but an occasional diversion brought relief from the incessant routine. Hardly had we arrived when the secretary of state for air, Sir Archibald Sinclair, descended upon us, accompanied by the officer commanding No. 12 Group, Air Vice Marshal Leigh-Mallory. "Archie" Sinclair, leader of the Liberal Party, appeared, at least in a sartorial sense, a man of the old school. Despite the cold, clammy air and the mud of Kirton, he wore, as was his invariable habit, a black jacket, striped trousers and spats, starched butterfly collar and bow tie, and a black homburg hat to match. In his carefully articulated speech he spoke kindly, congratulating me on the squadron's fine record (we had yet to establish one as night fighters). He was deeply interested in our new role, about which we conversed at length. I pleaded with him to give us airborne radar (AI) and suitable aircraft with adequate endurance and armament to ensure successful interception and combat at night. I begged him, too, that as long as we had to make do with Hurricanes he would see to it that our eight .303 guns were armed with the most effective ammunition. At present they were loaded with an even mixture of "ball," armor-piercing, tracer, and "De Wilde"—the last, which made a flash on striking the target, was the most deadly. I argued that since by night our chances of intercepting the enemy, let alone engaging him in combat, were so slender that we needed a high proportion of the most lethal ammunition available—De Wilde. This, said Sir Archibald, was not, unfortunately, possible. The De Wilde factory had been demolished during a raid in September, and supplies were not freely available.

We discussed the possibilities of a radar set for single-seater fighters. In theory it was feasible, but no one believed that in the dark the pilot alone could concentrate at once on flying his aircraft mainly by the seat of his pants, listening to the controller's directions, and watching the radar cathode tube. So I banished this idea from my mind, but held fast to my request for maximum striking power. The logic was so simple; we were not going to intercept often, so the expenditure of De Wilde would be limited; but when we did chance to intercept we should possess the best possible means of knocking down the enemy. Oddly enough, my argument never got through to the great ones until months later.

Leigh-Mallory was listening carefully. Though not born a fighter pilot (he was originally in army cooperation) he was always deeply interested in what his fighter pilots had to say. Douglas Bader, the famous legless pilot, was the most influential though not the only of Leigh-Mallory's soothsayers, and his persuasive views on tactics led to a bitter quarrel between L-M and Keith Park, who commanded 11 Group. I had met them both some years before the war started and admired them both in their different ways. When I took over 85 Squadron in June it was in 12 Group under Leigh-Mallory and I got to know him better. Then we had moved south into 11 Group, where I had more chance of appreciating the great qualities of Park. Now we were back again in 12 Group with L-M. I had a feeling that he had an avuncular interest in me, perhaps because he and his brother George (lost near the summit of Mount Everest in 1924) had, as kids, known my mother when she lived at Hartford Hall in Cheshire.

On the morning following the departure of those eminent gentlemen I was nearly killed by enemy fire—not, I hasten to say, in some heroic combat, but while chatting quietly on the ground at Caistor, our satellite airfield, with Jim Marshall, one of our flight commanders. He was a likable fellow, about twenty-two, tall, thin, and smily. He seemed to take a pleasure, which I shared, in teasing me, keeping always just within the limits of respect for me as his boss. I could always count on his loyalty and valued his advice. He had fought with the squadron in France.

As we chatted, Jim suddenly dived at me, dragging me to the ground with him on top of me. I went down wondering what on earth had incited this apparently unprovoked offense of striking a senior officer when I caught sight of a Heinkel streaking just above the hedge less than a hundred yards away, the rear gunner pouring forth tracer which zipped just above our heads. We quickly recovered from our surprise, jumped to our feet, and yelled, "Start up!" I could move as fast as anyone on one leg and a stick, but before reaching my Hurricane I was dismayed to see the fitter standing on the wing holding part of the engine cowling in his hand. "Button her up, quick!" I shouted, but it took him another two minutes. Jim was away well before me. Then I was off, the loose straps of my parachute and fighting harness clacking noisily in the slipstream against the outside of the fuselage until, once airborne, I had time to buckle them up. At "naught feet" I scoured the local countryside, without result. Jim, however, caught that brave Heinkel and sent it down, but not before it had bombed Kirton, demolishing our squadron offices. Luckily our adjutant, Tim Moloney, and the orderly-room staff had gone for lunch. That evening Tim wrote solemnly in the squadron diary: "85 has been bombed at Seclin, Merville [in France], Debden, Croydon, and Kirton. Total casualties, 1 killed."

The damp soil of the Caistor "satellite" airfield was soon churned into a quagmire, so we returned to Kirton, there to install ourselves permanently and persevere with the conditioning of our pilots to night-fighting tactics and procedure, where the weather, be it said, was an ever-present menace. Fortunately those pilots were not yet as aware as the few of us already "night-operational" of our almost hopeless task, lacking, as we did, the proper equipment, above all airborne radar and an effective armament. Our morale, notwithstanding, was high, and it received a little extra boost when, one black night at the end of October, Sammy Allard, more by luck than by his own or the controller's judgment, intercepted an enemy aircraft. Not that this fluke was any reflection on his skill. A good-humored Yorkshireman with a fine head of flaxen hair and a ready if slightly mocking smile, he was another veteran of the Battle of France. As a pilot, by day or by night, he had no equal in the squadron.

Sammy, patrolling unconcernedly, suddenly saw tracer, from an invisible source, piercing the darkness. He then sighted the navigation lights of two aircraft, no doubt our own, for the tracer was flying in their direction. Sammy closed immediately on the source of the tracer, and although unable to discern the shape of an aircraft he could clearly see its exhaust flames, upon which he opened fire, only to be blinded by his own tracer and lose sight of his target.

The very next night, as black as the last, Sergeant Geoff Goodman, while on patrol, was surprised to see tracer flying all around him. Like Allard, he fired back at the point from which it came, but his aggressor made off unseen in the dark.

Yet again, some nights later, Sergeant Berkley had a somewhat different encounter. Berkley, a newcomer to the squadron and no veteran of the earlier fighting, soon showed his prowess as a pilot. Hardly more than twenty, he was a tall and soft-spoken Irishman whose well-trimmed mustache added to his charm. Patrolling high up under the nearly full November moon, the blaze of incendiaries attracted his attention. Down he went, hoping to pick out the enemy bomber against the dazzling carpet of light, but it was he, unfortunately, who became the victim of this maneuver, offering himself as a silhouette to the enemy, who showered him with tracer. And talking of tracer, it must be remembered that for every glowing tracer bullet there are four or five more, invisible, of ball and armor-piercing, as well as the Luftwaffe's answer to our own De Wilde—7.92mm chromium-tipped bullets which exploded on impact.

Although these fleeting incidents marked the very beginnings of our career which would transform us into a specialized night-fighter squadron, they did teach us a lesson or two. Young Berkley's attempt to spot the enemy aircraft silhouetted against the fires started by incendiaries was soon to become a regular tactic, when British cities were consumed by fire sent down upon them by Kampfgruppe 100 in their new role of a *Beleuchtergruppe*, fire-lighters and incidentally the first Pathfinders.

The other lesson was that of exhaust flames. Those seen by Sammy Allard and Geoff Goodman came almost certainly from the twin Fafnir engines of a Dornier 17Z, now being used by the Luftwaffe as a night fighter. The defect of this otherwise excellent power unit was its short exhaust pipes, the flames from which could easily be seen. It was likewise with our Hurricanes, but the time had come at last to change the exhaust system. We flew our Hurricanes to the Rolls-Royce works at Hucknall, near Nottingham, where in little more than the twinkling of an eye, the company's fitters removed the old "kidney-type" flame-belching exhausts and replaced them with "stub" exhausts, short and flat, one for each of the twelve cylinders. By cooling and damping the flames they rendered them invisible. In return, they gave an exhaust note more deafening than ever, with a racy, staccato crackle when the engine was throttled back for landing. Those were beginners' lessons —more difficult ones were yet to come. Slowly, ever so slowly, we were creeping forward, but a long, dark road still lay ahead.

During these nights, when not on patrol, my place was on the flare path beside the Chance floodlight, connected by field telephone to the operations room and the control tower. A radio set kept me in touch with the pilots navigating tentatively in the dark sky above. Well wrapped against the cold in a sheepskin jacket and wool-lined flying boots, I could keep a close, if blind, eye on them, listen for signs of trouble, and transmit messages to them.

It was on a clear moonlight night in November, while the floodlight was illuminated, ready for François de Labouchère to come in and land, that another aircraft, invisible but with a decidedly odd exhaust note, flew low overhead. "Switch off, quickly," I told the floodlight operator, certain that it was not one of ours. Then to François I called, "Turn out your navigation lights. Enemy aircraft in vicinity." Then I rang the control tower. "It's okay," replied the duty officer. "It's one of our bombers preparing to land. He's just dropped a message." At that moment the "message" exploded—a 50-kilogram bomb, I should say—and the aircraft was back, machine-gunning vigorously in our direction. The floodlight operator and I both dived under its solid steel chassis. There then followed several moments of acute suspense. François, who had evidently not understood my message, was on his final approach, navigation lights still burning—a sitting duck for the enemy air gunner—while I peered out from beneath the floodlight calling him repeatedly on the radio, "Turn out your lights," but still he did not heed the message. "We'll have to get out and switch on the light," I told the operator, and we crawled out into the open. The floodlight threw its beam down the flare path and the suspense became unbearable. At last François touched down; I gave him a few more seconds to run out after his landing, then, "Out with the light!" I called to the operator.

The enemy aircraft was back, and I could now recognize the silhouette of a Dornier 17, its exhaust flames clearly visible. By some miracle no one, apparently, inside it had sighted François, who was now taxiing back towards the floodlight, his navigation lights still burning. I threw off my jacket and raced towards him, signalling to him to leave the motor running, jump out and—tapping frantically on his nearest navigation light—to switch them both off. He understood at last and a moment later was on the ground beside me. Above the crackle and slipstream of the motor I shouted in his ear, "Give me your helmet and parachute!" Though neither fitted properly, I somehow got into them.

At that moment the Dornier came back, very low this time, raking the airfield with machine-gun fire and sending François and me headlong for cover—he beneath the fuselage of the Hurricane and I under the tailplane, both of which, being covered in fabric, gave no protection whatever. However, it felt better to be under something, no matter what! Then the Dornier was gone, and a moment later I was up in the cockpit and roaring off the ground in hot pursuit of the intruder. Directed by the controller, I chased him, flat-out, eastwards into the breaking dawn, but having too much start on me he was gone.

The fun we had that night, if at times somewhat undignified, was all the same exhilarating. It could have been more so had our good friend François had more practice at the game. He had actually sighted the Dornier, closed in behind it, and followed it (his navigation lights on), but, unsure of its identity, he was afraid to open fire. Otherwise, as Tim Moloney noted in the diary, "85's first night victory might have been a Frenchman's."

On November 6 a signal came in from 12 Group headquarters, ordering the squadron to move to Gravesend, east of London on the southern bank of the Thames estuary. With it came a personal message from L-M: "Sorry you are leaving 12 Group again." That was nice of him.

We were not, however, quite ready to leave. I could not yet declare my outfit "night-operational," because of François and Emile. The language problem was still bugging them, and it was not safe to let them loose in the dark against the enemy. They persevered meanwhile in mastering the "patter" between pilot and controller. It would not take them long. No. 85 Squadron was heading in the right direction.

This was far from being the case that morning of November 6, with a Heinkel 111, registered number 6N + BH, of Kampfgruppe 100. It had taken off from Vannes, loaded with six 250-kilogram HE bombs and two Flam. 250s to attack Birmingham. At the controls was Feldwebel Hans Lehmann. The rest of the crew were all *Feldwebelen*, too: Otto Paul, Ludwig Meyerhoffer, and Heinz Bitte. They climbed up through solid cloud on a compass course, heading northeast via the Saint Malo beacon, intending to intercept the directional *X-Geraet* beam from the Cherbourg transmitter. But that night they were out of luck. Lehmann soon realized that the gyro (automatic) and magnetic compass readings differed by 90 degrees. Reckoning that he must be somewhere over southwest England, Lehmann let down, hoping to break cloud, find Bristol, and unload his bombs onto that vital and historic port. But Bristol was shrouded in cloud. The four *Feldwebelen* and their Heinkel were completely lost. Then, to his relief, the wireless op, Meyerhoffer, obtained a signal which he recognized as the Saint Malo beacon. Lehmann set course for it on his magnetic compass (which he trusted) and in time received the usual signal indicating that he was overhead. He then altered course for Vannes, sixty miles south, while Meyerhoffer signaled base that they were approaching. Oddly enough, Vannes did not acknowledge, nor was there any sign of the usual searchlight, pointing vertically to indicate the airfield. Down went the Heinkel lower and lower until Lehmann saw that he was over the sea, where he took the precaution of jettisoning his bombs. "Must be the Bay of Biscay," he told the others on the intercom. "We've overshot Vannes." He turned back northwards and soon, in the feeble light of dawn, discerned a coastline. His fuel tanks now nearly empty, Lehmann decided to put down on the first available beach. In the poor light he mistook the breaking surf for shingle and moments later the Heinkel splashed down into the sea. Lehmann, Meyerhoffer, and Bitte managed to get out and scramble ashore. But of Otto Paul there was for the moment no sign.

Beyond the shore stood a rampart of white cliffs. This, they all agreed, was certainly not the Brittany coast near Vannes; they must be in Spain. Two of the *Feldwebelen* set off to scale the cliffs, while the third stumbled along the shore hoping to find help. It was soon forthcoming, though not quite as the young German expected. He found himself confronted by a man in khaki, wearing the familiar tin hat of a British Tommy. The crew of 6N + BH had fetched up on the coast near Bridport, in Dorset, duped, as not a few of their comrades had been, by the Templecombe meacon, which they had taken for the one at Saint Malo. The police rounded up the other two, and later in the day the body of Otto Paul was washed ashore. It was buried with military honors, with an RAF contingent in attendance, at the nearby churchyard at Eype.

Technicians from Air Intelligence were on the beach soon after the ditching of the Heinkel. They watched in suspense as the receding tide uncovered the aircraft's markings, 6N + BH, and the emblem of a Viking ship. The Heinkel was unmistakably one of Kampfgruppe 100's, the first to come down in England. But before those keen-eyed detectives could examine the wreck, it had first to be salvaged.

This was not as simple as it looked. The army and the navy disputed the prize, the army arguing, "We captured the crew so the aircraft is ours," the navy insisting, "The aircraft's in the sea so it belongs to us." In the upshot, it was the navy that towed the Heinkel into deeper water to enable lifting derricks to approach and haul it out of the waves—which meanwhile had badly damaged the *X-Geraet* within. But for this foolish interservice squabble, many inhabitants of the Midlands city of Coventry might have been saved from death.

Air Intelligence meanwhile made another scoop. The Y-Service once again picked up some unusual signals which Dr. Jones immediately identified as a form of navigational beam. He gave it the code name "Benito" and, as usual, asked his colleague Dr. Cockburn to devise a suitable jamming apparatus. It was to be called "Domino." For once Cockburn was not pressed for time; there was no evidence to show that Benito was yet in operation with the Luftwaffe. The doctor and his team at Swanage were still working feverishly to perfect Bromide, the *X-Geraet* jammer. Unfortunately they would have to wait for certain vital elements, thanks to the navy-army conflict which had committed 6N + BH's *X-Geraet* to the corrosive influences of the sea.

The November moon was waxing—the bombers' moon again—and Londoners were bracing themselves against another series of mass on-slaughts. But the dozen or so enemy aircraft picked up by our coastal radar crossing the Channel early on the night of November 14 were certainly not heading for London, any more than the hundreds of others which, a little later, came streaming in over the south and east coast. Coventry, not London, was the Luftwaffe's target that night.

Those dozen aircraft in the vanguard were from Vannes. It was KGr 100's job to blaze the trail for the hordes which followed. So clear was the night that the KGr 100 crews, beyond checking their *X-Geraet* from time to time, hardly needed to use it until the final run-up to the target, upon which they showered, with telling accuracy, thousands of incen-diaries. Within an hour the center of Coventry was blazing so furiously that the following waves of bombers, before they crossed the English coast, could already discern the conflagration as a distant pinpoint of light, beckoning them on to the slaughter. Ordered to concentrate on aircraft and engine factories, they dealt them many a crippling blow.

Yet one entire unit, LG 1, according to the confession of one of its captured aircrews, was ordered to drop their load of bombs not on factories, but on working-class districts. The Luftwaffe killed more than 550 Coventry citizens that night and sorely injured another 800. But neither this fearful massacre nor the demolition of their factories and their splendid cathedral could damp the spirits of the survivors. To the city council's offer to evacuate ten thousand, only three hundred responded. Within a few days, Coventry's factories were turning again; such were the exigencies of war. Years were to pass before the city could build a new cathedral.

That night four of 80 Wing's Bromide jammers were in position to foil *X-Geraet* and the precision bombing it provided for the fire-lighters of KGr 100. Not one of the jammers was effective, and it was not until the experts of Air Intelligence at last discovered the needed clues from the sea-spoiled *X-Geraet* of the Bridport Heinkel, 6N + BH, that it was found that Bromide was wrongly tuned. A simple adjustment assured it thereafter a highly successful future.

The Luftwaffe's savage assault on Coventry marked the beginning of a new offensive against British industrial cities. It signified, too, quite clearly, the end of Hitler's dream (and Goering's too) of knocking out London and driving its citizens to mass hysteria and insurrection. But for all that, London remained an envied target. Three nights after Coventry, hundreds of bombers came back for yet another devastating attack on the great city. The worst, for the time being, was over.

In their paralytic attempt to defend Coventry and, once again, London, the night defenses, fighters and AA, did little to impede that murderous fire attack. A few night fighters sighted enemy bombers but failed to bring them down. The AA guns hit one or two. Another bomber collided with a balloon. To these feeble efforts 85 Squadron could make no more than a symbolic contribution. Three or four of us, all through the night, took turns to patrol. I did a couple of stints of an hour or so but, like the others, returned empty-handed.

On November 18, I signaled 12 Group, "All pilots night operational." The following night 85 Squadron nearly lost its commanding officer.

I took off on patrol about two hours after nightfall and climbed up into a sky luminous with stars and the waning moon to 15,000 feet, where I settled down on patrol, guided here and there by the controller. All was quiet in the sector and nothing disturbed the calm of our brief exchanges: "Hello Wagon Leader, vector [steer] oh-one-sixty, angels fifteen [height 15,000 feet]. Over." "Wagon Leader oh-one-sixty, angels fifteen, over,'' I acknowledged; thus we chattered while I admired the glory of the heavens. Over an hour had gone by when the controller's voice, this time clearly anxious, sounded in my earphones. "Wagon Leader, pancake [land] immediately. Low fog is rolling up fast towards the airfield. Hurry. Over." At that height I had not noticed the fog, but now, as I banked the plane and looked down into the dark vault below, I saw what looked like a sheet of white, some miles long, unfurling inland from the coast. I put the nose down and, with a vector from the controller, began a long, fast dive toward the airfield. It was going to be a close race.

The fog won; it was more than halfway across the airfield as I swept low overhead, and it had already blotted out the flare path. A passing thought struck me—climb up and bail out—but a stronger impulse— get down somehow—prevailed. I tightened up my harness straps. Wheels down, flaps down, and I descended in a left-hand turn straightening up in line with where I calculated the flare path must be. The red light on the hangar roof passed just beyond my right wingtip. It was the last friendly object I saw before plunging into the dense white mass below where nothing was visible beyond my Hurricane's nose. The rest was going to be delicate, but the wings spread out on each side of me felt as if they were my own; somehow I knew that they would bear me down safely to the ground, which could not now be far below. Peering ahead into the gloom, I waited for the flare path to show up. Suddenly it was there, glowing faintly, not stretching away in front of me but at 45 degrees to the right of my line of flight. It was too late to turn; I was too low, my airspeed too slow. I could only keep straight on, sightless, into the fog. After throttling back the engine I was conscious of a long, long hush as, carefully feeling the controls, I lowered the plane towards the hidden surface of the airfield, waiting hopefully for my wheels to touch. Before they did, the right wing dropped violently—a nasty trick of the Hurricane as it stalled—and the plane dropped out of my hands, crunching into the ground, smashing the undercarriage and careering along for some way before lurching to a stop. My head hit the windscreen, but my harness held the rest of me fast. For a moment I sat there, thanking God briefly but fervently for seeing me through. Then I called the controller, telling him I was down on the airfield but where I could not say. More moments passed until I heard voices and the whirr of engines—the ambulance and fire-tender, no doubt. Calling to them now and again—"Hey-oh! I'm here!"—I meanwhile inspected my poor broken Hurricane. The undercarriage was crumpled, the propeller bent, and clods of earth had damaged and dirtied the underside of the wings. It might have been so much worse.

The base commander, Stephen Hardy, tall, massive, gentle, and ever concerned for the well-being of us pilots, was there. "Glad to see you alive," he said. "I thought you'd bought it." He drove me to the mess, gave me a beer, and, after we had chatted, said, "Now go off to your room and sleep it off." Unaccustomed to lying between the sheets, I could not sleep—I dressed again and walked back to the pilots' room, where I lay down on a spare bed and pulled a blanket over me. Back in my natural habitat, I soon dozed off.

Tim Moloney, who fussed over us all and faithfully chronicled the squadron's activities, noted a little stuffily: "One of the major problems facing the hardworked adjutant is trying to make his commanding officer get enough sleep." Tim, perhaps, had reason to complain. But now I was so fully engaged in this occult practice of night fighting, sleep, more than ever before, would have to be sacrificed. Anyway, I had by now lost the habit.

While, that night, I patrolled in vain, ending up in a heap on the ground from which I emerged with but a bump on the head, a remarkable young man in his early twenties, John Cunningham, scored a memorable victory. John was a flight lieutenant in No. 604 (County of Middlesex) Squadron. That he was one of the most skillful pilots in the RAF there was no reason to doubt. But with his cherubic countenance—rosy cheeks, fair curling hair, and engaging smile—it was hardly thinkable that he had the makings of a redoubtable night-fighter pilot and a scourge to the enemy. His prowess was to become legendary.

John's victory that night was a near classic, a model for the future. His aircraft was a purpose-built night fighter, the first of such yet built—a twin-engined Beaufighter, fitted with Mark IV AI, the latest in airborne radar, and armed with a formidable battery of four 20mm cannons and six .303 machine guns. The one missing element, indispensable to a fully classic combat, was GCI—ground-controlled interception; that is, inland tracking by radar. (The coastal radar chain, effective as it was, could only "see" outwards, over the sea.) Failing GCI, it was the searchlights which helped to direct John on to his target. Spotting a searchlight cone some distance away, he made towards it. His radar operator, Sergeant Phillipson, "flashed his weapon"—a code expression which, apart from its connotation for the vulgar-minded, meant "switched on his radar set." Phillipson, his eyes riveted on the cathode tube, soon obtained a clear, firm "blip," the tiny shadow which betrayed the presence of an invisible enemy aircraft.

The chase was on, with the radar operator guiding his pilot in behind the enemy until, on the intercom, John said quietly, "Okay, I can see it"—a shape in the dark from which there emanated four clusters of twinkling flames, which led John to think that they came from each engine of a four-engined bomber. With his thumb he pressed the firing-button on the control column; the terrible salvo from the Beaufighter's cannons and machine guns blinded him. When he ceased firing he could see no further sign of the enemy. Twenty minutes later a Junkers 88, the only hostile bomber down that night, crashed in flames near Selsey Bill in Sussex. Its crew, who had bailed out, confirmed that they had been shot down by a night fighter. John's only error, a minor one, had been to mistake the exhausts, two to each of the Junkers 88's twin motors, for those of a four-engined aircraft. "Exhaust patterns," when we had learned to identify them, were to be a help in aircraft recognition.

85 squadron was at last on the move, to Gravesend, on the eastern outskirts of London. On the way there I stopped off at Debden, our earliest haunt, where we were taking over some of the Hurricanes of 73 Squadron, itself on its way to the North African front. Those aircraft, and the ones we already possessed, were being given, somewhat tardily, a new look—daubed with a lusterless black paint which robbed them of much of their pristine allure and left them with the guileful, somber countenance of a hunter who stalks his prey in the dark.

It was November 22 and incidentally my twenty-sixth birthday, which I celebrated with a few friends that evening at the White Horse in the nearby town of Saffron Walden. I had the faint impression that I was getting on in age. Officially (though there were notable exceptions), twenty-six years was the limit laid down for commanding officers of day-fighter squadrons, twenty-eight for night fighters. But finally it was not age that counted so much as reflexes and a contempt for fear. I was bent on getting my ex-day-fighter squadron off the ground again and into the night air. We raised our glasses (filled with mild beer) and drank to 85's success.

The following day I flew on to Gravesend, where the squadron, pilots and ground crew, were now foregathered in full strength. We were pleased to be thrust into the forefront of the defense, between London and the enemy. But how were we going to acquit ourselves, so inadequately armed as we were for night combat? I dared not envisage the future, but could only pray that our high spirits would see us through. They did, though we had still to endure months of frustration and calamity before we were able to approach the success of John Cunningham and Sergeant Phillipson, in their AI Beaufighter.

ove: Peter Townsend at the controls of a Vickers Vildebeest in Singapore, 1936. Photograph taken by Lieutenant
lonel W. W. Stewart of the 2nd Gurkha Rifles.

Above: Masts of a C.H. (Chain Home) radar station. Such stations could detect an aircraft at well over 100 miles from the coast. In fixed positions, they could see nothing of an aircraft once it had crossed the coast.　　*Imperial War Museum*

Right: G.C.I. (Ground Control Interception) Mobile Station. Designed for inland radar cover.
　　　　　　Imperial War Museum

Above: Balloons: attached by a steel cable to the ground, they could rise several thousand feet above, forming a defensive barrage against air attack. Here they are being inflated.   *Imperial War Museum*

Below: Day battle: 85 Squadron climbs to meet the enemy. Hawker Hurricanes in formation. The first British fighter plane to exceed 300 mph, Hurricanes are credited with destroying more German planes than any other aircraft during the Battle of Britain.   *Imperial War Museum*

Some of the aircraft used by the RAF fighter-pilots during 1940–41.

Right: Supermarine Spitfire (used mostly for day-fighting). An aircraft noted for its speed and manoeuvrability, it could reach a speed of 375 mph and fly above 33,000 feet.

Imperial War Museum

Right: Boulton-Paul Defiant, with 4-gun rear turret. Designed originally as a day fighter.

Imperial War Museum

Right: Bristol Beaufighter with Mark IV AI (Air Interception) radar.

Imperial War Museum

Top: Douglas DB7 medium
bomber before conversion to Havoc
night fighter. Eight Browning
.303 machine guns were installed
in the nose.
Imperial War Museum

Middle: Havoc Mk II Turbinlite
(''Helmore'')—the flying
searchlight. Sent to 85 Squadron
for trials, it did not prove
a success.
Imperial War Museum

Left: A Havoc of 85 Squadron
cross-country from Hunsdon,
Herts. Photograph taken by
T. A. Williams.

Above: Operations Room, Fighter Command Headquarters, Bentley Priory, Stanmore, Middlesex. Above: Controller and assistants. Below: W.A.A.F. plotters.   *Imperial War Museum*

Below: 85 Squadron fighter pilots. *Left to right:* Sergeant Webster, Sergeant Goodman, Sergeant Bentley, Squadron Leader Townsend (with top tunic button undone and recovering from a wounded foot), two Polish pilots Sergeant Gray. In the background a Hurricane with "kidney type" exhausts.   *Imperial War Museum*

Above: Jim Marshall in the cockpit of a Hurricane.

Imperial War Museum

Below: 85 Squadron night-fighter pilots relaxing at the dispersal point. (Debden, near Saffron Walden, Essex, March 14, 1941)

Imperial War Museum

Above: At the dispersal point, wearing dark glasses to acclimatize before going on patrol. *Left to right:* Bill Carnaby, Jim Marshall, Peter Townsend, Geoff Howlitt—with Kim, the Squadron mascot. *Imperial War Museum*

Below: Night patrol just before takeoff. The pilot, James Wheeler, settles into the cockpit of his Hurricane VY-X. The hexagon emblem of 85 Squadron is visible. *Imperial War Museum*

E LUFTWAFFE

e of the aircraft used by the Luftwaffe in attacks on London and provincial
sh cities, 1940–41.

e outbreak of World War II the Luftwaffe had an estimated strength of
00 men and 5,000 aircraft, while the RAF had about 100,000 men and 2,000
aft.

Left: Messerschmitt 109. Never
fully operational as a night
fighter, the Me. 109 was a
single-engined aircraft; the Me.
110 a twin-engined two-seater
fighter bomber.

Left: Heinkel 111 medium bomber
taking off. (The Heinkel, Dornier
and JU-88 bombers had a bomb-
load of 1,100 pounds)
Imperial War Museum

Right: Dornier 215 (a variant of the Dornier 17)
Imperial War Museum

Right: Junkers JU-88—twin-engined day or night fighter bomber with a top speed of 280 mph. It largely replaced the JU-87, which sustained heavy losses during the Battle of Britain due to its low speed of 210 mph.
Imperial War Museum

Right: Captured Focke-Wulf 190 in front of the control tower, West Malling, July 5, 1943.
Imperial War Museum

LONDON ON FIRE

Firemen battle against the flames caused by high explosive and incendiary bombs, 1940–41. In one concerted attack on December 29, 1940, fires raged all night and a quarter of the City (the square mile around St. Paul's) was destroyed.

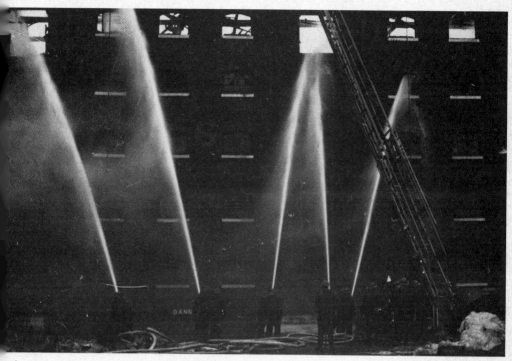

Above: Surrey Commercial Docks—No. 6 warehouse. September 1940. Economic targets like docks, goods depots, power stations and railways were always vulnerable to attack.   *London Fire Brigade*

Below: Incendiary bomb, Piccadilly, London. October 11, 1940.   *London Fire Brigade*

Above: Blackfriars Goods Depot
ablaze. Firemen at work from
Blackfriars Railway Station, EC4.
October 16, 1940.

London Fire Brigade

Right: Fire Blitz, Southwark
Street, SE1, on December 29, 1940,
when thousands of incendiary and
high explosive bombs were rained
on London.

London Fire Brigade

Pimlico, SW1, April 16, 1941. *Above:* Ebury Street: houses and gas main alight. *Below:* garage on fire in Bessborough Place.

London Fire Brigade

ft and above: Firemen working in Queen Victoria Street, London EC4, May 10/11, 1941.   *London Fire Brigade*

ow: No. 23 seen collapsing in flames.   *Guildhall Library*

Above: General view of Ludgate Hill, EC4 (with St. Paul's in the background) showing firemen playing hoses on the burned-out buildings, May 12, 1941.   *BBC Hulton Picture Library*

Below: Firemen damping down smouldering debris in Newgate Street, EC4.   *Guildhall Library*

SCUE

e Home Front, volunteers gave their services to organizations involved in
e and salvage work, among them the Civil Defense, ARP, WVS, and Salvation
y. Despite bombed hospitals, medical staff carried on their duties as usual.

Above: London's first night air
raid. An Anderson shelter on which
a bomb made a direct hit. Although buckled, it withstood the bomb
and blast. August 25, 1940.
BBC Hulton Picture Library

Left: The inhabitants of this shelter
on waste ground in Fetter Lane,
EC4, were not so lucky when it
received a direct hit on October 9,
1940. The occupants were mostly
old people from tenement houses
nearby. By 1941 air-raid shelters
had been provided for about 20
million civilians.
Associated Press

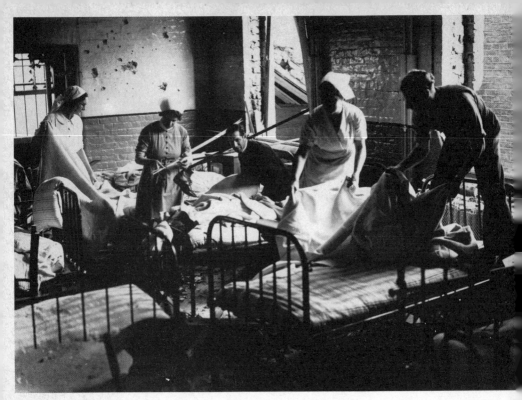

Above: A damaged ward at Forest Gate Hospital, Tower Hamlet Road, Essex, October 2, 1940. Fortunately, th[e] patients had been moved to a shelter before the bomb fell.   *Associated Pres[s]*

Below: Newborn babies being evacuated from the maternity wing of a bombed southeast London hospital, September 16, 1940.   *Associated Press*

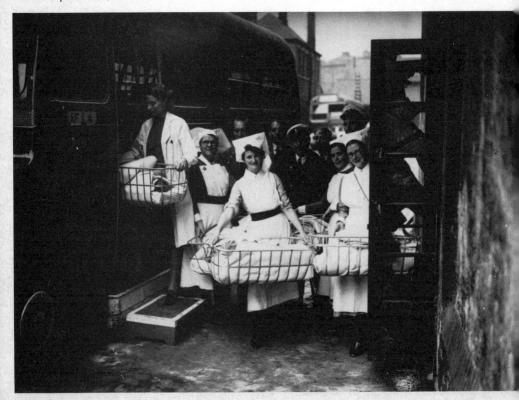

Above: Rescuers assist a patient extricated from the ruins of St. Matthew's Hospital, Shepherdess Walk, London, N1. October 9, 1940.
Associated Press

w: Nurses from the same hospital manage to smile
ey salvage bedding. *Associated Press*

Below: Damaged wing of St. Thomas's Hospital, London, after an air-raid attack, May 16, 1941. *Associated Press*

Above: Digging for survivors off the Strand, WC2, 1940. (On the right is the Savoy Chapel.)

    BBC Hulton Picture Library

Right: Soldiers help clear the damage resulting from a high explosive bomb on the Bank Underground Station, January 11, 1941. The bomb penetrated the carriageway and exploded in the booking office at 8.05 P.M. 57 people were killed, including 1 policeman, and 70 people were injured. January 1941.

    BBC Hulton Picture Library

Left: Rescuers find a survivor at No. 7 Budge Row, EC4, one of several people brought out alive after an air raid.

Guildhall Library

Below: A welcome cup of tea from the Salvation Army for families salvaging furniture from bombed houses in Dulwich.

BBC Hulton Picture Library

Above: A wounded boy is carried from his home by a rescue worker after being trapped for an hour in his bedroom after a raid on Ilford, in the suburbs of London. *Associated Press*

Below: Using oxygen and artificial respiration, rescuers attempt to resuscitate a woman victim of a South East a raid. She recovered and was taken to hospital. *Associated Pre*

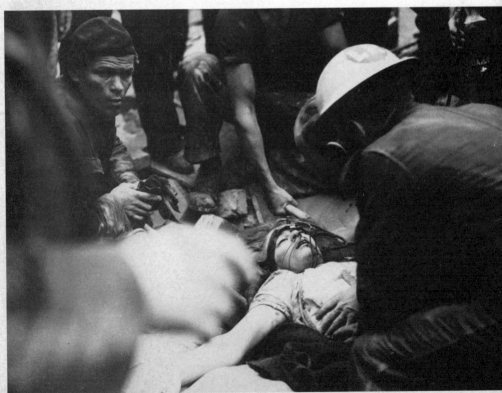

*: One of the last bombs to fall on London in World War II was a V-2 rocket which landed on busy
gdon Market in the city on March 8, 1945. 380 people died. But that is another, and no less heroic, story of the
ears after the period of this book.

BBC Hulton Picture Library

AFTERMATH

The area around St. Paul's was laid waste in the Blitz—yet despite a bomb that fe
into the crypt, damaging the High Altar on the way, the cathedral itself remained
largely intact and an inspiring symbol of the endurance of the British people.

Above: Perhaps the most famous wartime picture of St. Paul's, ringed by flames. *Daily M*

Below: Fallen masonry on the High Altar and a hole in
the east roof caused by a high explosive bomb: 6 A.M.,
October 10, 1940. *Guildhall Library*

Below: The crypt can be glimpsed through the b
crater in the cathedral floor. *Guildhall Li*

bove: A view from the cathedral roof looking over the ruined city towards Paternoster Row.   *Guildhall Library*

Below: Madame Tussaud's, Marylebone Road, NW1, September 9, 1940. Many waxworks were lost.
BBC Hulton Picture Library

Above: Street scene, Balham, London, October 17, 1940. (Note the ironic sign on the right.)

BBC Hulton Picture Libro

bove: Londoners walk along a narrow pathway between bombed buildings in Goswell Road, E1, after one of the *worst* night attacks of World War II—December 29, 1940.   *Associated Press*

Below: Similar damage in the West End looking down Piccadilly from the Circus (with Eros removed for safety throughout the war), October 14, 1940.   *Associated Press*

Above: The historic Guildhall in the city after a night raid, December 29, 1940. The giant mythological figures of Gog and Magog were lost in the debris of the Great Hall. (A crown belonging to one of the figures can be seen in the center of the picture.) Monuments to Wellington, Nelson, Pitt, and Chatham were among those damaged.

Guildhall Library

Below: Liverpool Street Station, London, damaged by two high explosive bombs (January 1941) which exploded simultaneously at Nos. 135 and 151 Bishopsgate at 8.20 P.M., causing approximately 60 casualties, of which 38 were fatal. *Guildhall Library*

Above: Among the many beautiful Wren churches destroyed in the London Blitz was St. Mary Le B Cheapside. Originally burned down in the Great F of London, 1666, it was subsequently rebuilt by S Christopher Wren, c. 1680. The church was gutte a night raid on December 8, 1940. (It has now be restored.) New "Bow Bells" were recast from th damaged in the Blitz. *Guildhall Libr*

Below: Central Criminal Court ("Old Bailey"), E Barristers' entrance. High explosive bomb, May 1 1941. *Guildhall Libr*

Left: Churchill surveys the damage at the House of Commons, Palace of Westminster, SW1. May 1941.

Popperfoto

Below: Many provincial British cities were also bombed—among them ports and industrial targets like Coventry, Leeds, Liverpool, Hull, Glasgow, Manchester, and Plymouth. Coventry in the Midlands was particularly badly hit and its medieval cathedral reduced to a shell. Like St. Paul's in London, Coventry Cathedral became a wartime symbol, and when the cathedral was rebuilt after the war, the new building was imaginatively linked to the ruins of the old.

The Photo Source

LIFE GOES ON . . .

Throughout the Blitz, the inhabitants of London and provincial British cities went
about their daily tasks much as usual, and shops, offices and theaters remained ope
Hitler's and the Luftwaffe's inability to break the morale of the British people was
of the factors that brought about an eventual cessation of the bombing.

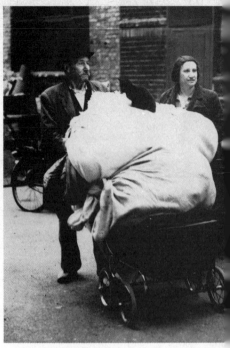

Above: Shoppers buy bread from a damaged bakery
in an area bombed earlier that day, August 23, 1940.
Associated Press

Above: A couple bombed out of their home pile
belongings onto a pram—with a black kitten for
September 15, 1940.　　　*Associated*

Below: King George VI and Queen Elizabeth inspect bomb damage at Colindale Avenue, Hendon,
September 27, 1940.
Associated Press

ove: Londoners sleeping in the tube during a night
1, September 27, 1940. (By 1941 London Under-
und stations had bunks for 725,000 civilians.)
Associated Press

: Miss Ellen Wilkinson, Parliamentary Secretary to
inistry for Home Security, photographed with some
children in a London tube station shelter during a
f inspection, October 10, 1940.

Associated Press

Above: An Eastender at his bombed house,
September 28, 1940.   *BBC Hulton Picture Library*

Below: Suburban homes on the outskirts of London the
morning after a raid. (Censorship prevented the exact
location being indicated on many wartime photographs.)

BBC Hulton Picture Library

Above: Despite the presence of a huge bomb crater, passersby still feed the pigeons as usual in Trafalgar Square. October 13, 1940.

Associated Press

Right: The bombed library of Holland Park House (near Kensington High Street) with business apparently going on as usual. November 1940.

18

MOURNFUL NIGHTS AT GRAVESEND

G ravesend. The very name was enough to give one the willies, particularly when we were all trying hard not to think of the ever-present possibility of dying an untidy death, our body splattered amidst the burning, twisted remnants of our aircraft. Our brief sojourn at Gravesend was to be an ordeal. Yet there was one agreeable feature: we were lodged far from the airfield, the pilots at Jeskyns Court, a pleasant manor house, the ground crews at a place with the droll name "Laughing Water." While the main reason for this was that there existed no accommodation at the airfield for either man or beast, there was another, connected with our role as "specialized" night fighters. It was now recognized that after the night's work, ground crews and pilots deserved to sleep far from the thunder of day-flying aircraft.

At the break of day, when informed by the controller that the squadron was "released," we would return to our quarters for eggs and bacon, then to bed, to sleep for six hours or so. When the brutal awakening came, we felt little appetite, still drowsy as we were, for the lunch being served to the few daytime men of the administrative staff, who, among ourselves, were known as "penguins." Why? Because they had cold feet and couldn't fly. Really, we meant them no wrong, for they included veterans like our beloved Tim Moloney, who, aged nineteen in World War I, had risked his neck and still sported his air gunner's single wing above the medal ribbons of that war. Others, of a younger generation and undecorated, were condemned, through some defect of eyes or lungs or heart, to serve as "wingless wonders." They were good men, with few exceptions; it was those exceptions who occasionally provoked our disparaging epithets—penguins or wingless wonders.

At lunch, the conversation, more than the food, revived us for the next stage—night air tests during which we tried out our black, sleuthy-looking Hurricanes. The proper functioning of the engine and radio was naturally of prime importance. By instinct, we were tempted by the thrill of a few aerobatics, a loop perhaps, and a few slow rolls. We resisted, however, for such maneuvers upset the gyrocompass and artificial horizon, knocking them off their supports, their gimbals—another of those strange, romantic words which belong as much to aviation as to *Alice in Wonderland*—

> 'Twas brillig and the slithy toves
> Did gyre and gimble in the wabe . . .

Toward sunset, we came to "readiness," the start of a twelve-hour period of alert spent in a Nissen hut, with its hemispherical corrugated-iron roof and concrete floor, upon which were aligned a number of iron bedsteads furnished with a thin mattress and a couple of rough blankets. Though it mattered little to me upon which bed I lay, some pilots were more possessive. One night I noticed a bed with a parachute lying on it and a notice warning: "Hemingway, his bed." Paddy Hemingway, quiet-spoken with a thin mustache that fitted him well, was another veteran of the Battle of France, and a close friend of Jim Marshall's. An excellent pilot, he showed a remarkable aptitude for being shot down, bailing out, and walking or swimming away intact. So far, he had a preference for water. Fished out, *in extremis*, from the North Sea during the Battle of Britain, he jumped down again, a few days later, into Pitsea Marshes. His career as an involuntary parachutist was not yet ended. Meanwhile his parachute lay there, stating a claim to "his" bed.

We were summoned, one by one, to the Air Ministry medical establishment for eye tests. It was then that I met a charming man, Air Commodore Livingstone, an ophthalmologist, who explained to me the mysteries of night vision, quite a different optical process to seeing by day. From him I gathered that when you walk out of a lighted atmosphere, strange things happen to your eyes. The "rods" are slowly flooded by a liquid, "visual purple," until, after about fifteen minutes, your eyes are capable of piercing the darkness. The process resulted in "visual acuity." Some had it, others not. I responded satisfactorily to the tests of Dr. Livingstone, who then got talking about contact lenses. They were something new. Though I had no need of them myself, the doctor told me that he knew several pilots, bombers mostly, who had faced the flak of Berlin and the Ruhr without a qualm, but who cried out in agony at his attempts to fit them with contact lenses. Each one of us has his own kind of courage. It was henceforth ordained that pilots awaiting their turn to patrol must wear dark glasses so that their eyes might already be adapted to "night vision" before takeoff. This did not discomfort us in the least, for our Nissen hut was permanently illuminated by the glaring light of a number of kerosene lamps. They burned with a small but disturbing roar which denied us the opportunity of dozing, let alone sleeping, however lightly.

Outside our Nissen hut, our swarthy Hurricanes waited, like tethered horses. Since we departed singly on patrol, a "scramble" (takeoff) at night was a less hurried affair than by day. It was as well, for the surface of Gravesend airfield was plastered with a thick layer of mud through which, after discarding our black glasses, we had to plod in order to mount our own personal charger. Then, right foot in the stirrup (a retractable step), which scraped off its small share of mud. Left foot, then right, onto the wing, where you left your slimy footprints, and finally, swing the right leg over into the cockpit and onto the seat—the mud deposited there rubbed off eventually on your bottom. Once in the cockpit—your night vision, thanks to the black glasses, perfectly adapted—the engine fitter helped to strap you in, shining his torch on the quick-release fastenings, the instrument panel, and, inevitably, straight into your eyes, whose carefully nurtured night acuity would vanish in an instant.

The nicety of preadapting your eyes to night vision, while appreciable, was not all that important. The pilot, once in his cockpit and set for the takeoff, had but to peer forward along the long nose of his Hurricane and point it into the dark sky. Soon after takeoff the eyes became transformed so that they could see like those of a cat.

The mud problem, however, persisted. What had been scraped off on the rudder bar and the cockpit floor gradually dried out into dust, which, on opening the cockpit hood, was blown by the slipstream into your eyes. The coating of mud remaining on your boots eventually froze solid when you reached the subzero temperature of your patrol altitude.

That was the personal side of the mud problem. There was another, more serious. On takeoff, as the aircraft forged ahead under full power across the airfield, the propeller whipped up mud, sending it flying into the air intake, clogging the radiator and spattering the underside of the wings and fuselage. Mud was the most likely culprit when Paul Arbon's

Hurricane crashed on takeoff. Paul, a pale-faced and slightly plump young man, was nicknamed "Dopey"—why I never understood, because there was nothing about his flying that suggested he was particularly dim-witted. On the contrary, he was an able pilot and loyal friend. When his engine cut just as he was lifting his Hurricane off the ground, it careered into a Nissen hut occupied by ground crew. Dopey emerged from the wreckage unhurt, but five men inside the hut were injured when the three tons of Hurricane descended upon them.

Gravesend, true to its name, witnessed the very nadir of our fortunes. We soon found out that our new VHF radio sets were not reliable. If the causes were obscure, the effect played on the morale of our pilots. Map reading in the total dark of the blackout being out of the question, the night-fighter pilot depended on the ground controller to guide him home. "Homing" by radio was his assurance of a safe return to base; if deprived of it for some reason, he was hopelessly lost—unless lucky, as I was the night that my radio "packed up" somewhere over Kent. The slender crescent of the moon gave but a dim light, but visibility was good. I soon picked out the coastline, then laboriously followed it up the Thames estuary until I spotted the red flashing beacon of Gravesend. These lighthouses were sited some five miles from the airfield and flashed in Morse the two "letters of the night." Site and letters were changed nightly. They were a godsend to us, but the Germans were for a long time puzzled by them, occasionally bombing them out of sheer frustration. Had the weather been thick that night, my last hope would have been to bail out—still a chancy business, for it was impossible to know where you would fall, on *terra firma* or in the drink, where in the icy water you were likely to perish. Many unfortunate Luftwaffe crews, equipped though they were with dinghies, radio, and survival rations and pills, suffered such a fate. Their bodies were washed up in numbers on the east and south coast. For both sides, weather and sea were common foes.

On the night of December 8, the Luftwaffe, more than four hundred bombers strong, returned to the assault on London. They blasted the city with hundreds of tons of high explosive and more than a hundred thousand incendiary bombs, raising fires which inflamed the sky above and shed enough light on Gravesend to read a newspaper. Many of us, myself included, were dispatched during that awful night to do battle with the hidden enemy, but in vain. The controller positioned me to patrol at 16,000 feet between the estuary and the city itself. It was tormenting, in all that immensity of black sky, to look down on London three miles beneath me, consumed by fire and torn by the blast of bombs and land mines whose fiery deflagrations rent the darkness below. For two hours, while the enemy was killing hundreds of our people, I searched in vain, desperate and ashamed at our impotence to defend the defenseless.

Having landed, taxied in, and switched off, I jumped down from the cockpit, sick at heart, and walked through the mud to the floodlight. That night the wind was westerly and the flare path was laid out so that we landed towards London. Sergeant Calderwood was approaching to land. A ruddy-faced young Irishman with a pleasing brogue, he was a steady pilot and, as we were about to see, a man of selfless courage. His approach seemed normal, but as he flashed past the floodlight I could see that he was going too fast. His wheels touched well down the flare path; he squeezed the brake lever on the control column, slid, wheels locked, across the mud, and tore into the tangle of barbed wire forming the airfield defenses. The Hurricane's tail reared into the air as it overturned and came finally to rest on its back.

With others I ran to the scene, but in our frantic efforts to reach the Hurricane and its pilot the clawing barbed wire ripped our clothing and held us back. A strong smell of petrol was in the air, and I well knew that a crashed Hurricane could lie inert for a minute or two and then burst into flames. The suspense was agonizing. Hung up in the barbed wire, I was quite close to Calderwood, but incapable of getting closer. I told him, "Hold on, the firemen will soon cut you out." Never did his Irish brogue affect me more than when he answered calmly, "Don't worry about me, take care o' yourselves." He might have been incinerated within the next few minutes, but thankfully the Hurricane did not go up in flames. The firemen extricated our Irishman, redder in the face than usual after hanging on his straps for twenty minutes upside down.

Two nights of foul weather brought a short respite to London and the provinces. We nevertheless continued to patrol. With the low-lying clouds, full of lightning and reflecting the searchlight beams below, flying was extremely unpleasant, not to say risky. Around midnight, Sergeant Hutton, a quiet, stolid young Yorkshireman, took his turn to patrol. He had not been gone more than half an hour when I was informed that an aircraft, probably a Hurricane, had crashed in Tilbury docks, just opposite us on the north bank of the river. After a roundabout journey by car through Deptford Tunnel I at last found the place, a deep, gaping hole in the soft ground wherein were embedded all but a few remnants of a Hurricane. Men had been working with flares and a lifting rig to haul out the wreckage—and with it the body of poor Hutton. After some hours, the foreman said to me, "It's no good, we'll never reach him. All we can do is to fill in the hole." "Keep on trying," I pleaded. "He deserves a decent burial." This Hutton finally received when, ten days later, his body was recovered.

Some people say "Never two without three." Such was to be 85 Squadron's misfortune during those ghastly nights at Gravesend. Sergeant Howes, a calm, loyal member of our band, had fought with the Squadron in France and been shot down. Now he was back with us, but stayed barely long enough to meet up again with his old friends. One freezing night just before Christmas, when clouds hung low, having apparently lost control of his aircraft, he dived into the ground. The cause of the tragedy may well have been icing; or it may have been that he was confused by lightning and searchlights. We were never to know, for our good friend died without a word on the radio. They had carried his body away before I reached the burnt-out wreckage of his Hurricane, beside which lay a charred, pathetic-looking flying boot.

Gravesend was giving us a cruel time, but there was no dismay, not even among the youngest, like Sergeant Gray, who looked more like a boy of sixteen than a skillful and determined night-fighter pilot. His daring exploits in bad weather sometimes alarmed me, and I would wait anxiously on the flare path for his return. Another youthful but more seasoned pilot was Jim Bailey, who had fought by day in Defiants and was lucky to be alive. You would never have imagined that he was the son of his millionaire father, Sir Abe, for Jim usually had at least one hole in his trousers and drove around in a rickety little Morris 8. His fair hair was perpetually disheveled and he was always laughing—at what or whom I was not always sure, but I often suspected it was me. He had flying in his blood; his mother was a well-known and intrepid aviatrix.

With Jim Bailey came his friend Bill Carnaby, another survivor of the carnage of the Defiants. Tall, dark, thin, and taciturn, Bill was the very opposite of his friend Jim, but a most welcome addition to our ranks, whose remaining gaps were being filled by seasoned volunteer pilots. Another was Dudley Honor, who had fought valiantly in Greece.

Shot down behind the enemy lines, he made good his escape and was taken off from an isolated beach by an RAF flying boat.

Gus Gowers was another old hand who returned to 85 Squadron. He had fought in France and in the Battle of Britain, when he was shot down. Burned on the face and hands, he was taken to Caterham Mental Hospital, a wing of which had been given over to the RAF. It was there, on my own release from the hospital, that I had visited Gus. His face was still black and his burned fingers like claws. Yet for all that he could not get over the joke of ending up in a loony bin. Neither, sadly, as soon became apparent, had he yet got over the shock of his terrible wounds. Soon after he came back to us he confessed as much to me; he could not take it—yet. He left us for a temporary ground job and I never saw him again. Later, while leading a day-fighter squadron over France, Gus was killed.

The same fate overcame our French friends, Emile and François. The language problem having proved too difficult, they left us for day fighters. Before leaving, Emile wrote to me: *"Nous étions parmi vous absolument comme chez nous. L'escadrille était notre 'Home' . . . maintenant plus que jamais nous sommes certains d'avoir la victoire."* (Among you we were absolutely as if among our own. The squadron was our "Home" . . . now we are more than ever certain of victory.) Emile was killed leading an RAF squadron over Dieppe in 1942. François disappeared during an offensive patrol over his own country.

One evening, after putting my Hurricane through the usual "night test," I returned to Jeskyn's for a bite before the hour of "readiness." There, sitting in a chair in the drawing room, I found an elderly-looking gentleman, his wavy gray hair parted down the middle, his narrow rubicund face aglow with good health. My attention was immediately drawn to his pilot's wings and the medal ribbons below them—the Military Cross and two campaign medals of World War I. "Good evening, sir," I said politely. "Good evening, sir," he replied, with an embarrassed smile. It was only then that I noticed the thin stripe of a pilot officer on his sleeves. He went on, "You must be the CO of Eighty-five Squadron. I'm reporting to you for flying duties. My name is Wheeler."

James Wheeler was a prodigious personage. As a young soldier in the first war, the two smaller fingers of his left hand had been shot away. He managed to hold the throttle lever perfectly well with his remaining two fingers and thumb, and like this had done thousands of hours' flying as an airline pilot. Although I never discovered his exact age, it was somewhere well into the forties. We continued to call each other "sir" for a while. Then I came to call him James and he, to my relief, dropped the "sir."

Our losses and our pains and frustrations never dampened the spirits of the wonderful team of which I happened to be the leader. We should have to keep on groping in the dark with our dear Hurricanes until equipped with proper, "specialized" night fighters. The only type at present in existence was the Beaufighter, for which priority naturally was given to the six Blenheim night-fighter squadrons. The Beaufighter, its teething troubles remedied, promised to be a scourge for the enemy's bombers. The night after Sergeant Howes died, John Cunningham and Sergeant Phillipson scored another decisive victory, this time against a Heinkel 111 of Kampfgruppe 100.

19

FOUL WEATHER

December was what Londoners, with tactful understatement, were calling a "light month," although it was to end with a holocaust. They all, the Callow family included, were able to enjoy a short breather while the Luftwaffe was concentrating its night offensive against our ports and industrial cities.

Sheffield was one of them. The city came under heavy attack on December 12 and again on the 15th. It was bad luck on Melve Callow, the wag of the family, that she arrived that very day in Sheffield with friends to attend the twenty-first-birthday party of a football star, Bill Pickering. She had hesitated before going, but her mother encouraged her: "Go on, Melve, it will make a nice change for you." So Melve dressed up in the beautiful pale blue costume she had recently bought and was saving for the party.

When her train pulled into Sheffield station, Melve saw that it was in ruins—hit during the raid three nights earlier. She and her friends made straight for Bill Pickering's house, where guests were already arriving. As a precaution, each one was first shown down to the basement shelter. Then up to the ground floor again, where the party started. Just as it was in full swing the sirens began wailing, and all but a few of the guests trooped down to the shelter. Melve was among those who stayed outside to keep company with one of her London friends, Harry, who had been injured in the London bombing and was on crutches.

At the height of the raid a bomb demolished the house next door, sending an avalanche of debris down the shelter stairs and blocking the entrance. Ironically, those few who had stayed outside were unhurt;

they all, except for the lame, unfortunate Harry, began digging with their bare hands to free the trapped revelers, who, as they staggered out bleeding and disheveled, threw their arms, for support, around the first person they met. By the time they were all out, Melve's beautiful pale blue dress was torn and stained with blood and dust. Ambulances took the shelter victims away, leaving Harry with his crutches and Melve in her rags, sitting disconsolately among the rubble. "Blimey," complained Melve, "they might bleedin' well have taken us with them." Next day, still in her rags, she hastened back to London.

A few nights before Christmas, the Luftwaffe turned once again on Liverpool and its docks on the River Mersey, which, with Glasgow's Clyde-side docks, were the terminus of Britain's lifeline with America and Canada. They were back the following night in greater strength— three hundred bombers with the usual mixture of high explosive and incendiaries. The series continued during two more nights, when it was the turn of Manchester to be ravaged by blast and fire. Next day was the eve of Christmas, with its message of goodwill among men, which men, whether at war or not, had always so barely heeded. During the festival itself, however, the bombardment was interrupted—more, probably, because of the forbidding weather, which kept us, on our side, pinned to the ground, than for any feelings of goodwill that Hitler and his bloody henchmen may have felt for the British.

Christmas and Boxing Day over, the Luftwaffe, on Friday, December 27, came to London bringing their gifts of oil bombs, explosive, and fire. The night was well chosen, for city workers had gone for the weekend, leaving offices, shops, and warehouses unwatched. At Gravesend a dense haze reduced horizontal visibility to zero and clamped us to the ground. Once again powerless to intervene, we could only watch the white vapor trails streaming behind the bombers heading up the estuary for London, hear the sickening thud of their bombs, and gaze sadly at the fiery glow lighting up London's sky.

That raid was a prelude to the great city fire of Sunday, the 29th— a night yet more favorable to the fire-raisers when the Thames, the source of the firemen's water supply, was at its lowest, a thin river bounded on each side by a broad stretch of stinking slush, through which the firemen had to haul their connecting hoses in order to draw on the saving water.

The raid was made by fewer than 150 bombers and by 10:00 P.M. was called off because of bad weather over the Luftwaffe's bases. But Kampfgruppe 100, which led it, navigating on *X-Geraet*, its Heinkels loaded with incendiaries only, accomplished its mission as "pathfinders" with precise and deadly effect. Although the Germans were already alive to the disturbing influences of Bromide, the RAF's jammer, it failed to upset their aim that night. They laid down a carpet of fire within a radius of about one mile from St. Paul's. Visible from afar, despite the broken cloud drifting over London, it beckoned, as at Coventry, to the rest of the pack, who had only to stoke the flames with their high-explosive and incendiary bombs. The burning city kindled into a huge brazier. Nothing like it had been seen since the Great Fire of 1666, when the diarist John Evelyn wrote that he witnessed "a blood red sky, painted by a myriad of seething fires."

Nearly three centuries later, young Ray Callow, doing his duty as a messenger that night, had a similar vision: "It looked as if the whole city was on fire and the sky above as well." It did not seem to him that London could be saved. But the firemen were as ever, fighting back against the devouring flames. Ray's brother Johnny was there. It was not until towards the end of that brief, devastating raid that the bells went down at the Earldom Square substation. "Numbers one and two pumps!" The keen rivalry between Johnny's No. 1 pump and his friend Steve Needham's No. 2 put them on their mettle as they raced each other up the Old Kent Road, heading for Blackfriars Bridge. At one moment Pat Mahoney, the number-three man in Johnny's team, cried out, "Hey, look, up there!" Above, they could clearly see aircraft silhouetted against the incandescent sky. Then they were crossing Blackfriars Bridge and, turning right, came to Ludgate Hill, to be faced with the inspiring, unforgettable spectacle of St. Paul's Cathedral, its famous dome with the cross high aloft, standing proud of the surrounding smoke and flames—London's cathedral, the symbol of London's indomitable resistance.

The main load of bombs dropped within that circle around St. Paul's marked by KGr 100's incendiaries. A strong westerly wind fanned the flames until between the cathedral and the Guildhall there raged an impassable sea of fire. More conflagrations were devouring the area bounded by Moorgate, Aldersgate, Old Street, and Cannon Street. Many of London's ancient and cherished architectural treasures were vandalized that night. Bombs struck the County Hall and the Tower of London, and the Guildhall, heart of London's pride and tradition, was half consumed by fire. Eight Wren churches were shattered and burned. But in the midst of all that desolation Wren's great masterpiece, St. Paul's, stood up defiant and practically unscathed.

Johnny and his team's evening out ended in anticlimax. Although hundreds of pumps had converged on the city, some fires were so fierce that they had to be left to burn themselves out. Ordered to stand by, Johnny's team did so until dawn, when the fire control officer told them, "You can push off." Neither wet nor dirty, they drove back, dejected, to the substation, there to be greeted with jibes: "Well, mates, where've you all been? Out on a beano or something?"

Dejected, too, were the pilots of 85 Squadron, who had flown off into the night in an attempt to engage the enemy with the aid of the system called "Layers." While the AA guns held their fire, cat's-eye fighters were stacked up at intervals of 500 feet to patrol above the blazing city in the hope of spotting an enemy bomber against the flames. But the bombers seen that night from the ground by Pat Mahoney and his comrades of No. 1 Pump remained, in the confusion of smoke and cloud, invisible to our pilots above.

Thus 85 Squadron made its last vain effort in 1940 to defend London by night. Our failure did not come from want of trying; we had put in more hours of flying than any other squadron. It was due to lack of the right tools. In an attempt to bolster up the ineffective night defenses, weird devices, brainchildren of the boffins, had recently been tried. One was the aerial mine. Carried by old-fashioned Handley Page Harrow aircraft to 20,000 feet—it took them an hour to get there—the mines, which dangled from a parachute on the end of 2,000 feet of wire, were sown across the path of approaching enemy bombers. An ingenious but fruitless idea. A more crazy one was proposed by the navy, experts at sowing mines at sea, but less realistic about their possibilities for ensnaring enemy bombers. The sailors' plan was to release scores of free balloons, each with an explosive charge attached, to drift with the wind towards the advancing bombers. But the wind bloweth where it listeth: the drifting explosives might end up anywhere. The idea was soon abandoned, fortunately for the continued well-being of our own fliers.

Yet another idea, one for use on the ground, was the decoy fire devised by Colonel John Turner, onetime director of Air Ministry Works and Buildings and affectionately known, if I am not mistaken, as "Concrete Bill." The purpose of his decoy fires, called "Starfish" sites, was to draw the main bomber force away from the fires raised by the pathfinders of KGr 100. Starfish sites had harvested a good number of bombs and were to gather many more.

With all these thoughts and visions of impeding the enemy came the news that we were to be reequipped with Defiants, the two-seater former day fighter with a four-gun turret. Although the news stirred no particular enthusiasm among us, we felt willing to try any machine which might be an improvement, as a night fighter, on our well-loved Hurricane day fighters. The Defiant was clearly not the ultimate solution, but a stepping-stone, perhaps, to something better. Despite my deep and lingering instincts of a day-fighter pilot, flying a single-seater, single-engine plane, I felt certain that only a machine fitted with radar, with an operator to work it—that meant a two-seater twin-engined aircraft—could provide the answer to interception at night. The proof had been amply demonstrated by John Cunningham and John Phillipson in their Beaufighter. Before reaching that ideal we would have to grope blindly in the dark and cold winter skies for many a night, disappointed by our continuing failure, but by no means demoralized.

As the year drew to a close, with London still smoldering, the British prime minister, Winston Churchill, far from being dejected, felt on the contrary that "all this clatter and storm" was a stimulant to further effort. Looking back on 1940, he saw it as a "tremendous year," if the most deadly, in British history. The "citadel of the Commonwealth" had defied the enemy's attempts to take it by storm.

Beyond the seas, it is true, her positions were dangerously menaced and her army, air force, and, above all, her navy and merchant navy were stretched to the limit. But they still held on and when occasion arose, as it did more and more, fought back. Malta, hitherto defenseless, but a potential thorn in Italy's side, was reinforced by convoys sailing in the face of the Italian navy and air force.

The Italian invasion of Greece, to whom Britain had pledged her aid, however slender it might be, had been repulsed by the Greek army. Suda Bay, the best harbor in Crete, was occupied, with the Greeks' assent, by the British navy, which sailed on a few days later to cripple the Italian fleet at Taranto.

On the far shore of the Mediterranean, in North Africa, the 25,000-strong British Army of the Nile had repulsed the Italian advance into Egypt, taking 38,000 prisoners. With their meager, dispersed forces the British were so far holding their own in the eastern Mediterranean, while their naval "Force H" took care of the western end.

Only one thing, Churchill said, ever frightened him: the German U-boat menace, and that was not quite all. At the end of October the German pocket battleship *Scheer* broke out, via the Denmark Strait, north of Iceland, into the Atlantic. A month later she was followed by the cruiser *Hipper*. Both warships began to prey on British convoys. During a five-month cruise, *Scheer* sank sixteen merchantmen. *Hipper*, intercepted by the Royal Navy early in her career, had to run for Brest. But the cruisers *Scharnhorst* and *Gneisenau* and the battleships *Tirpitz* and *Bismarck* were lurking in port, waiting to join the marauders.

The U-boats presented a more deadly peril. Invisible when they chose to be, evasive, and in great numbers, they had the immense strategic advantage of ports on the north and west coast of France. The British, on the other hand, denied ports and airfields in the neutral Irish Republic, had to divert their convoys around Northern Ireland through the Northern Approaches, to Liverpool's Merseyside and Glasgow's Clydeside. These two ports, as Churchill said, were now of mortal significance.

During one week in September, U-boats sank twenty-seven ships. In October, twenty out of a convoy of thirty-four were sent to the bottom by U-boats. Imports of oil, food, and equipment declined, but still the massacre of the brave merchant ships went on until, one night in December, when the U-boat scourge had reached its most cruel, Churchill called a meeting in the downstairs War Room in Whitehall. Only the Admiralty and senior naval officers were present. Out of that tense discussion came the decision to go over to the offensive. From now on RAF Coastal Command and naval antisubmarine craft would relentlessly hunt the U-boats in the very waters they had chosen to hunt our convoys. The Battle of the Atlantic entered a new phase.

Churchill, himself half American through his mother, kept in constant touch with the American president, Franklin D. Roosevelt, signing himself nostalgically as "Former Naval Person." Ceaselessly he apprised the president of Britain's grievous losses in ships bringing arms, equipment, and food to the beleaguered island. The mortal danger to Britain, he wrote, was the diminution in shipping tonnage. "We can endure the shattering of our dwellings and the slaughter of our civil population," he wrote, but unless there were ships enough "to feed the island, import munitions and move armies . . . we may fall by the way."

Churchill had to face the stark fact that Britain, up to November 1940, had paid $4.5 billion in cash for American aid and was nearing the bottom of the barrel. Only $200 million was left. He told the president: "The more rapid and abundant the flow of munitions and ships which you are able to send us, the sooner our dollar supply will be exhausted." This did not deter him from placing an immediate order for two thousand combat planes a month, confident, as he said, that the Americans would not limit their generous aid only to what Britain could pay for. "You may be certain," he promised, "that we shall prove ourselves ready to suffer and sacrifice to the utmost for the Cause and that we glory in being its champions."

Months earlier, Eleanor Roosevelt had remarked, with exceeding candor, to her husband: "You must remember, Britain represents our first line of defense." Now the president, on December 17, was almost repeating her words, as he told a press conference, "There is absolutely no doubt in the mind of a very overwhelming number of Americans that the best immediate defense of the United States is the success of Great Britain defending itself." Both for that reason and the survival of democracy, he concluded, America should do everything possible to help the British.

Thus was born, or rather reborn, the idea of Lend-Lease, for it originated by a U.S. government statute dating back to 1892, permitting the secretary of war to lease army property "when, in his discretion, it will be for the public good." The new Lend-Lease Bill was prepared for Congress. Churchill described it as "the most unsordid act in the history of any nation." President Roosevelt, "our great friend," as Churchill called him, in his "fireside chat" on December 30 told the American nation: "There is danger ahead. . . . If Britain should go down all of us in all the Americas would be living at the point of a gun. . . . We must produce arms and ships. . . . We must be the great arsenal of democracy."

Thus Britain was now free to plan, unshackled by debt and doubt for the future. Churchill explained, "What we had was lent or leased to us because our continued resistance to the Hitler tyranny was deemed to be of vital interest to the great Republic."

It is always remarkable how one particular topic can be the subject of so many divergent opinions—especially when the political gentry are involved. By the end of 1940, Churchill was certain of ultimate victory, however bitter the struggle. His gallant if exacting ally General de Gaulle confided to his close collaborators, *"La guerre est gagnée"*—the war is won. Almost the same words were used by the German foreign minister, Ribbentrop, in a letter to Germany's ally, the Russian dictator Stalin: "The war has been won by us," he wrote. "It is only a question of how long it will be before England . . . admits to collapse." And Stalin expressed his readiness to share in the resultant spoils of this now overdue event. Shortly afterwards, Hitler, unrivaled as a political double-crosser, issued, in mid-December, his Directive No. 21, headed "Operation Barbarossa," whose purpose was "to crush

Soviet Russia in a quick campaign before the end of the war against England.'' The Fuehrer, on New Year's Eve, wrote to his friend the Italian dictator Benito Mussolini, assuring him, ''The war in the west is itself won. A violent effort is still necessary to crush England.''

But it was Molotov, the poker-faced Russian commissar for foreign affairs, who, with Churchill, undoubtedly had the best grip on the situation. After days of stormy meetings with Ribbentrop and Hitler in Berlin, he gave a farewell banquet. Just as Ribbentrop rose to answer a toast of friendship, the sirens started wailing and the guests hurried down to the basement shelter, where the two foreign ministers continued their talks. Churchill later wrote: ''We had heard of the conference beforehand and though not invited to join in the discussion did not wish to be entirely left out of the proceedings.'' Indeed, RAF bombers were at the rendezvous. While they cruised overhead, the explosions of their bombs reverberating to the depths of the shelter, Ribbentrop kept repeating to Molotov that Britain was finished. ''If that is so,'' replied the commissar, ''why are we in this shelter and whose are those bombs which fall?''

20

ICING UP

E arly in the new year, 85 Squadron migrated to Debden, our familiar habitat north of London where we enjoyed the luxury of metaled runways. There, thanks to the dense fog, which kept us grounded, we were able to preen our ruffled feathers. During this month and the next, fog, ice, snow, and low-lying cloud were to prevent both the enemy and ourselves from flying—the kind of weather when one said, "Even the birds have to walk."

Bad weather was an obstacle, a physical one, to which we were now well accustomed. The arrival in our midst of Defiants, with air gunners to fit, was more a psychological problem. The Defiant, powered with the same Rolls-Royce Merlin engine as our Hurricanes, was a sound aircraft. But it was considerably slower than the Hurricane and, of course, a two-seater. We had fought successfully by day and fumbled by night as single-seater pilots in a high-performance machine. Now we were obliged to fly an inferior machine, not as captains of our own little ship, but as taxi drivers to the air gunner behind, ensconced in his four-gun turret. I tried to believe that this combination would improve our results as night fighters, the ultimate aim. Despite my own unspoken doubts and theirs we were agreed to go ahead and try. If we could do better at night in Defiants than in Hurricanes, that would be our reward. "The prospect of losing the Hurricanes," our adjutant wrote in the squadron diary, "was directly responsible for many impromptu aerobatic displays." But our Hurricanes were not immediately taken from us. While we practiced by day and by night in Defiants, we flew Hurricanes on operational night patrols—as usual in vain, even on the nights of the 11th and 12th, when London came under heavy attack. On the tarmac that night I was chatting with Sergeant Calderwood. Pointing southwards towards a red glow in the sky, he remarked, "Look at the moon rising—what a marvelous sight." "That's not the moon," I told him, "it's London burning."

In mid-January our commander in chief, Air Marshal Sholto Douglas, paid us a visit. Of medium stature, eagle-eyed, eagle-nosed, and extremely sharp-witted, he was a chief to whom you could speak your mind with the certainty of being listened to attentively. We gathered about him in the pilots' room and he talked to us in turn. When I presented James Wheeler, Sholto paused a moment in front of this gray-haired veteran with First World War medals. "How old are you, Wheeler?" he asked. "Thirty-five, sir," replied James, unabashed. "Really?" pursued Sholto. "You must have been a pretty remarkable child in the first war."

James was still a remarkable man. With his age and experience I always knew I could count on his help when needed. That night, with the cloud base at 300 feet, the Germans were droning thousands of feet overhead on their way to bomb the Rolls-Royce works at Derby. Although he had grounded us because of the weather, the controller telephoned asking tentatively for a "weather test." My maxim being "Never ask others to do anything you can't do yourself," I took the hairiest weather tests upon myself. Tearing down the runway in my Hurricane and up into the dark, I was immediately enveloped in cloud. Climbing still, I soon broke out into a crystal-clear sky studded with stars. So beautiful was it that I would gladly have stayed there all night, but as the low cloud made operations impossible, my immediate problem was to get down safely to the airfield. Rather than take the risk of going blind down through the cloud and ending up in a heap on the ground, I spoke to the controller: "Wagon Leader calling, please ask Pilot Officer Wheeler in officers' mess to go quickly to control tower and call me." James, off duty and peacefully sipping a beer, responded immediately. Five minutes later he called me. "Hello, Wagon Leader." "Hello, James," I replied. "Please fire off a few rockets"—they rose to 1,000 feet—"to help me position airfield. Tell local searchlights to project horizontally so that I can see the ground." One after another, rockets came shooting up through the cloud layer and faded out. At the fourth volley I was close enough to the airfield to begin my descent. Confident in our joint technique, I let down into the cloud. Seconds passed and then suddenly I was in the full glare of the horizontal beams, and trees and telegraph posts were slipping past just below. And there was Debden's flashing beacon. The rest was easy; our artisanal method had worked perfectly. It only remained for me to offer James a final beer.

The main satisfaction we got from our Defiants was giving our faithful and efficient ground crews an occasional joyride. They were always close to us pilots and shared in our tribulations. But we made slow progress in becoming operational on the new aircraft. Snow and fog kept us grounded for days on end. There was another reason, too: a rumor had reached me that we were soon to be reequipped with Havocs, the British name given to the American twin-engined Douglas DB7, originally a high-performance medium bomber but now being converted in Britain into a night fighter with AI and a battery of eight machine guns in the nose. Confirmation soon came from Air Vice Marshal Leigh-Mallory, now commanding No. 11 Group, who had been following our problems closely and heeding my repeated pleas for better equipment. It looked as if we were on the verge of becoming "specialized" night fighters.

The era of the Defiant was, for us, over. It was not to be despised as a cat's-eye night fighter, and as such the Luftwaffe found it a troublesome and determined adversary, especially in attacks from below, when the plan view of the bomber offered a larger target to the Defiant's air gunner. This solid but shapely machine made a useful contribution to the gradually increasing respect among the Luftwaffe for British night fighters. If the Defiant did not find favor with us, it did help to convert us from the single-seater mentality to the two-seater. There remained yet another step, from single-engined aircraft to twin-engined, with AI—the answer to the night-fighter's prayer.

In mid-January, John Cunningham, with Sergeant Jimmy Rawnsley, now his radar operator, downed another enemy bomber. Their interception was an all-time classic: perfect cooperation of the GCI, whose controller, Flight Lieutenant Brown, put John within AI range of the enemy, and AI, which enabled Rawnsley to guide his pilot to within visual distance. GCI stations were going up all over the country. Our own, in the Debden sector, was at Waldringfield, in Suffolk. We had already started working with it, but in Hurricanes we still lacked the missing link, AI, which, once ours, would connect us directly with the enemy. As we waited for Havocs we continued, in Hurricanes, our lone patrols as long as snow and fog did not keep us and the Luftwaffe earthbound.

Just before the month ended, their majesties the king and queen paid us the honor of a visit. The king and queen moved tirelessly among their bombed-out subjects and fighting men, who took courage from their so genuine concern for their well-being. Douglas Bader's 242 Canadian Squadron had come over from nearby Duxford for the occasion. Douglas, five years my senior, was a human phenomenon. With one leg amputated above the knee and the other just below, he was yet one of the greatest of our fighter pilots. The officers and men of our two squadrons were ranged stiffly inside a hangar. Just before the arrival of their majesties, Douglas (whom I had first known during the day fighting) confided to me, "Look, old boy"—his standard opening gambit—"the one thing I can't do is stand properly to attention. So if I overbalance, please come to the rescue." As the royal inspection proceeded I waited nervously for Douglas, tin legs and all, to crash to the ground. Luckily, by parting his feet slightly, he remained upright.

It was a long tradition, originating probably from the RAF's origins in 1918, for "fighter boys" to wear the top button of their blue uniform tunic undone. When one or two pilots had asked me, "Should we do it up for the king?" I replied, "No, let's keep up the old tradition." So all our pilots' top buttons remained undone. Douglas evidently had a more proper respect for royal protocol; all his pilots' top buttons were done up. When he came to our pilots, the king, who had a keen eye for details of dress, stopped in front of Sammy Allard and asked him, "Why do the pilots in your squadron wear their top buttons undone and the other squadron's are done up?" Sammy, with his disarming grin, replied, "It's an old tradition, sir. Perhaps the others are too shy of your majesty." Standing behind the king, our dear commander in chief, Sholto Douglas, went very red in the face.

"Come February, fill dike, be it black or be it white." True to the old adage, February gave us a generous downpour of both, keeping Luftwaffe night bombers and RAF night fighters out of the sky. Only two major raids were made that month, both on the Welsh port of Swansea.

Our most insidious enemy was, as usual, the weather. Geoff Howitt, caught in a snowstorm, managed to grope his way into Gravesend—of all places. Sergeant Webster, an exceptionally able young pilot, ran into double trouble, a snowstorm and engine failure. By a miracle he survived a crash landing.

Suddenly one night the sky cleared and sparkled with stars. Back came the Luftwaffe, though not in force. "Dopey" Arbon was first off on patrol. The GCI controller put him on to an enemy bomber, guiding him so accurately that, in the clear sky, he came close enough to sight it. He opened fire, only to see the enemy aircraft dive away and disappear. I was next off. Hardly having lifted away from the airfield, I was fired upon by some unseen enemy lurking in the dark. I called for a vector and the sector controller gave me a course to steer, which, lacking the accuracy of the GCI, failed to put me on the track of the intruder. Such incidents only increased our frustration and made us long all the more for Havocs. They also warned us that German night fighters, on offensive patrol, were prowling in the dark around us. We had not forgotten that semicomic adventure at Kirton four months ago. The German offensive patrols were operating out of Schipol, in Holland, and although mainly on the lookout for returning RAF bombers, would not hesitate to attack anything in the air or on the ground. Ju. 88s and Dornier 17s had been converted into night fighters, each with a forward-firing 20mm cannon and machine guns.

In Germany, night-fighter pilots had not yet caught the public imagination. Their defensive cat's-eye night fighters, in Me. 109s and Me. 110s, operated, like us, by single patrols, limited to only thirty minutes to an hour, with no more than three per night. We were worked harder, naturally, since our country was under heavier attack. Controlled by R/T, with searchlights indicating the raiders, the German pilots, like us, realized that it needed a lot of luck to bring off an interception. The general opinion was that night flying was at best a thankless job, at worst a nightmare and costly in pilots' lives. Stronger opinions were held by Italian pilots: night fighters were useless, AA guns being more effective. A pilot of the Regia Aeronautica who had gone up in pitch dark against an RAF attack on Turin thought he was lucky to get down alive. However much we could sympathize with all these feelings it was meanwhile clear that besides the pursuit of our bombers, German night fighters on offensive patrol were also interested in us. If the compliment was hardly deserved, it was all the same rather flattering.

There came to us at this time, to gain experience, a wing commander from the Air Ministry named Hamilton, tall, charming, and, after years spent behind an office desk, slightly haggard. To have quit its safety for the glorious uncertainties of night fighting proved that he was a brave man. I was watching on the tarmac one night as, navigation lights on, as was the rule, Hamilton approached to land. Suddenly out of the darkness came a long burst of machine-gun fire, followed by the roar of a zooming aircraft—another of those German night fighters. He missed our friend, who wisely extinguished his lights and after waiting awhile landed intact.

The cold of these winter nights put us to almost unendurable torture, and our black, long-suffering Hurricanes as well. At high altitude the temperature inside the cockpit was no more than a few degrees above the arctic temperatures outside. Various means were proposed by our thoughtful scientists to alleviate our discomfort: for our flying boots, innersoles filled with a chemical which, when water was added through a little hole, gave off heat. A nice idea, but the thick innersole made the boots a tight and uncomfortable fit. More popular were "hot potatoes," bags filled with the same chemical which you slipped into any available pocket. They too were somewhat cumbersome. We tried an electrically heated flying suit, only to discard it, for it was too bulky for the small confines of the cockpit. German Me. 109 pilots did likewise with theirs. The Sidcot flying suit (a relic of the First World War) helped to keep the cold out of those who liked to wear it, but in the cockpit it was hampering. I preferred to pile on as many sweaters as there was room for. Silk and wool were the best thermal insulators. Generous Americans, moved by our country's resistance, sent over "Bundles for Britain," no doubt in the same Atlantic convoys that were bringing our Havocs. Among them, apart from balaclava helmets, scarves, and other woollies to wear on the ground, was a kind of home-knitted sleeve which could stretch from the leg over the knee and up to the thigh. It took up no room and greatly helped to save our lower limbs from frostbite. In one of my own, the left leg and foot—which, in the day fighting, had stopped a hefty German bullet—the blood circulation was not so good and the cold numbed it up to the knee. A pair of silk stockings, sent by my mother, went a long way to alleviate the problem. To protect their hands, some pilots wore leather gauntlets, but I preferred myself to feel with my fingers the touch of the controls and switches. Woollen mittens over thin silk gloves kept my hands warm enough.

In the intense cold at high altitude our Hurricanes suffered, too. You could feel the throttle lever and controls stiffening in the freezing air. Ice forming on the air intake and propeller blades made the engine falter and sent vibrations through the aircraft and into your body, which was part of it. Ice building up on the leading edges of wings and tailplane altered their profile and impaired their lift, leaving you with a horrible sinking feeling which you could not control unless you dived down to a lower altitude. But this maneuver, while a remedy to one problem, provoked another. The humidity in the air lower down formed an opaque layer of ice on the thick frozen glass of the bulletproof windscreen. Coming in to land one night in February with my windscreen completely obscured, I had to open the hood, slide my left hand forward along the side panel of the windscreen, and scrape the ice off the front of it with my nails in order to see the flare path.

We possessed but one remedy to prevent icing: a thick, sticky brown paste which was rubbed on the propeller, the air intake, and the leading edges of the wings. It was the invention, so they said, of an imaginative but not too realistic boffin, who, remarking that snowdrops did not freeze up, concocted this paste from their flowers. It sounded like a tall story.

The Germans too, of course, endured similar problems from the bitter cold. For clearing snow from the runway they found the trimotor Junkers 52, if there was one available, effective as it taxied up and down, blowing away the snow in the slipstream of its three engines. A more serious problem was the icing up, in flight, of their planes. Several had crashed, some of them in Britain. German de-icing equipment was not standard, some aircraft being fitted with pulsating systems to prevent formation of ice, others with a system that blew hot air through pipes in the leading edge of wings. These somewhat sophisticated systems were supplemented by a special de-icing paste hardly likely, with the Germans' know-how in synthetic chemistry, to have been made from snowdrops. It was rubbed on by hand by the ground staff, but some aircrews, not trusting their technical men, did the dirty work themselves.

While both air forces quailed before the rigors of winter, the Luftwaffe, as they pursued their mission of destruction against our cities and ports, had to face perils as bad as, if not worse than, those of the elements. The RAF's radio counteroffensive had sown much confusion among the enemy. The jammer Aspirin had thoroughly calmed the Luftwaffe's enthusiasm for *Knickebein*: aircrews could not trust that particular beam navigation system any longer. The precision of *X-Geraet*, the beam used by the fire-starting Kampfgruppe 100, had been so blurred by our Bromide jammers that those celebrated Luftwaffe pathfinders were evidently no longer happy in their work, fiddling with their frequencies in the middle of an attack in an effort to escape from Bromide, and on one occasion dropping parachute mines which could not possibly be aimed to mark the target with any accuracy.

The Luftwaffe's latest and most sophisticated beam system, *Y-Geraet*, fitted in the Heinkels of Kampfgeschwader 26's 3rd Staffel, proved a fiasco from the start. Since its signals had first been detected in November 1940 by the RAF's Y-service, Dr. Cockburn had been working on his jammer, named "Domino." The BBC, with its powerful television transmitter at Alexandra Palace in south London, was also in the plot, re-radiating the Germans' signal and causing turmoil with their ingenious but vulnerable beam. Meacons, those cunning, deceptive radio beacons, kept plaguing the enemy bombers.

It was probably one, or perhaps more, of these snares set by the RAF's 80 Wing that led, on the night of February 15, to a remarkable happening at Debden. With a few stray enemy aircraft about, I had been sent up to patrol. A couple of hours later the controller called me in to land—"as soon as you can," he added. "The weather's closing in." Once I was down he telephoned me at the dispersal point: "It doesn't look as if there will be any more 'trade' tonight," he said, "and the weather's getting worse. So Eighty-five can go to release." That meant we were free. But "release" or not, I invariably spent the night at the dispersal point. Except that night, when thanks to a recent dose of flu I felt particularly exhausted. I decided to catch up on some sleep in my room in the mess and confided the night watch to Jim Marshall and Paddy Hemingway. I bade them a peaceful night.

In my bedroom I lay back between the fresh, clean sheets, for once relaxed and without a care in my head. Toward midnight, as I tuned in my Murphy portable radio, there came to my ears the distant throb of engines. It grew closer and the familiar note made me conclude that it was an odd Heinkel on the way home. Then the aircraft was overhead; the sound of its engines diminished, as it apparently came in to land. I changed my mind—it must be one of ours, lost. Some minutes later the engines were turning at full throttle and their sound faded into the night. This time I thought "God bless him, he's on his way again." After listening to the news I switched off and went to sleep.

Tim called on me early next morning. "I suppose you know what happened last night," he said, ready to spring a big surprise. "Yes," I replied drowsily, robbing him of the initiative. "A Heinkel landed." "How the hell did you know?" demanded Tim. I did not, for certain, but I soon found out.

Those two amiable types, Jim and Paddy, were watching, each with a cigarette dangling from his lips, as the aircraft approached and swept into the flare of the floodlight, which someone had obligingly ordered to be switched on. "Gosh!" exclaimed Jim. "It's a Whitley." "Don't make me laugh," retorted Paddy. "It's a Wellington." The aircraft taxied round and stopped, its engines still turning, outside the control tower. Out came the duty pilot, "Ace" Hodgson, a young New Zealander, so zealous a pilot that I called him "the Ace" and the name stuck. He found himself confronted by a tall young man in unfamiliar uniform who put his hand on the Ace's shoulder and addressed him in an equally strange language. Only then did Hodgson realize that the man was a German, his aircraft a Heinkel 111. The two enemy airmen then retired hurriedly in the direction from which they had come.

Four officers of the Local Defense Regiment, responsible for guarding the airfield, happened to be present, watching events from the roof of the control tower. Hodgson shouted to them, "We're covered by the rear gunner! Don't shoot!" They were anyway in no position to do so, each one of them having left his revolver in his bedroom. It was related that the "airman of the watch" climbed into the Heinkel and asked the pilot if he needed refueling. If that was indeed the case the German pilot was chivalrous enough to allow him to get out before he taxied back to the runway and took off.

I was rent with chagrin and frustration on hearing the full story. Here we were, trying vainly for the last four months to shoot down a German night bomber, and we had failed to capture this one alive. It only needed someone to park a car, an ambulance, or a fire tender in front of the Heinkel. But it is easy to be wise. . . .

Early the following morning, Leutnant Florian, pilot of another enemy bomber, a Ju. 88, and his crew were flying home after bombing Liverpool when, thanks to faulty D/F bearings, they lost themselves completely. The Leutnant landed at Steeple Morden, in Bedfordshire, where he, his crew, and their Ju. 88 were captured.

21

THE ENEMY CAMP

The Luftwaffe bomber crews were becoming more and more aware of the dangers facing them in the night skies over Britain. The ceaseless interference with their radio beams was disconcerting enough. But that was far from being the end of their troubles. British AA fire was more intense and accurate than ever, and particularly unpleasant now that the guns (thanks to their GL radar) were firing unaided by searchlights and their shells bursting without warning in the dark, and dangerously close. Searchlights were no more the helpful beacons by which the Luftwaffe could identify the target. They were more powerful, more numerous, and (thanks to their SLC radar) remarkably accurate, working in groups of six and forming a cone—remarkably efficient, the Germans found to their discomfort.

Balloons and their cables were a real if less frequent menace, particularly to the Luftwaffe mine-layers, whose favorite waters were Plymouth harbor, the Thames, the Firth of Forth, and the Mersey. Gliding down through the barrage to drop mines was a nerve-shattering experience, which the mine-layers did not always survive. One of them, a Heinkel, on hitting a cable, was blown to pieces by its own mine.

Although our night fighters had not yet made any marked impact on the Luftwaffe, its bomber crews had sometimes sighted us and knew we were searching for them. The news that was getting back to them of our occasional successes was beginning to make them jumpy, to the point where one crew member confessed that on each mission he felt obsessed by the fear of night fighters. His problem, at present, was largely psychological.

When, having run the gauntlet of these several hazards, the bomber crews returned safely to base, their aircraft were still not entirely secure. Sabotage of German aircraft was on the increase and had caused some crashes. Telephone lines were another target for the saboteurs—even little boys on their way to school, a pair of tweezers in their trouser pocket, were tempted to commit such villainous crimes against the Reich.

But the morale of the young night-bomber crews, mostly in their early twenties, was high. Hitler had declared that there were no more islands, and they felt buoyed up by the certainty of invasion, come springtime. What made them believe that? "Hitler has said so" was the invariable answer. It was the answer I got from twenty-one-year-old Werner Schulz when I talked to him back in May 1940 on a southbound train from Scotland. "The war will be over by Christmas," he told me with a confident smile. "What makes you think so?" I asked him, and he replied, still smiling, "Our Fuehrer has told us." The Fuehrer had proved to be a false prophet—not for the last time—and the older hands were feeling less confident; the air-sea blockade was not having the desired effect, U-boats were too few, and British industry seemed unexpectedly resilient to the night-bombing offensive. It was when Luftwaffe prisoners were driven across London on their way to the RAF interrogation center at Cockfosters that they received their most brutal shock: they could not believe that they were really in London. Dr. Goebbels's propaganda had assured them that every window was shattered and the city in ruins. Ruins in plenty there were, of course, but London was then the biggest of all cities, and the Luftwaffe men, to their bitter disillusionment—for their efforts by day and night had been very considerable—made their own discovery that business went on as usual, with shops and theaters open and taxis and red buses plying the streets. It was not like that in Berlin, and they were worried lest Berliners might not stand up to the kind of punishment that the Luftwaffe had dealt out to London.

For the aircrews who made it back to base, there were, however, certain compensations. They thought—unkindly, for they were overwrought and living from day to day—that the only good things in France were food, champagne, and public brothels. There were, as well, other compensations in plenty, in the form of decorations, which, to keep up the spirits of the men, both air and ground crew, were dispensed with a lavish hand. So lavish in fact that jokes were going round. While the Iron Cross Second Class was highly prized by the young, the older hands despised it. Everyone, they said, was bound to receive one, sooner or later, with the rations. The Iron Cross First Class, however, was rightly respected. And yet there were odd cases like that of a certain *Feldwebel*. On watch at a dummy airfield one night, he waited until the RAF was overhead, whereupon he took a lantern and ran here and there, hoping to attract the *Englaender Bomben*. But since the wary RAF bombers refused to be tempted, the valiant *Feldwebel*, so the story ended, was still running. This astonishing act of devotion earned him the Iron Cross First Class.

Petty conflicts between Luftwaffe senior commanders and Goering, whom they considered (rightly) more of a politician than an airman, were often provoked by Goering himself. Dashing from base to base as fast as his bulk would allow, he delivered pep talks and bestowed medals upon all and sundry. This naturally annoyed the commanders in question, and none more than Hugo Sperrle, the monocled and massive general commanding Luftflotte 3, which operated at night over Britain. Between Goering and Sperrle it was well known that there was little love lost. After Goering had paid a surprise morale-raising visit to one of Sperrle's bases, distributing Iron Crosses, Sperrle himself arrived next day. Not to be outdone by the *Reichsmarschall*, he promoted nearly everyone to *Feldwebel*, including one man whom Goering had raised to *Unteroffizier*, a superior rank, the day before. Thank God that in this bloody and bitter struggle, on one side and the other there was occasionally something to make us laugh.

22

CRY HAVOC!

At Debden one morning early in February I had watched as a clean-lined, mid-wing, twin-engined monoplane landed on its tricycle undercarriage. That was its most striking feature; instead of a tail wheel at the end of the fuselage there was a nose wheel at the front. It was the first Havoc I had ever seen—not for our own keeping, but a demonstration model. And what a demonstration! Its pilot, Squadron Leader Salter, took me for a ride during which he proved that the Havoc could perform the rolls, loops, and stalled turns which were the normal repertoire of a single-seater fighter. While night fighting did not call for such antics, the Havoc's behavior was encouraging. Not one of us, except James Wheeler, had ever flown a twin-engined aircraft. Salter further cheered us by saying how much easier it was to land with a tricycle undercarriage than to make a "three-pricker" with the conventional landing wheels.

Hardly had Salter left when a technical officer arrived to lecture us on the mysteries of AI and the technique of night interception controlled by GCI. Though much diligent practice was needed to master it, the system was quite straightforward. The night fighter was scrambled under the directions of the sector controller, who then handed it over to the GCI controller. If he was already busy guiding a preceding fighter to intercept, the following one was kept waiting in the "cab rank." The GCI controller called him when the next "customer" (from the Luftwaffe) showed up, and guided him to within AI range—a few miles. Then, "Flash your weapon," the controller would order, and the night fighter's radar operator would take over, guiding his pilot to approach the "customer" from astern. If all went well the moment came when the pilot announced, "Okay, I can see it." The rest was up to him.

The technical officer had only just departed when, next day, Sammy Allard and his pilots of A Flight hurried north to Church Fenton, there to do a short conversion course onto "twins"—Blenheims, as it happened.

Meanwhile our first Havoc was delivered, but no one yet dared touch it. On Sammy's return I sped myself to Church Fenton to be "converted"—by no one less than Group Captain George Stainforth, who, in a Schneider Cup Supermarine S6 (forerunner of the Spitfire) had, in the early thirties, exceeded 400 mph; he was one of my boyhood heroes. In the hands of such a master, and despite my instinctive dislike of twins, I was quickly converted. Yet, after the sensitive, powerful Hurricane with its single throttle lever, "spade-grip" control column, and one mighty engine cowled in the long nose which you pointed where you willed, it felt odd to be sitting behind a screen of Perspex with nothing in front but thin air, between two propellers turning like windmills, each controlled by a separate throttle lever, and holding a "spectacle-grip" control column to maneuver the unwieldy aircraft. But once used to her size, I found the Blenheim handled well. After a twenty-minute solo I was heading south again for Debden, there to find that a second Havoc had arrived. Still no one took to flying it, the reason being that the electricians were fitting and testing the AI and the armorers were busy on the guns—eight Brownings mounted in the nose cockpit, which was destined, in the original bomber version, for the bomb aimer. In the roof of his cockpit was an escape hatch, which for our purpose could be removed for inspection of the guns.

The look of the Havoc pleased me. After admiring it I climbed up into the cockpit. What a change from the Hurricane's cramped, uncomfortable interior. The floor of the Havoc's cockpit was neatly laid with a green carpet and the knobs of different levers—throttle, airscrew pitch, and mixture—were variously colored in green, red, and yellow. What luxury! Only one thing disturbed me—the tips of the propeller blades whirled round within a few inches of the pilot's ears. Climbing into an airplane cockpit was one thing; getting out—in a hurry—was quite another problem. I did not fancy the prospect of bailing out of a Havoc.

While the armorers worked on the guns and the electricians on the AI and radio, installing, adjusting, and testing them and making them ready for the next phase of the battle, we kept plugging away, patrolling in our Hurricanes, only too conscious that they were nearing the end of their career with us. It had been distinguished enough by day, but by night dogged by failure and disaster. We owed our casualties to the weather, not to the enemy, and had inflicted none on him. However,

> The heights which some men reached and kept
> Were not attained by sudden flight,
> But they, while their companions slept,
> Were toiling upwards in the night.

On the night of February 25 I took off on patrol from Debden and climbed up beneath the black dome of the moonless sky. Visibility was good. The sector controller gave me a vector of 090 degrees—due east—and told me to go over to Channel B—the GCI frequency. Pressing the second of the four little red buttons on the control box at the left of the dashboard, I called the GCI controller. He put me to "orbit" at 12,000 feet above the balloon barrage at Harwich.

A quarter of an hour before I left Debden, a Dornier 17, U5 + PM, had taken off from Merville—incidentally, 85 Squadron's base during the Battle of France. At the controls was twenty-one-year-old Leutnant Heinz Patscheider, the youngest of the crew. His wireless operator, Unteroffizier Paul Schmidt, was only two years older. The veterans of the crew were Feldwebel August Beysiegel, the twenty-seven-year-old air gunner, and the observer, Oberfeldwebel Martin Mummer. He was twenty-eight and before joining the Luftwaffe in 1936 had worked first as a hairdresser, then as a policeman. That night of the 25th he was making his fifty-first flight over Britain. On this particular mission the Dornier carried sixteen 50-kilogram high-explosive bombs and a quantity of incendiaries. The crew had orders to attack our night-fighter airfields.

After crossing the French coast at 6,000 feet, they continued climbing across the North Sea until, at 12,000 feet, they made a landfall just south of Harwich, where I had been circling patiently for half an hour until receiving the order "Vector two-one-zero"—south-southwest. That was the last I heard from the controller, although he was to hear more from me. After I had flown some minutes on a course of 210 degrees the piercing silver-blue shafts of nine searchlights suddenly shot up into the sky, and there, in the apex of their cone, glistened an aircraft steering east—too far away to identify, but I gave the tallyho! (aircraft sighted) to the controller and veered east at full throttle in pursuit. Before I could close with it the aircraft reached the coast and made out to sea. The searchlights groped after it, lost it, and doused, leaving me peering into the dark and cursing the ill fortune which had always been our lot. The crew of U5 + PM were at the same time cursing the British searchlights from which they had just escaped. They decided on a ruse which, they hoped, would deceive the searchlight crews into taking them for a "friendly."

A moment later I sighted the two navigation lights of an aircraft coming toward me. "Suspecting trickery," as I later recorded in my combat report, I turned in toward it. The moment it recrossed the coast the searchlights once more pierced the darkness and held it. I closed in, taking care to remain concealed, out of their beams, and began to stalk the mysterious plane. The dazzling glare of the lights cast shadows on it, making identification difficult. To see better, I flung back the hood, but the blast of the slipstream loosened the friction buckle on the chin strap of my helmet and the controller's voice was drowned in the bluster of the engine. I kept the hood open, for I had to be sure that the aircraft was not "one of ours." There had been tragic cases of mistaken identity. At first I took it for a Ju. 88, with its long engine cowlings. Then, still carefully avoiding the searchlights, I slipped past astern and saw it had twin rudders. A Dornier 17? Or conceivably one of our Hampdens? If so, it had no right to be burning its navigation lights above 5,000 feet. But there were foreign pilots flying with us who sometimes disregarded the rules. I moved out to the left and it was then that I saw, unmistakable, on the side of the fuselage, the black German cross. The plane was a Dornier 17. In company, we had covered a lot of ground, they with their navigation lights on, cruising blithely along in the searchlights, I lurking in the surrounding shadows.

The rest happened quickly. Coming in from their left and slightly above, still concealed from the searchlights, I held on until the last moment, then pressed the firing button. A short burst—thirty rounds from each gun—and it was over. The effect of the De Wilde was terrible; the Dornier's controls were hit, its incendiaries set on fire. Still held fast by the searchlights, the span of its wingtips marked by its red and green navigation lights, it spiraled steeply earthwards streaming smoke and sparks, the air gunner adding to the fireworks as he poured tracers wildly into the dark. Then the stricken aircraft reared up steeply, followed by the tenacious searchlights, until, as it seemed to be poised motionless at the apex of their beams, there streamed from it three parachutes. I waited hopefully for the fourth, but Paul Schmidt's parachute got tangled on the tailplane and was torn to shreds. Down went the Dornier again in a steep spiral, to crash with its load of bombs and its navigation lights still burning, near Sudbury, in Suffolk. I saw a great explosion and flames. Then—surprisingly—a stick of exploding bombs which fell across the fire. A following Luftwaffe bomber had mistaken it for a burning English target.

The Home Guard soon rounded up the Dornier's crew, Patscheider with a broken leg, Beysiegel and Mummer unhurt. The body of Paul Schmidt was discovered not far away. I felt sorry, and still do, that he had to die so young.

That combat was 85 Squadron's first—and last—night victory in Hurricanes. I owed it jointly to my comrades of 85 Squadron, pilots and ground crew, who had never once flinched before the cruel elements, the disappointments and dangers which had been our lot. As fate would have it, I was appointed the executioner, and as such I am glad that three of my victims were reprieved at the last moment.

We fighting on our side and they, the Germans, fighting on theirs could never be certain of the extent of our lease of life. Fate, without warning, could foreclose it. Faith is a surer companion than Fate, with her unpredictable caprices. Three nights after the Dornier, she played me a curious trick.

It was toward midnight that I took off in my Hurricane on patrol. The controller vectored me northwards, here and there, round and round, in pursuit of an elusive enemy aircraft. The weather, already doubtful, was steadily deteriorating. But it was not primarily to the elements that I owed my embarrassment that night. After an hour without the foggiest idea of my position, I called for a fix. No answer. I called and called again; still silence. The cockpit lights, I realized, were fading—I pressed the switch of the navigation lights, but neither red nor green showed up at my wingtips. Fearing the worst, I tapped a letter or two on the Morse key to try the downward signaling lamp; it made not the faintest blink. The battery was flat. I could neither speak nor show myself to anyone, nor could anyone communicate with me. Circling, I peered down into the murk below, but could see not the slightest helpful sign or feature, beacon or coastline, below. Visually and aurally, I was cut off from the earth. The only way to return—safely or not, I could not tell—was to bail out. I steered west away from the sea for ten minutes to allow for a reasonable chance of falling on dry land, then made ready to go over the side. It was only then that a strange white light, diffused by the cloud and haze, shone far below. In a moment it was gone; then it reappeared and I dived towards it. Out it went again. When it next appeared I was clear of the drifting cloud and saw a pair of navigation lights approaching it and another pair or two circling above. There was an airfield below, with aircraft waiting to land, which was what I wanted to do so much myself. With no lights or radio to identify myself, I could only choose a convenient aircraft, slip in behind it, and follow it down to land in its wake, praying that the floodlight would shine on till I touched down. It did, and I taxied back to it. A man ran forward and climbed up to the cockpit. "Sorry," I shouted to him. "I'm in trouble. I'm from 85 Squadron." "We'll see about that," he shouted back, thrusting a pistol into my back. "Taxi back to the tarmac." Which I did, while he still jabbed me with his pistol. I could hardly blame him, after our adventure with the Debden Heinkel, for his unfriendly welcome. My Hurricane was no positive proof that I was British; many had been captured by the Germans in France. But in the silence which followed after the engine was switched off, when he could hear my English voice, he became more affable and I soon proved my identity. I discovered that I had landed at Langham, in Rutlandshire, sixty miles from Debden.

I flew back to Debden next day, thankful to have survived yet another brush with death. I did not believe in Fate, despite the tricks, some of them subtle, that she seemed to play on us. I ascribed these inexplicable happenings, were they good or bad for my personal well-being, to God. In those dangerous times, few airmen, if they possessed any feelings, could not but feel an awareness of God, or whatever else they liked to call that power beyond our understanding. Many call it Fate, who at least passed for a woman. But to bow to Fate and attribute all happenings to her seemed to me too abjectly submissive. Rather than trust in Fate I preferred to believe in God. That required Faith, a challenge which put one to the test, for in our simple terms it meant courage, tenacity, morale—positive qualities—as well as resignation to cruel adversity. When, after my return to Debden, I landed that night from patrol in driving rain and nil visibility, I felt it more proper to thank God (yet again) rather than to congratulate myself.

March was a stern and testing month during which we worked zealously to achieve the status of "specialized" night fighters. Yet we were to taste once more the bitterness of grief. Continued and uneventful night patrols in Hurricanes only spurred us to greater efforts by day in Havocs—powerful yet docile aircraft which our pilots quickly learned to handle. More and more Havocs were arriving, thanks to James Wheeler's tireless commuting between Debden and the aircraft depot at Burtonwood, near Liverpool. A specialist radar officer, Pilot Officer Cordingley, a soft-spoken and ingenious university graduate, was appointed to our squadron. Radar operators arrived in a steady flow to be teamed up with one or another of our pilots. The one who came to me was George Barker, just commissioned, of short and solid build and an incorrigible joker. He was just my man, for, oversensitive and solemn as I may have been, I was quickly transformed when others made me laugh. There were not all that many who did, but George was one. I was glad to have him as a joker, and he produced some of his best in the most precarious situations. Joking apart, he was a highly skilled professional.

Another amiable joker was Charles Maton, who had faithfully served Sir Abe, James Bailey's father, as private secretary. He was not paired with young James—as well, maybe, for there was an age gap. Charles joined the veteran James—James Wheeler—and never had we a more lighthearted yet competent team, who kept us in high spirits and embellished our reputation.

The ground crews worked like beavers during these days, for the Havoc, like all new aircraft, was plagued by teething troubles and lack of spares, to the point where our excellent technical chief, Warrant Officer Stammers, was forced to cannibalize one or two aircraft, robbing them of parts to keep the others flying. Although my personal aircraft was never decorated with any device other than the squadron and individual markings VY-0 and the squadron's white hexagon, whose unknown origin dated from the First World War, some pilots, now there was more room available on the front of the fuselage, began naming their aircraft. One day, in a dark corner of the hangar, I noticed a dilapidated Havoc from which most of the working parts had been removed. The broad white letters of its proud name, *Queen of the Air*, had been scratched out and below it in chalk was scrawled Bitch of the Deck.

One disquieting defect of the Havoc's instrumental panel was the inaccuracy of the petrol gauges—main tanks and reserve. Returning one morning after a practice flight with George, I dived down to take a close look at the dummy airfield, planted with wooden stakes and other obstructions, near to Debden. As we skimmed over it at "naught feet," both engines cut dead. "Now what are you going to do?" I heard George chuckling on the intercom. My hand was already on the fuel cock, twisting it so violently onto "Reserve" that I nearly broke my wrist. Our surplus speed from the dive gave the engines, after a few embarrassed coughs, time to pick up. George was still laughing. "We nearly had it that time," he called over the intercom.

Our AI-GCI interception training was in full swing, with one Havoc acting as target, the other, working with the GCI, as defending fighter, when it was decreed that these exercises should continue under the supervision of the experts at Catterick, in Yorkshire. At the prospect of quitting, if only temporarily, the warm and lively ambiance of Debden, and wasting time in the process, I flew north to Catterick on the morning of the 13th to protest and plead. Shortly after lunch a mess waiter called me to the telephone. It was Tim, at Debden. "I'm sorry, I have bad news," he began. "Sam Allard, the Ace, and Walker-Smith have just been killed in an accident." Shattered, I returned forthwith to Debden.

A squadron commander was obliged to make a formal report on every accident. I talked to the few witnesses available and gathered that Sammy was to fly to Ford, in Sussex, there to collect a Havoc from 23 Squadron. Sergeant Walker-Smith accompanied him, to fly the new Havoc back to Debden. The Ace had begged Sammy to take him along for the ride—there was just room for two in the rear cockpit. An armorer told me that after loading and checking the guns, he had trouble fitting the inspection panel on top of the fuselage back into place. Sammy told him, "Let me help," and between them they succeeded, as far as they could tell, in securing the panel. The other vital witness was a gunner of the airfield defense manning a machine gun at the windward end of the runway. As the Havoc, on takeoff, roared low over his head, he noticed a black object fly from the aircraft, but did not see it fall to the ground. He watched, horrified, as the Havoc, after a steep, short climb, stalled and went into a spin.

I inspected the wreckage—a chore I hated but was compelled to do. The only recognizable part of the Havoc was its tail unit; and on the leading edge of the fin were two slight dents, two feet apart, which intrigued me. Searching further, I came upon the gun-inspection panel. I picked it up and walked back to the tail unit. It fitted exactly the two dents on the fin. It had evidently become detached and by a chance in a million, had come to rest balanced exactly across the tail fin. Its resistance, with the engines at full power, had forced the tail down and put the Havoc into an uncontrollable climb until it stalled and spun into the ground. Most of us, Sammy, the Ace, and Walker-Smith included, had often had occasion to thank God for deliverance. Now in our immense chagrin at their death it was hard to understand His mysterious ways.

Sympathy, at once heartfelt and practical, was immediately forth-coming from our commander in chief, Sholto Douglas, and our group commander, Leigh-Mallory. "L-M" informed me that the squadron was released to complete its day and night training on Havocs. How long would it take us, L-M asked, to become operational on the new type? I promised we would be ready for the night of April 7. That would give us three weeks, precious little considering the vagaries of the weather and the dearth of spare parts. Our rehearsals for the opening night increased in tempo, especially with the technique of GCI-AI in-terceptions. We had flown our last night patrols on Hurricanes. We missed them, of course, and although our contribution to the night defense of the realm had been practically negligible, it was now nonexistent—just at the moment when the Luftwaffe resumed in earnest its night offensive against the Island.

Their strategy being to complement the U-boat blockade, the Ger-mans' renewed and savage attacks were directed mainly against our ports. The first to suffer was Cardiff, at the beginning of March. Lon-don's turn came next when on each of the nights of the 8th and 9th, 150 bombers were over the docks and city and the dead in London were numbered in hundreds. Hundreds more civilians died when Portsmouth, Plymouth, Bristol, Liverpool, Glasgow, and Hull were all sorely hit with high explosive and incendiaries. Nor, in the industrial Midlands, were Birmingham and Coventry spared. Inevitably it was again Lon-don's turn. A sharp attack on the night of March 15 was the prelude to a mass assault by nearly five hundred bombers on the 19th which left 751 Londoners dead and hundreds more badly injured—a massacre not of the British plutocracy whom Goering had bombastically claimed was his target, but of the poorer folk of the east and southeast of London.

Woolwich took heavy punishment. In the Arsenal, stores and work-shops were demolished and set ablaze. To the south, where the ground rises toward the Common, military barracks—the Cambridge, Con-naught, and Grand Depot, known to many an earlier generation of the army—were shattered as well as the lives of scores of young soldiers within their walls.

Less than fifty yards away, Mulgrave Road School, hit by oil bombs, went up in flames. Not that this caused too much sorrow to Ray Callow, who had been evacuated there after his own school, Burrage Grove, had been hit. But Ray, home from duty in the Town Hall, that night witnessed a sight which brought such horror to his young eyes that he still remembers it vividly. A heavy bomb damaged a house in Eaton Road, not more than thirty yards from the Callow home, where soldiers, back on leave, were chatting and playing cards with friends. Rescue squads found six of them dead—without a scratch on them. Blast had snuffed out their lives. A seventh, an elderly lady, had been killed by flying debris. Ray was watching when stretcher men carried her body out. They rolled it off the stretcher and tipped it into a kind of metal all-purpose coffin; Ray caught a fleeting glimpse of the dead woman's face, the mangled features, the hair clotted with blood and brick dust. That was the most awful sight ever engraved on the mind of young Ray.

At the AFS substation at Earldom Square the girl operator pushed down two bells—"Numbers one and two pumps, Lewisham!" Many pumps had already reached the blaze when Johnny's No. 1 pump and Steve Needham's No. 2 reached the unimaginable shambles—scattered and burning wares from market stalls, from clothes shops, grocers, fruiterers, toyshops, and the rest. Charred remnants of fruit and vegetables, clothes, boots, smashed dolls, and smoldering teddy bears lay strewn everywhere. For two and a half hours Johnny and his men helped fight the blaze while the chief fire officer directed operations, shouting orders: "Numbers one, two, and five in there, then out and across to the right . . ." Walking backwards with an eye on the pumps as they moved with the flames, the chief fire officer had just shouted, "Now you, get in there!" when his voice fell silent. He had "got in" himself, into a bomb crater full of muddy water. As he crawled out, dripping from his tin hat downwards, the firemen dared not laugh—not until they were on their way back to the substation.

The Luftwaffe immediately followed up that slaughter of London's poor with a heavy two-night attack on Plymouth's dockland, Devonport. There came a lull of two weeks ending in early April with more violent assaults on the west coast ports, Bristol, Liverpool, and Glasgow, at the receiving end of Britain's Atlantic lifeline. Then, as a change from mauling our ports and their stubborn, unconquerable people, nearly 250 Luftwaffe bombers flew off into the night of April 8 to hammer Coventry, whose people, as ever, had no more intention than any other citizens in the land of bowing before the would-be conqueror.

On their side, the would-be conquerors and notably the Luftwaffe, seriously disturbed by their failure to crush British morale, blockade British ports, and destroy British industry, were having a hard think about improving their methods. The problems facing them were accumulating night by night. To begin with, the German aircrews found the blackout over Britain embarrassingly effective—all but those red flashing beacons which showed us the way to go home but continued to puzzle the enemy.

Then there were decoy fires, "Starfish," the creation of Colonel Turner. German observers had their own pet decoys and were extremely wary of them. It was when decoy fires appeared to be part of the target that they looked like any other blaze, well worthy of a stick of bombs. When isolated they deceived no one; they had an unreal look, too compact, the flames too yellow instead of the lurid red of a real blaze belching smoke. A rumor spread among the Luftwaffe that shortage of firewood was forcing the British to give up decoy fires. There, they were overhasty; Starfish decoys were yet to fool the Luftwaffe and collect many more bombs destined for vital targets.

The blackout, Starfish sites, and red flashing beacons were relatively minor worries compared with the failure, thanks to Aspirin jammers, of *Knickebein* to guide the Luftwaffe bombers to their targets. At this check to his favorite gadget, Goering fumed, venting his anger on his unfortunate *Gruppe Kapitänen*. Yet it was none of their fault. Goering should have sent a rude letter to the astute Dr. Cockburn, inventor of Aspirin. Cockburn's Bromide jammer, though increasingly successful against the *X-Geraet* of Kampfgruppe 100, had not yet put an end to its fire-raising pathfinder activities. Crack unit as it had always been in navigation, its crews, in broad moonlight, were able to identify and mark their target with precision. As for *Y-Geraet*, the crews of the specialist unit 3/KG 26, were so bothered by Cockburn's Domino jammer that out of eighty-nine raids, it fuddled them completely in all but eighteen. Accumulating gradually, too, were the successes of British night fighters and AA guns. Their results, if modest and still perhaps more psychological then material, were regular, night after night.

It was not easy for the Luftwaffe to remount or intensify its offensive. One factor might have tipped the balance against the British: a four-engined bomber. Goering, with characteristic lack of foresight, had rejected the idea in the mid-thirties. Since then the four-engined Focke-Wulfe 140 had been built and with its long range and reliability was plaguing our Atlantic convoys. But it did not threaten Britain as a long-range bomber. Only now was the four-engined twin-propeller Heinkel 177 coming into production. It could carry two "Max" 2,500-kilogram bombs. It was still full of bugs and anyway was conceived, like the

Focke-Wulfe 140, for reconnaissance and extreme long-range bombing.

Meanwhile the Luftwaffe confined itself to tactical considerations: London was best approached from the west, with the Thames, the Serpentine, parks, and railway termini as landmarks—much more peaceful than from the east, following the Thames estuary, where AA was thick on the ground. With night bombing so inaccurate, raids were to be concentrated during the period of the bombers' moon to give the best possible chance of target identification and accurate aiming. The bomber should approach "up-moon," more easily to identify the target by its silhouette or its reflection on water. But there was a danger: the bomber itself would be clearly silhouetted, for the benefit of the night fighter which might be on its tail.

There was a funny idea in the minds of some Luftwaffe night-bomber aircrews that British night-fighter pilots were drawn from owners of sports cars. It is true, in my own case, that I owned an MG in Singapore in 1936 and a sporty little Standard with wire wheels a few years later, but my present model was a solid Rover saloon. RAF "types" were generally fond of sports cars, but night-fighter pilots did not possess a monopoly. The respect for our night fighters was growing, be it because of our supposed preference for sports cars or our growing professionalism as night fighters. Luftwaffe crews were now beating it for home at 5,000 feet, well below our normal patrol heights, in the hope of avoiding us.

They were arming themselves, too, with peculiar devices, with the intention of discouraging our unwanted attention: things like a towed kite, or jets of petrol which ignited automatically, or grenades pushed down a chute at the bottom of which was a trigger which fired them— and God help the bomber if the grenade got stuck at the bottom of the chute, where it was sure to explode prematurely. As for the front end of the bomber, one in every *Staffel* was now being fitted with an improved balloon-cable-cutting device, a projecting pole, like the horn of a narwhale, from the end of which a wire extended to each wingtip, where a small explosive charge would sever any balloon cable deflected in its direction. Aerial balloon-sweeping was to be confided to one unlucky crew of each *Staffel*, who would clear the way for the following aircraft. The tactic looked unlikely to be a great success. Finally, the most sensible idea of all, was a system to boost the speed of a bomber in emergency: gas or compressed air was fed into the supercharger, enabling the aircraft to make a sudden spurt and leave the pursuing fighter standing. For this reason, perhaps, the system was called "Ha-

ha.'' These were some of the bright ideas of the German boffins, which, like those of our own, were seldom put into current use.

The spirits of the Luftwaffe bomber crews were high, buoyed up as they were by hopes of the coming invasion of Britain and by letters from their loved ones in Germany which told of increasing movement and ferment in the Fatherland with the approach of spring. Rumors were circulating of a new "secret weapon," the *Seilbombe*, a sort of kite loaded with explosive and designed to be towed behind low-flying aircraft for the purpose of cutting high-tension cables and telephone wires in Britain. With all this invasion fever went a sincere if mistaken belief in the "humanity" of the Fuehrer, Adolf Hitler, ridiculed though he was on the British side. Germans believed that Hitler, onetime corporal in the German Imperial Army, knew so well the horrors of war that he wished to spare his country yet more suffering. An admirable sentiment were it true. But it was not. Hitler was only too ready to sacrifice the lives of German soldiers, sailors, and airmen, of their families and sweethearts, to his ambition of becoming master of Europe, perhaps of the world.

The Luftwaffe lost a hundred men over Britain during March. That did not discourage them. On the contrary, a more insidious influence was creeping into their hearts, tending to weaken their will to fight. Quite simply, it was the easy living that they enjoyed at their bases in France, good living with plentiful food and wine and girls. Few were the French girls who consented, but there was no lack of German girls, serving like our WAAFs in the Luftwaffe. They were nicknamed *Blitz-mädchen*, aged between eighteen and thirty-five and working as telephonists and radio operators—cheerful girls, conscientious, intelligent, and discreet.

Naturally, Paris was the big attraction for all, but serious restrictions opposed a visit to the City of Light. Only soldiers and civilians having urgent reasons were considered. A permit was needed for the person and his car. Luftwaffe men had to report to the provost marshal of the Luftwaffe at 62 Rue du Faubourg St. Honoré, where they were allotted permits and lodgings. The curfew fell for NCOs at 11:00 and for officers at midnight. Regulation dress was required "fully buttoned up." Luftwaffe men could travel free on the Métro, first class where it applied. But they had orders to keep aloof from French civilians; they were prohibited from dancing, from smoking in the streets, on the Métro, and in buses, from sitting on bar stools in public places. Forbidden also was allowing French women to ride in service cars, and walking arm in arm with the opposite sex. Good manners were required in every situation, and a soldierly bearing.

Such were the enemy, the young men we were fighting. But they were not always so restrained as their code of discipline might suggest. Some, who fell on our side, told of the fantastic orgies they had enjoyed. Others, less fortunate, their mutilated bodies washed up on our shores, had in their pockets French money, tickets for the Paris Opéra, the Empire, the soldiers' theater in the Avenue Wagram, the Champs-Elysées, the Avenue Montaigne. They had their fun when they could get it, as we did. We occasionally spent a night at the Coconut Grove, or at Kate Meyrick's 43 Club. But London, unlike Paris, was being bombed. At least our rare visits to the city, when bad weather at the airfield permitted, enabled us to share in a small way the lot of Londoners. We amused ourselves as the bombs crashed around. On the way home one night a canister of incendiaries just missed the car. All that was good for us, for it helped to close the great gulf between us as we patrolled miles up in the darkness and those who were taking it below.

Usually Luftwaffe crews visiting Paris put up at the Monty Hotel. Nearby was the well-known Lotti, where the Gestapo were lodged, and it was a dire experience for a Luftwaffe man when the Monty was full and he had to spend the night with the Gestapo at the Lotti. Captured Luftwaffe crews, greatly fearing the Gestapo, were at this time particularly reticent in interrogations. Happy in their expectation of a German victory, they all the same dreaded an eventual investigation by the Gestapo on their talks with their RAF interrogators.

23

BRITAIN'S STRUGGLE ON DISTANT FRONTS

The first half of 1941, Churchill recalled later, imposed more stress and brought greater problems upon himself and his colleagues than any other period during the war. Britain still alone, surrounded by German-held Europe but loyally supported by the Commonwealth and aided by her great friend, the United States, was fighting both the Axis powers, Germany and Italy, on several fronts. On the home front she was holding out, thanks mainly to the bravery of her citizens, against the repeated onslaughts of the Luftwaffe. Far away, on other fronts, she was striving both for survival and for conquest— in the Atlantic and the Mediterranean, in North Africa and East Africa. Meanwhile there were sinister portents of a new Axis front developing in the Balkans, with its threat for the safety of friendly Greece, and of Yugoslavia, whose friendship had yet to be proved.

Britain's own fate depended ultimately on the Battle of the Atlantic. As long as British merchantmen and those of other nations brave enough to share the perils of the cruel sea could reach British ports and discharge their cargos of food, arms, and equipment (including our Havocs), Britain could hold out indefinitely. Of that Churchill was sure, even if it came to a German invasion, still considered as a very present threat. Our army, our Home Guard, and our air force, both bombers and fighters, had increased immensely in strength. As for the navy, it could always be trusted to defend the waters surrounding our island.

In the broad Atlantic and the northern approaches, where the navy and the RAF's Coastal Command kept watch over the convoys, the task was far harder. Despite constant vigilance, sinkings of merchant ships were, in Churchill's words, "awe-striking." The Kriegsmarine's U-boats were now hunting in "wolf packs," with disastrous results for the convoys. Early in April, a wolf pack sank ten ships out of a convoy of twenty-two. The U-boats were not alone. While the German pocket battleship *Scheer*, after five months of ravaging British convoys, had returned to Germany, the battle cruisers *Scharnhorst* and *Gneisenau* had broken out into the North Atlantic and the cruiser *Hipper* was still at large. Between them, in two months, they sent twenty-nine merchantmen to the bottom, often without stopping to pick up survivors. These grievous losses did not go without retribution. In March five U-boats were sunk, one of them, U-47, commanded by the ace Prien, and two others, U-99 and U-100, by two other distinguished commanders. With the appalling figure of 350,000 tons of shipping already sunk, the Battle of the Atlantic was far from over. The Mid-Atlantic was the danger area, and in April, Churchill remembered: "Somehow we had to contrive to extend our reach, or our days were numbered." It was then that the United States Navy came to the rescue, when President Roosevelt extended its zone of patrol eastward to cover more than half of the American side of the ocean. The U.S. Navy—though the United States was a nonbelligerent—could, and did, report enemy movements in its zone to the Royal Navy.

In the Mediterranean, naval supremacy was essential to British plans in Greece and North Africa. Since November, RAF squadrons fighting alongside the Greeks had helped in the rout of the Italian armies. In early March 1941, Churchill decided to aid Greece more fully. The forces, ground and air, sent to Greece and Crete would have to be taken from the North African front, itself unmistakably threatened by the Germans. The transport of these reinforcements would put a further strain on our Mediterranean fleet, heavily engaged in escorting convoys from the west and east, through to Malta, the British naval base some eighty miles south of Sicily. That beleaguered island had been bombed fifty-eight times during January; in the months to come, Luftwaffe units from Sicily and Pantellaria Island would attack it on an average of two or three times every day.

Thanks to the complaisance of Bulgaria, Romania, and Hungary, German forces had been transiting those countries and massing on the northern frontier of Greece. By the end of January, the Luftwaffe was installed on Bulgarian airfields and within striking distance of Greece and Crete.

Yugoslavia, whose regent, Prince Paul, uncle of the young King Peter II, had made a secret deal with Hitler, was not to be caught so easily in the German snare. The uprising, led by Air Force General Simovic, forced the regent to abdicate. King Peter, after making good his escape by sliding down a drainpipe, appeared at divine service in Belgrade Cathedral on Friday, March 28, to be wildly acclaimed while the crowd insulted the German minister and spat on his car. Hitler, enraged, brooded vengeance against those heroic people.

That same Friday the British Mediterranean fleet scored a signal victory against the Italian fleet off Cape Matapan, at the southern tip of Greece. Meanwhile, British, Australian, and New Zealand troops were taking up positions alongside the Greek army. All waited for the blow to fall.

Some hundreds of miles south across the Mediterranean, on the shores of Africa, the British Army of the Nile, with strong Australian support, was again on the move. After its victory at Bardia, it advanced westward, capturing Tobruk, with thirty thousand prisoners. Tobruk, with its port, was an invaluable prize. The British and Australians then pressed on another 250 miles across the desert and on February 6 captured Benghazi, where the bearded Italian general, Bergonzoli, nicknamed "Electric Whiskers," surrendered. The Italian army had by now lost 130,000 prisoners, hundreds of tanks, and over a thousand guns. It no longer existed.

But, as in Greece, so in North Africa; German troops were massing to fill the gap left by the Italians, disembarking at Tripoli in Libya. The German general, Erwin Rommel, soon to earn the name "the Desert Fox," was preparing to counterattack.

The task of General Wavell, commander in chief of the British Middle East command, was one that would have daunted a lesser man. By March 1941 his armies were facing the enemy on fronts as widely dispersed as Greece, North Africa, Ethiopia, and Somalia; other formations stood ready for action in Palestine and Kenya. By January 1941 the 4th and 5th British-Indian Divisions were engaged in a new offensive against the Italians in the Sudan, pushing them back eastwards into Ethiopia, where, led by General William Platt, they continued the pursuit into northern Eritrea. There, before the stronghold of Keren, some eighty miles from the Red Sea, they were temporarily halted by obstinate Italian resistance.

A thousand miles to the south, in Italian Somalia, on the shores of the Indian Ocean, General Alan Cunningham, at the head of the 11th African Division and the 1st African Brigade, was in mid-February advancing inland. His army, supported by aircraft of the South African Air Force, put the enemy to rout. After entering Mogadishu, Somalia's main port, Cunningham's forces then veered northwest across desert and hills into Ethiopia, and then overwhelmed the Italians at Harrar and Diredawa. Since the start of the campaign he had covered nearly a thousand miles of difficult terrain and accounted for more than fifty thousand of the enemy for the loss of five hundred of his own men. After a pause at Diredawa to regain their breath, Cunningham's forces continued another two hundred miles into the mountains toward the capital Addis Ababa, which they entered on April 6.

Meanwhile, far to the north, General Platt's 4th and 5th British-Indian Divisions with, overhead, the South African Air Force and RAF squadrons from Aden, had fought a hard and costly battle to defeat the Italians at Keren. They then entered the pleasant town of Asmara, and on April 8 captured Massawa, on the Red Sea. With the elimination by the Royal Navy and the Fleet Air Arm of the entire Italian naval force in the Red Sea, the days of Mussolini's new Roman Empire were numbered.

While British and Commonwealth forces fought on with varying fortune across this immense battlefield of the Atlantic, the Mediterranean, Greece, and North and East Africa and over Germany itself, it was hard not to feel that the part of my squadron in the struggle was insignificant. I often thought of my brothers—Michael, a destroyer captain fighting somewhere on the high seas, and Philip, commanding a battalion of the Gurkha Rifles in India. His fight against the Japanese was yet to come.

Yet paltry by comparison as our own efforts may have been, we were doing our utmost to strengthen the night defenses of our cities, and above all, London. For the home front was paramount. If, after all the valiant fighting on other fronts, Britain yielded, her hopes of beating Hitler would collapse around her. Britain was a fortress, the only one still inviolate, from which, sometime in the future, sallies could be made against the foe. Hitler himself had in January said as much to his military chiefs: "The British can hope to win the war only by beating us on the Continent. The Fuehrer is convinced that this is impossible." More than three long years were yet to pass before Hitler was to discover that he was mistaken. In the meantime, Britain must at all costs hold out.

24

THE HOME FRONT: THE NIGHT BATTLE APPROACHES ITS CLIMAX

On April 7, as promised, I reported 85 Squadron at readiness for operations that night. Incidentally, as commander of a twin-engined squadron, with its increased establishment, I was now given the rank of Wing Commander (Acting)—"Wing Co." If sounding rather less gallant than "squadron leader," "wing co." had a friendly ring about it which I enjoyed.

After days and nights of training, the squadron at last took its place alongside the "specialized" night-fighter squadrons—25, 29, 68, 219, 600, and 604, all of them equipped with Beaufighters. No. 85, with its Havocs, was the ugly duckling and not quite so well off as the Beaufighters in performance and armament, let alone experience. But we were of the same mettle as the rest, and only time would show how well we could do. Completing the regular night-fighter force were eight "cat's-eye" squadrons flying Hurricanes and Defiants. Given moonlight, visibility, and GCI control, the "cat's-eyes" continued to inflict losses on the enemy. No. 23 "Intruder" Squadron operated over enemy territory.

I was among a few others who on the night of the 7th made their first operational patrol in a Havoc. The enemy was headed for Liverpool and no "trade" came our way, nor again on the night of the 8th, when the Luftwaffe attacked Coventry. The following night witnessed the beginning of a dramatic change in our fortunes. After six months of futile searching in the dark we suddenly, scientifically, that night found three enemy aircraft.

It was Geoff Howitt and his operator, Sergeant Reed, who, on April 9, won the squadron's first victory on Havocs. A waxing moon near to full and the air as clear as crystal made for better sighting, not only for the night fighter but for the enemy upper and lower rear gunners on the lookout. After the GCI—call sign Cranford—had guided Geoff for some time out to sea, a good blip came up on Reed's cathode tube and at 9,000 feet he guided his pilot in from astern, when Geoff had a good "visual" of a Heinkel 111, its crew evidently unaware of their impending fate. An excellent pilot, cool and matter-of-fact, Geoff sent a deadly stream of fire into the bomber; he could see the flashes of his De Wilde bullets as they struck home, tearing off bits of metal, which flashed past dangerously close to the Havoc. The Heinkel dived steeply and crashed into the sea. One enemy aircraft destroyed.

Jim Marshall and his operator, Sergeant Hallett, were next off that night, and the GCI soon put them on the track of a "bandit" which, after Hallett had taken over on the AI, Jim sighted in front, but 1,000 feet below at an altitude of 14,000 feet. Throttling back gently to prevent the engines from streaming visible flames of late-burning gas, Jim lost height and closed in behind his target. But the Heinkel's gunners had seen him and replied to his fire. Through streams of tracer he could see his De Wilde striking the left wing of the Heinkel. It pulled up, dived steeply, and disappeared from Jim's view, and from the cathode tube. One enemy aircraft damaged.

An hour before midnight I took off with George Barker seated before his radar set. Behind him in the rear cockpit stood Sergeant Bailey, a young Australian and an airman to the bone; his father had been a crewman with the famous pioneer pilot Charles Kingsford-Smith, yet another of my boyhood heroes.

That night I had decided on an experiment, impressed as I had been by the Defiant's ability to attack with its hydraulic four-gun turret from underneath the enemy.

I had rigged up in the rear cockpit of my Havoc a Vickers K machine gun; the mounting could only take one, hand-operated at that. Bailey, a radar operator by trade, had volunteered to come with me as gunner. We climbed away into the night in great fettle, as was always the case with George chuckling in the backseat. None of us dreamed that the joke, in the end, would be on us. At 14,000 feet, Cranford put me onto a "bandit." After some minutes, George had a blip, and after a five minutes' chase I sighted a Ju. 88 three hundred yards in front and above. I was overtaking fast, so rather than throttle right back and risk being spotted from my engines' exhaust flames, I made a series of S-turns before slowly closing in from below and astern. Then, dazzled by the diffused moonlight on my plastic Perspex windscreen, I lost sight of the bomber. George immediately took over and soon brought me back into visual contact. As we continued to close, all three of us saw flashes just beyond our own left wingtip—very probably exploding grenades, a gadget occasionally used by the enemy. He had evidently seen us. Now very close, I opened fire, but while George reported De Wilde strikes, my own view was completely obscured by the blinding flashes of my eight forward guns, while smoke and cordite fumes filled my cockpit. As the enemy dived, turning violently left and right, I followed and at 11,000 feet began stalking him again. But he could still see us, thanks to our searchlights, which firmly held me but only occasionally flickered on him. We now came under intensive and accurate fire. George reported hits on our right wing and engine and more on the left wing; also that his microphone had frozen up and he had exchanged it for Bailey's, which left him and Bailey connected to each other like Siamese twins and both of them plugged into Bailey's socket. I stuck on the enemy's tail, but during my violent evasive action to dodge his flying bullets, Bailey was floored and George unseated. However, he managed to grab the Vickers gun and pump a few bullets into the Junkers' belly as we finally slid below it. George—and I could still detect his chuckle—then shouted: "The bloody gun's jammed!" I now gathered myself for another front-gun attack and this time approached, unobserved, to within close range. When I opened fire we all saw a mass of De Wilde strikes and a fair-sized explosion in the right engine. Then our stubborn enemy, lurching clumsily to the right, went down in a long, steep dive until he disappeared from both visual and radar contact. We had been trying to kill each other for the last half hour.

In making out my combat report I claimed the Junkers as probably destroyed; a Junkers 88 did crash in our sector, its survivors saying it had been repeatedly attacked by a night fighter. But the evidence was not conclusive. Our Junkers may have fallen into the sea; bodies of Luftwaffe crews were continually being washed up on our shores. If ever it got back, then the crew would be able to spread the story that our night fighters were around and that they were becoming more dangerous. Psychology in war is a powerful factor. The Luftwaffe high command was becoming increasingly worried at the losses of its night bombers. The crews themselves were suffering more and more losses among their friends. Two and sometimes three sorties in a single night were putting crews under mounting stress, which could only be aggravated by their growing fear of British night fighters. One unhappy young radio operator of 3/KG 53 was so obsessed with a fear of night fighters that, imagining his Heinkel 111 was being continually followed, he kept screaming false warnings on the intercom to his pilot. His fears were finally put to rest when the 20mm cannon shells of a Beaufighter tore into his Heinkel and killed him.

In my own Havoc we were lucky to land intact, at about half past midnight. George had warned me of the strikes on our aircraft, but he could not tell that the oil tank of the right engine had been holed. The oil pressure held up, just, until landing. By then the oil tank was empty and the engine on the point of seizing up. The enemy gunner, after raking the right wing and engine, had been obliging enough to lift his gun over my cockpit before putting more bullets into the left wing. For George the biggest joke of the night, apart from his and Bailey's tangle in the rear cockpit, was the stray bullet which somehow had made its way through one leg of his trousers.

When I took off next night, April 10, it was with George alone. The good Bailey, after his adventures of the night before, was in no hurry to accompany us. We all agreed that in theory the rear-gun attack from below was in certain situations a valid alternative—Defiants were still proving it—to the front-gun attack. But a single hand-operated rear gun fired from an open cockpit was clearly not the equal of the Defiant's four-gun hydraulic turret.

My thoughts on this subject were, I believe, influenced—already— by the conviction that our eight forward-firing .303 guns were, at night, far from adequate. Aiming at and hitting one's target at night, even under the benign light of the moon, was far more tricky than by day. Darkness dulled the visual senses and other reflexes as well. This considered, I had pleaded since Gravesend, four months ago, for the most lethal armament possible. The Havoc's battery of eight .303 machine guns installed in the nose had that grave disadvantage of blinding the pilot, at least until the guns were fitted with "flash eliminators"—a kind of cone fitted to the end of the barrel. And it was too feeble. The Beaufighters with nearly as many machine guns—six—plus four 20mm cannons seldom missed. I demanded four cannons to be fitted as soon as possible. In the meantime our numerous night interceptions too often ended, for want of firepower, in inconclusive combat.

As I took off with George just after midnight the following night, April 11, we felt surer of ourselves as a regular crew of pilot and radar operator. George's humorous asides were, as always, stimulating. Vectored by Cranford onto a raid, George soon picked it up on his AI cathode tube until I sighted, above and slightly to the left, a Ju. 88. It took me a few more minutes to stalk in, unseen, to close range. Then I opened fire, and while the reassuring flashes of my De Wilde were visible, the tongues of flame from my guns made it impossible to hold my aim through the reflector sight. I released the firing button in time to see tracer coming from the Junkers, which swung violently to the left and went down in a steep dive, streaming little jets of flame, like bright red-and-yellow silk handkerchiefs, until it was lost to my own visual and George's radar view. One Ju. 88 damaged. A disappointing combat, for he looked a "goner," as I wrote in my combat report, "on the way down." I could only wish him *bon voyage* on the way home.

That brief affair over, I climbed up again on an indistinct vector of 330 degrees from Cranford and heard no more from him. But from George came a sudden tallyho. We were close to the summit of a towering, moonlit mass of cumulus cloud. Before George could utter another word, a Heinkel, easily recognizable, suddenly appeared from the shadows, a hundred yards away and on a converging course. We both swerved violently to avoid collision, and I grabbed the throttles back, hoping to slip in behind him. But he, understandably frightened, was already diving ahead of me into the shadowy canyon of cloud and was quickly lost in its depths.

In mid-April came a signal concerning me personally. It informed me that I was to be posted to 11 Group Headquarters. Although the news was disappointing, I was prepared for it. I had been on active operations day and night since the war began twenty months before and commanding 85 Squadron for nearly a year. Moreover, I was well aware that my physical and nervous resources were running low. However, I could not accept the prospect of leaving 85 at this moment when, after all our vain searching in the dark, we were now beginning to catch the enemy night after night. But problems still remained to be solved with the maintenance and armament of our Havocs. I hastened off to 11 Group to plead with L-M, and he, always ready to listen, allowed me a stay of execution until mid-June, with a kindly word of advice: "Take it easy a bit."

During the first half of April, the Luftwaffe—except for a heavy raid on Coventry—had pursued its strategy of "strangulation" with night attacks on our ports—Liverpool and Glasgow, Bristol, Birmingham, Belfast, and Tyneside. It was perhaps a heavy raid on Berlin by RAF

Bomber Command, whose navigation and bomb aiming were often praised by Luftwaffe prisoners, that provoked massive retaliation by the Germans on London. On April 16—"the Wednesday," as Londoners would remember it—nearly seven hundred bombers assaulted the capital, killing over a thousand of its citizens and injuring more than twice that number, besides hitting thirteen churches and eighteen hospitals. A captured German bombardier, when asked to describe his feelings about killing hospital patients, replied: "Well, they were already half dead, so I have no regrets." Mass aerial bombardment of unarmed and anonymous innocents was surely the most callous and degrading of all kinds of warfare.

"The Wednesday" saw London's most murderous raid to date. The attack of over seven hundred bombers on April 19, "the Saturday," caused as much slaughter in the capital. These two horrible massacres were a measure of the continuing failure of the British night defenses, despite their unrelenting efforts, to protect the civilian population. While the night fighters for their part were inflicting increasing losses on the enemy, they were still not enough to deter him.

Leaving London to mourn its dead, the Luftwaffe turned again on our ports. Night after night through the rest of April and into May the Germans mercilessly battered the ports on their hit list, adding Sunderland for good measure. Thus did they hope to reduce them to rubble and render them useless. But the people of the ports held out, and their repair and restoration services kept the docks in operation.

Our progress in 85 Squadron was encouraging, at least by comparison with the past, although it was already evident from the number of inconclusive combats that our Havocs needed more clout than their eight machine guns, with their blinding flash, could provide. On that Wednesday night, guided by GCI, Sergeant Berkley and his operator, Sergeant Carr, peering into his cathode tube, intercepted a Heinkel. Berkley fired a long burst, saw the unmistakable strikes of his De Wilde bullets, and for a few more fleeting seconds watched the Heinkel diving until it was swallowed up in the night. Another inconclusive combat. James Wheeler and Charles Maton, thanks as ever to the magic of GCI and AI, found and did battle with a Ju. 88, but their discomfort at being held in the searchlights as they came into range was increased by a stream of tracer from the enemy. James fired and saw the flashes of his De Wilde on the Junkers, which dived away smartly and disappeared. One more enemy aircraft damaged.

While the GCI and AI were regularly working the miracle of guiding us to within sighting distance of a black bomber in the dark, the ensuing combat, so often inconclusive, began to weary and frustrate us. The enemy was hit—that could be seen by the flash of the De Wilde bullets as they struck—but he was not hit hard enough. Paddy Hemingway, however—his operator was the Australian Bailey, more at home at his radar set than as third man in my own Havoc—managed to strike a decisive blow, despite the blinding flash of his guns, on an unidentified enemy bomber. Its final plunge into the sea was confirmed by the Observer Corps.

Our commander in chief, Sholto Douglas, had most kindly invited me to call him direct at Fighter Command Headquarters if I had problems. I had already done so on a number of occasions, thereby incurring the displeasure of his technical staff officers concerned. Throughout April I had pleaded with him to send us flash eliminators for our guns. Even more insistently I begged him to have our Havocs fitted with 20mm cannons. This he promised to do at the very soonest.

It was already May, and the squadron moved thirty miles south to a new airfield, Hunsdon, with long, brand-new asphalt runways still smelling of fresh tar. During the first week of the month, four more combats followed, two ending with the enemy "probably destroyed," two classed as "damaged." Since October 1940 we had spent six months groping blindly for the enemy in the dark, with but one successful combat. In the past four weeks, with Havocs, AI and GCI, we had downed two of the enemy with four "probables" and six damaged. For the fourth month in succession we topped the list of "night hours flown," and felt certain at last that we were on our way to attaining that standard set by our onetime commander in chief Dowding, who on the very eve of 85's conversion from day to night fighters, had vowed that Fighter Command would never rest "until we can locate, pursue, and shoot down the enemy by day and by night." By night we were not yet there, but things were slowly improving.

During the first nights of May, the Luftwaffe, having failed for months in its attempts to subdue Liverpool and Glasgow, came back repeatedly as if in a last, desperate attempt to have done with the job. Its blows fell, too, on Belfast and Barrow-in-Furness. On the 8th the Luftwaffe struck out wildly at Nottingham, Hull, and Sheffield. With other squadrons we were able to help parry these blows. On the 9th we patrolled as usual, but no enemy came to tarnish the silver moonlight which illumined Britain that night. A silent night like that had often presaged, in the past, a coming storm.

25

GERMANY'S DISTANT FRONT:
DRANG NACH OSTEN

Indeed, the Luftwaffe was preparing, on the personal orders of Hitler, for exactly what it did not know. Although its losses of night bombers were higher than ever—190 aircrew killed or captured in April—they, at least the younger ones, still believed in the invasion of Britain and thereafter victory. The older ones, less sanguine, were, when captured in Britain, only too glad to be out of the war. Those on active service were sustained, meanwhile, by the appeal of passing pleasures, to judge by the entry cards to this or that brothel found in the pockets of dead or captured aircrews. A night, perhaps the last, in bed with a woman could help to divert their thoughts from the nightmare of dying in the darkness over Britain. So also, once their course was set for England, did their emergency foods sustain them: choco-cola to fortify the system and boost the blood circulation; coffee beans, real ones, unavailable back in the Fatherland, to stimulate the nerves. Peppermint helped to slake their thirst and "Pervertine" kept them wide awake. And chewing gum—there was nothing else so good for soothing the nerves. On our side we did not resort to such artificial stimulants, least of all that revolting delicacy chewing gum. We were stimulated enough by the desire to defend our island. Not that, for myself, I particularly desired to kill anyone; I just wanted to shoot out of our dark sky those black bombers which came to trouble and murder our people.

The German airmen felt surer of victory than we, who were thinking more of survival. So sure were they that in their letters home they told their family and friends to send no more parcels. They would be back home before the presents arrived. Yet none could deny that the strain of night operations was telling on them. Letters from home added to their anxieties—in the past they used to tell of laughable little British bombs falling here and there; now they related their accuracy and their devastating effect. Gas warfare remained a specter in the minds of many a Luftwaffe airman; antigas defenses in Germany were so lamentable that Germany might well get the worst of it. What most of them did not know was that the Luftwaffe was well armed in offensive gas weapons—gas bombs filled with lung gas, nasal irritants, and nerve gas—and that the Wehrmacht, in readiness for invasion, was as well if not better equipped.

In a more local context, German aircrews were by now only too painfully aware of the increasing threat to their lives from the British air defenses in general and night fighters in particular—not to speak of the traps laid to catch them, the radio jammers Aspirin, Bromide, and Domino, those false beacons called meacons, and Starfish, the decoy fires. But as brave soldiers of the Reich they flew on in the face of these embarrassing devices.

Another factor, more insidious, came to trouble their minds. Disturbing stories were circulating about Russia, Germany's ally for the past two years. Rumor had it that, incredibly, the alliance was about to break up and that Germany and the Soviet Union were on the verge of hostilities. Captured Luftwaffe men were beginning to wonder whether Germany could ever win the war. So far their apprehensions were the issue of vague imaginings, but the facts, unknown to them as yet, were on record.

As long ago as July 1940, Hitler had decided to invade Russia. When General Jodl confided the secret to officers of the high command staff they were amazed. As long as Britain remained undefeated it was unthinkable that Germany should fight simultaneously on two fronts. Nevertheless, planning for the Russian invasion began in October 1940. On December 18, the Fuehrer, in his Directive No. 21, had ordered that the German armed forces were to "crush England." He and his sycophantic generals gave themselves six to eight weeks to complete the operation, code-named "Barbarossa." The starting date was given as May 15. But the defeat of the Italian armies in North Africa, then in Greece, and Yugoslavia's spirited defiance, all of them forcing Hitler to intervene, obliged him to postpone the date to June 22—a five-week delay which was to prove fatal.

The most astonishing feature in the Russian affair, after Hitler's duplicity, was Stalin's stupidity. The Soviet leader, on March 20, 1941, was informed by the U.S. ambassador in Moscow of Hitler's planned invasion. Churchill too on April 3 tried to warn Stalin through the British ambassador, Sir Stafford Cripps, but the dictator showed no signs of alarm. In mid-April, at a public ceremony in Moscow, Stalin embraced the German ambassador, Count Fritz von der Schulenberg, before the assembled crowd of diplomats, saying, "We must remain friends." To the German military attaché, Colonel Krebs, he promised, "We will remain friends with you through thick and thin." Although, a week later, the Soviets were complaining to Berlin about Luftwaffe aircraft overflying their border territory, they remained conciliatory. "We shall not mind as long as it doesn't happen too often" was in effect their reply.

At the beginning of May, rumors were rife in Moscow of an imminent German invasion. They reached the ears of Stalin, of course, and worried him, as did reports of German troop movements on Russia's eastern frontier. But despite the warnings of the United States and Britain he refused to associate these ominous portents with the diabolical plans of Hitler. Stalin was determined that there should be no conflict between the two countries. In the meantime the massing of German troops continued on Russia's frontiers and the Kriegsmarine took up its war dispositions.

Rommel's counterattack on March 31 at Agheila, some 150 miles by road west of Benghazi, marked the beginning of a disastrous period for Britain. The British and Australians began falling back to Benghazi and a week later were in full retreat. The Australians defending Tobruk beat off two attacks and earned a message from Churchill—"Bravo Tobruk." But the enemy, leaving the port aside for the time being, pressed on eastward in the direction of Egypt. On April 12 the Germans took Bardia, a few miles from the Egyptian frontier, where they halted. Rommel, the Desert Fox, had achieved a brilliant operation; for the British, in Churchill's words, it was a disaster of the first magnitude. They were back where they had started in December.

He now directed the Royal Navy to intervene with all its might to impede the enemy. It must cut Rommel's supply lines to Tripoli; "heavy losses in battleships, cruisers, and destroyers must if necessary be accepted," the "Former Naval Person" added grimly. Tripoli must be bombarded from the sea, so also must German traffic on the coastal road leading eastward to Egypt, as well as being harassed by commando forces. Here again, losses must be faced. "The urgency is extreme," Churchill insisted, "especially should the German attack on Yugoslavia and Greece succeed.'' At that moment, in mid-April, it showed every likelihood of doing so.

The German Twelfth Army had crossed the frontiers of Yugoslavia and Greece on April 6. While Yugoslav resistance gradually collapsed, the Greek armies, though stiffened by 53,000 British troops from North Africa, were falling back before the overwhelming numbers of the Wehrmacht and the Luftwaffe. Churchill, harking back to the glory of ancient Greece, envisaged a last stand at Thermopylae, but the Greek army, after months of heroic resistance, no longer had the strength to stay with the British.

Wavell thereupon ordered the reembarkation of his troops—British, Australian, and New Zealander. As at Dunkirk so now on the beaches of Greece the Royal Navy and the Allied merchant fleet performed a heroic feat. With the Luftwaffe undisputed master of the air, evacuation could only proceed by dark. The sailors brought off some 42,000 men, more than half of whom were taken on to Crete, where the final act of the Greek tragedy would soon be played.

British participation in the Greek campaign was more an act of *noblesse oblige* than a response to a binding obligation. It touched people in the United States, and not least the president, who wrote to Churchill: ''You have done not only heroic but very useful work in Greece. . . .''

On May 4, Churchill, in his reply, was in somber mood. ''We shall fight on, whatever happens,'' he told Roosevelt, adding that if Europe, much of Asia, and Africa became part of the Axis system, that would mean ''a hard, long and bleak struggle'' by Britain, the Commonwealth, and the United States. Meanwhile, he averred, the British were determined to fight to the last for Egypt, Tobruk, and Crete.

As Churchill was in the act of writing to Roosevelt, the German Fuehrer, in Berlin, was crowing over his latest victories; his speech was well laced, as usual, with insults directed at Churchill. Hitler ended by suggesting that Churchill's ''abnormal'' state of mind could be explained only as symptomatic either of a paralytic disease or of a drunkard's ravings. It was a pathetic performance, particularly as the Nazi warlord himself was about to make the biggest strategic blunder of his life. Despite the attempts by some of his advisers to dissuade him, his landlocked mind was incapable of appreciating the awful predicament of Britain. Instead, he remained obsessed with his plan to invade Russia before turning, ''in six or eight weeks,'' as he said, to finish off Britain at this point at the nadir of her fortunes.

Churchill was the only man living who had the measure of this wicked, vainglorious, and foolish man. In sober, measured terms the British prime minister had, the previous day, spoken to the nation in that very personal way he had of moving us to the core of our being. After the recent disasters in Europe and North Africa, "we must not," he said, "lose our sense of proportion and thus become discouraged or alarmed. When we face with a steady eye the difficulties which lie before us, we may derive new confidence from remembering those we have already overcome." He went on to quote two verses of the poet Arthur Hugh Clough which, he said, "seem apt and appropriate to our fortunes tonight, and I believe they will be so judged wherever the English language is spoken or the flag of freedom flies." With millions of others I was listening intently. At this moment of our great tribulation the words of the prime minister and the poet fell superb and serene on the ear:

> For while the tired waves, vainly breaking,
> Seem here no painful inch to gain,
> Far back, through creeks and inlets
>   making,
> Comes silent, flooding in, the main.
>
> And not by eastern windows only,
> When daylight comes, comes in the light;
> In front the sun climbs slow, how slowly!
> But westward, look, the land is bright.

26

THE WORM IN THE APPLE:
THE FLIGHT OF
THE DEPUTY FUEHRER

Yet still another disaster was impending. The Luftwaffe through March, April, and May, backing up the U-boats, sank 179 ships. In early May, 40,000 tons were destroyed in the docks of Liverpool—that "tormented target." The offensive against the ports had reached its climax; after another heavy assault on Belfast and Glasgow, the Luftwaffe came back to London on the night of May 10.

The idea for the raid occurred during a boring and seemingly interminable tea party hosted by Hitler for a bunch of his cronies, at his mountain retreat, the Berghof, in the Bavarian Alps. It was Martin Bormann, Hitler's bull-necked private secretary, who raised the subject: the RAF had once again bombed Berlin. How about another reprisal raid on London? Orders went out to General Hugo Sperrle, the fleshy, sadistic commander in chief of Luftflotte 3, at his headquarters in the Hôtel Luxembourg in Paris: "Target London: all available aircraft." That meant five hundred or so, for a large reserve was already held back in preparation for Barbarossa. Sperrle, in 1937, during the Spanish Civil War, had planned the attack on Guernica, which killed thousands of civilians. London could expect no quarter in this special reprisal attack. Yet if Sperrle's motto was "Is there a foe that bombing cannot break?" London would give him a positive answer.

Targets were allotted: the Victoria Docks opposite Woolwich; West Ham, Stepney, Millwall Docks, and the West India Docks; and finally Battersea Power Station. Kampfgruppe 100 was to lead the attack with incendiaries, but since the Luftwaffe meteorology men, "weather frogs" as they were called, had forecast clear visibility under a full moon, they would not need their *X-Geraet* for the actual bombing—fortunately for them, for British Domino jamming sent it haywire. But the beam from Cherbourg was laid on all the same; it cut the intersecting beam from Holland over West Ham. By 6:00 P.M., Fighter Command, AA Command, and the Fire Service Headquarters at Lambeth had all been informed. What deeply concerned the firemen was that the Thames that night would be at ebb tide. Pump suction hoses lowered from Thames bridges might not reach the water; from the river embankment firemen would have to carry them across twenty yards of slimy, stinking mud before they could be immersed in the river.

Across the Channel in the Pas de Calais, around 6:00 P.M. Oberst-leutnant Adolf ("Dolfo") Galland, commanding 26 Jagdgeschwader, received an unexpected call from Goering in Berlin. Galland was to get his fighters into the air immediately. "But, Herr Reichsmarschall," Galland dared to object, "there are no enemy bombers flying in." "I'm not talking about aircraft flying in," bellowed the *Reichsmarschall*, "I'm asking you to stop one flying out—and shoot it down!" A few minutes later, half a dozen of Galland's Messerschmitt 109s were in the air searching for the mysterious aircraft. By 7:30 P.M. they had all landed back at their base with nothing to report.

Nearly three hours later—and by British "double summertime" the sky, with a rising moon, still glowed with light—eleven of Kampfgruppe 100's Heinkels were heading across the Channel on their *X-Geraet*, for London. By now the south-coast and east-coast radar stations were saturated with plots, duly reproduced in the operations map at Fighter Command, where our commander in chief, Sholto Douglas, gravely surveyed the attack massing on London. As the enemy converged on the capital, Sholto was puzzled by a single plot crossing the North Sea not far from the English coast and traveling considerably faster than the bombers. It crossed the coast near Alnwick in Northumberland at 10:23 P.M. A few minutes later, the Observer Corps post at Chatton, near Edinburgh, reported having sighted the aircraft flying low—a Messerschmitt 110. Impossible, replied the controller at Fighter Command—an Me. 110 could never get that far and return to base. He ordered a fighter up to intercept, but the plot, heading northeast, faded. It was about 10:45 P.M.

A couple of minutes after 11:00, KGr 100 was over West Ham, where, in moonlight nearly as bright as day, they bombed visually, opening an attack such as London had never yet endured. Unlike the great fire raid of December 29, which was concentrated on the square mile of the City around St. Paul's, the deluge of high-explosive and incendiary bombs spread, during the next five hours, to the heart of the City and northwards to Shoreditch; to St. Marylebone, Paddington, Kensington, and Battersea in the west; and south of the river to Bermondsey, Deptford, Greenwich, and Lewisham. Fire and destruction rained down without discrimination—on Lambeth Palace, where the archbishop was in residence, on the sick and dying in St. Thomas's Hospital; fires raged at Waterloo Station, St. Pancras, and Paddington, consumed the roofs of the thousand-year-old Abbey of Westminster, of Westminster Hall, and of the House of Lords; the chamber of the House of Commons was gutted. The Old Bailey, Gray's Inn Hall, and five Wren churches were among scores of historic buildings shattered by blast and fire. Faraday House, nerve center of London's telephone system, and St. Paul's Cathedral, surrounded by flames, were threatened for hours. Hundreds of private dwellings suffered the same fate, their owners imploring the firefighters to save their property and belongings instead of trying to rescue buildings which belonged to the ancient past.

The crying problem was water; 600,000 gallons a minute were needed to extinguish the conflagrations which raged in the one square mile of the City alone. The Thames at low tide could not provide enough; the 5,000-gallon static tanks sited here and there in the streets ran dry. Some pumps searched for water in the sewers of London, only to find the filters of their pumps were soon clogged with detritus. That night the Luftwaffe lit over 2,200 separate fires.

In the midst of this inferno, near the Royal Mint, a few streets away from the Tower of London, Chief Fire Officer Alfred Shawyer was instructing the pumps as they drove up. Shawyer, six feet tall and solidly built, had been a prizefighter before the war and had fought for Britain in the Golden Gloves tournament in New York. In his off-hours he had become a keen ballroom dancer—under the tutelage of no other than Johnny Callow. In the mid-thirties the two had become good friends, but in time their ways had separated.

At this moment, Johnny's No. 1 Pump, accompanied by No. 6, was heading for the conflagration in central London. When the bells had gone down at the substation the order was "The Minories!" "Where the hell's that?" Johnny asked his driver, Fred Cosh. "I'll show you," replied Fred; a cockney, he knew the City like the back of his hand. Driving flat out up the Old Kent Road, he came to the Bricklayer's Arms and turned right, dodging through narrow streets until he reached London Bridge. Before they were halfway across, Johnny began sniffing the air. "What's that terrible smell?" he asked Fred. "Oh, shut up, Johnny!" shouted Fred. "That's Billingsgate Fish Market. Round here I follow me nose." Past the fish market they sped, then had to pick their way down small streets strewn with debris, sometimes having to back and find another way among the crashing bombs and roaring fires. At last Fred came to a halt. "Here we are, the Minories, and next door to the Royal Mint. Plenty of money in there for us, Johnny!" he chuckled.

Johnny got down from the cab and, on heel and toe, his dancer's step, he strode toward the red-and-white-checked control van and confronted the control officer to ask for instructions. But instead he blurted out: "Blimey, Alf, if it isn't you!" And Alf Shawyer with a great laugh exclaimed, "Blimey, Johnny, it's been five years. What a place to meet again." It was neither the place nor the time for reminiscences. Johnny and his men unrolled their hoses, found a hydrant, and connected up. For the next four hours, under ceaseless bombardment and with barely enough water pressure, they fought the fire until it died. Alf Shawyer told Johnny, "Better knock off now, mate. Ta-ta, see you later!" "You bet!" shouted Johnny and drove off.

Badly mauled though the surrounding boroughs of Greenwich, Deptford, and Lewisham were, Woolwich received but one serious hit—once again on the long-suffering Arsenal, where high explosives and incendiaries kept firemen and rescue squads busy all night. Johnny's younger brother Ray did less running than usual that night, but was proud to be on duty when the London sirens sounded for the 545th time in the last nine months.

When, after seven hours of bombardment, the all clear sounded, London was still burning and smoldered on for several days. Its citizens were left to mourn nearly fifteen hundred dead and pray for thousands of injured. War, since it has existed, has forever been associated with massacres of the civil population. But since "this hellish invention," as Churchill had called it, of air warfare, the massacre of innocents was being perpetrated, on an ever-increasing scale, not by the drunken, dastard soldiery of yore who slew and pillaged with impunity, but, despite themselves, by sober young airmen of rare courage. The anomaly was a cruel one.

Night fighters were up in force all through that night of May 10-11; Fighter Command had declared, for reasons of moon and good visibility, a "fighter night." Cat's-eye fighters, Hurricanes, Spitfires, and Defiants, stacked up over London, Beachy Head (on the Channel coast), and other strategic points, reported many sightings and combats. Between them they claimed nineteen enemy bombers destroyed. AA guns, their shooting restricted by the fighter night rules to a height of 12,000 feet, claimed to have downed four more. The "specialized" radar night fighters, better suited to darker nights, when they could stalk the enemy unseen, shot down another four. Alas, the claim of enemy aircraft destroyed later proved to be wildly exaggerated. The Luftwaffe lost only eight aircraft that night. Of these, two were certainly accounted for by 85 Squadron.

First off from Hunsdon were Flight Lieutenant Gordon Raphael and his operator, Sergeant Addison. Gordon, a hardy, ascetic Canadian, suffered neither fools nor Germans gladly. With the burning city visible from Hunsdon, Gordon was in high dudgeon when, after preliminary directions from GCI and skillful guidance by Addison, he sighted a Heinkel 111. With no time to lose, lest the Heinkel see him, he closed in fast, his bead on the bomber's left engine—it was Gordon's private theory that hitting one power unit and the wing tanks gave better results. Tonight he proved his theory. The stricken Heinkel spiraled down steeply to the left, caught fire, and exploded before crashing.

No. 85's second victory was scored by Flying Officer Evans with Sergeant Carter as operator, an unassuming but thoroughly professional pair. The procedure GCI-to-AI-to-visual went smoothly, and Evans, though his Havoc presented a fine target in the moonlight, was not spotted by the enemy, a Heinkel, whose engines and fuselage he sprayed from short range. Evans's technique, too, was deadly. The Heinkel pitched forward and, streaming sparks, went down in a dive so steep that the Havoc could not follow. The Heinkel was already half consumed by flames before hitting the ground. The time was 2:30 in the morning of the 11th.

While, at the summons of ground control, the Havocs of my squadron roared down the runway and up into the night, I myself, for reasons I shall soon explain, remained unusually passive on the ground. From our dispersal point at Hunsdon we could see the immense, incandescent glow which rose above London, staining blood-red the fair moonlit sky. From where we watched, sixty miles north of the capital, it was an awful sight.

And while, all through that fiery night, the hundreds of enemy bombers bore down on London, saturating our coastal radar screens, Fighter Command Control watched, mystified, the plots of a lone aircraft flying northward out to sea. Later, it turned inland and the plots disappeared near Glasgow. At Bonnyton, north of that city, a crofter, David McLean, saw an aircraft burst into flames; above, in the glare of the flames, a man was visible, swinging on the end of a parachute. Some minutes later, back in his cottage, David was offering tea to the shaken pilot. A German, handsome with dark eyes and bushy eyebrows, he told McLean that his name was Albert Horn, *Hauptmann* in the Luftwaffe. Later, at the central police station in Glasgow, the German gave a different name: Rudolf Hess. If that was true, the man standing in the police station was no ordinary Luftwaffe pilot, but the deputy Fuehrer of the Third Reich and Hitler's right-hand man. He asked to see Wing Commander the Duke of Hamilton, at present commanding the Turn-house (Edinburgh) sector.

"Douglo" Hamilton, a shy and sparely built man with straight blond hair, was instructed by the commander in chief of Fighter Command to go over to Glasgow. There the duke was convinced that the German was indeed Rudolf Hess. He had come to Britain, he said, to discuss a peace plan.

Winston Churchill, as was so often his wont, had been spending the weekend at the house of Mr. and Mrs. Ronald Tree at Ditchley, near Oxford. Throughout dinner, the progress of that Saturday night's fire raid on London had been telephoned to him from the Home Security War Room. Dinner over, the guests were enjoying a movie, *The Marx Brothers Go West*, when the prime minister's secretary, Miss Shearburn, came and whispered to him, "I have a very urgent message for you." Churchill, absorbed by the antics of the Marx Brothers, did not budge for a few minutes. Then he left his seat to read the message, which had been typed out on a slip of paper. It read: "Rudolf Hess has arrived in Scotland." Churchill took the paper, glanced at it, then looked up, beaming, and said: "The worm is in the apple."

The reason why, that night, I had not taken off on patrol with the rest was that the 11 Group commander, Air Vice Marshal Leigh-Mallory, had insisted, a month ago, that I take it easy. Despite my own impulsive feelings, I had respected his advice; I knew he was right. I was completely whacked—I believe the Luftwaffe had their own word, *ausflugen*, "out-flown," flown to a standstill. As a pilot, I was no longer functioning properly; while the spirit was still willing, the flesh and its vital functions of vision and reflex were weak. That half-hour-long inconclusive combat with the Junkers 88 in early April was to me a disturbing sign, but one that I was not prepared to admit. On the other hand, when Leigh-Mallory had granted me another two months with the squadron, I already knew I was dead beat. I suspect he did too, for he had known me ever since, nearly a year ago, I had been given command of 85 Squadron.

When shot down for the second time at the end of August 1940, I was already nearing the end of my tether. Otherwise, I should never have rushed headlong into that swarm of Messerschmitts, knowing full well that they were bound to get me. Air fighting, like any other, may need courage, but it requires, too, intelligence and even prudence, as the great World War I German ace Manfred von Richthofen proved when, at the height of his career, he was killed because of forgetting that rule. The longer you kept fighting, the more you needed cunning rather than just plain dash and derring-do.

In air combat, skill alone—this I had acquired in nearly two years of day and night fighting—is not enough. Luck played a big part. I had enjoyed more than my fair share, ever since those first combats in early 1940. Time after time my aircraft had been hit; bullets had holed the wings and fuselage, they had zipped through the propeller past my head, between my legs even. One had exploded in the cockpit, bringing me down in the sea, yet unhurt; another had hit me, downing me once more. Luck—I would dare say God—had helped me survive the perils of the night, the cruel weather, and the enemy combined.

Not that, oddly enough, any of these things had particularly frightened me. In fighters, even night fighters, we had our own way of enjoying the funny side of danger, however hideous, and laughing at each other's stories over a pint or two of beer. But the trouble was that these hair-raising experiences accumulated to form stress, a word we ourselves only knew in its aerodynamic context, as applied to our beloved aircraft. But we too, our minds and bodies and nervous systems, were, without our noticing it, under increasing stress, which, if not relieved in time, would break us and plunge us into the dark, deep pit of depression and fear. Against them there was but one antidote, action. But action, like a drug, made such demands on the body that we came to living on our nerves alone. That was the beginning of the end.

In my case—there were hundreds of others—Leigh-Mallory, in his wisdom, had noticed this. He prescribed less action. Our medical officer had noticed too; he put me on barbiturates which were supposed to calm the nerves and induce sleep. But my body, hardened for months against fatigue and insomnia, fought the drug, which only made me feel worse.

As indeed did the reduced dose of action, which left me defective as a pilot, and a night-fighter pilot at that. I was no longer the pilot I had been. But I had been given a stay of command until mid-June. I must hold out till then, not overdoing it as was my habit, though pride or just plain foolishness, but taking my normal turn to patrol.

Unexpectedly, the nights were henceforth quiet; apart from a few sporadic raids the Luftwaffe bombers simply vanished in the darkness. The blitz was over. Britain had thwarted Hitler's declared intention— to eliminate her as a base for continuing the war. This she remained until the end, when his tyranny was overthrown.

EPILOGUE:
END OF THE LONG NIGHT

With *der Tag*, D-Day for Hitler's attack on Russia, fixed for June 22, the Luftwaffe, after that murderous blitz on London, was hastily transferring the majority of its units from the British to the Russian front. Thanks to the Germans' failure to "annihilate" Russia, the Luftwaffe did not return within the six to eight weeks envisaged by Hitler to finish off Britain. The enemy's pressure on the home front subsided and remained negligible for the next twenty months.

Meanwhile the Greek campaign culminated in disaster when the Germans overran Crete at the end of May. In the Atlantic the Royal Navy and the RAF were gradually gaining the upper hand. On May 27 the navy and its air arm sank the so-called unsinkable *Bismarck,* all set to prey on the Atlantic convoys. By July the worst of the Atlantic battle was over. The Japanese attack on Pearl Harbor on December 7 brought the Americans into the Pacific war. But it would be months before the tide of war turned, in 1942, against the Germans, with the Russian victory before Stalingrad and the British offensive at El Alamein in North Africa.

The last attack on London was, as Churchill affirmed, the worst. Had there been many more of that intensity, London, through sheer exhaustion of her civil-defense resources, might well have been unable to "take it" any longer. But London had made it—so had every other British city. A popular ditty, sung by those lovable Cockney comedians Flanagan and Allen, went:

We've won it, we've done it
We've beaten them at last
Up in the air . . .

"Down on the ground" would have been a truer line.

All the same, our night defenses had increased immeasurably in strength since August 1940, and in all sectors. In the Wizard War we had sown confusion among the enemy, as we had with rather less refined means, with Starfish sites. Our antiaircraft guns and searchlights no longer amused the enemy night bombers with their harmless fireworks displays; they were now recognized as a real menace. Our night-fighter squadrons were regularly clawing the enemy out of the night sky—not that eight out of five hundred downed on that night of May 10 was anything like the hiding we gave them during the day battle in 1940. But Sholto Douglas was confident that, with further raids, our night fighters would get the better of them. Thank God for London and the rest of Britain's great cities, his theory was not put to the test.

No. 85 Squadron, which had grown up, not without pain, from cat's-eye fighters to AI fighters, kept on with its good work. I made my last night patrol with the squadron early in June, then departed to join the night operations staff at No. 11 Group.

My successor as commander of 85 Squadron was a likable, debonair, and moustachioed stranger, "Scruffy" Saunders. Alas, he stayed with them only four months until he and his operator, Pilot Officer Austin, were shot down during a night combat over the North Sea. A similar fate put an end to the young lives of Sergeant Berkley and his operator, Sergeant Carr, over the Thames Estuary. Following Scruffy, the squadron passed into the able hands of Gordon Raphael until, in 1943, John Cunningham (still teamed with his operator, Jimmy Rawnsley) took his place and led the squadron, now equipped with the sensational De Havilland Mosquito, on to battle with enemy night bombers and night fighters, too, over their own territory.

It was in April 1943, as "station master" at West Malling, a day-and-night-fighter base in Kent, that I finally got even with that Heinkel which had landed at Debden and escaped. Our resident night-fighter squadron, No. 29, had been operating against "lightning raiders," single-seater Focke-Wulfe 190s which climbed high over France, dived down on London, and loosed off one or two bombs. Towards midnight the sector controller called me in the control tower: "All is quiet now, you can relax." I returned to my room in the mess and lay on my bed, but this time fully clothed—in case. Ten minutes later an aircraft with an odd exhaust note passed low over the mess. I called the duty officer, "Curly" Clay (he was quite bald), and asked him, "What's that aircraft that has just landed?" A moment later he reported, "It's one of ours." "Curly," I said, "please take another look." This time he came back to the telephone and, in a voice which had risen several octaves, stammered, "It's a Focke-Wulfe 190!" "Grab it!" I told him. "I'll be with you in a minute."

When I arrived at the control tower I found, parked on the tarmac, a black Focke-Wulfe 190. In the control room on the first floor stood a German pilot and on each side of him one of our men pointing a bayonet at his tummy. In the minute or so before I had arrived the little Hillman van in which sat two girls of WAAF had driven out to the aircraft, which had stopped on the flare path. They believed it to be one of our returning bombers. Just in front of it, the driver turned and switched on the illuminated panel on the roof which said "FOLLOW ME." This the German did, comprehending nothing. As he reached the tarmac and switched off, the AA liaison officer climbed onto the Focke-Wulfe's wing and, short of a revolver, stuck a pencil into the pilot's back and said something resembling *"Handen hoffen"*—hands up. Thus was thirty-year-old Feldwebel Otto Bechte taken prisoner.

In another room on the first floor of the control tower I listened as our interrogator questioned him, without understanding a word apart from his repeated reply *"Ich bin ein deutsche Soldat."* Suddenly the door was flung open and Paul Arbon, who happened to be there, I cannot remember why, announced, breathless: "There's another one just landed!" With Paul following I spun, hardly touching the steps, down the spiral staircase, and ran outside just in time to see the "Beaverette"—a small armored car—driving off toward the Focke-Wulfe, still on the flare path, its propeller turning. I yelled after them, "Don't shoot!"—to be answered by a sharp burst of machine-gun fire. In a moment the Focke-Wulfe was on fire; the pilot, on fire too, was climbing down from the cockpit when Paul and I arrived. We leapt on him, knocked him to the ground, beat out the flames of his burning flying suit, and dragged him away from his aircraft. As it blazed, the flames fanned by the still revolving propeller, our firemen were playing their foam hoses on it. The German pilot, meanwhile, still on the ground, yelled and struggled like a madman so that Paul and I had to use all our strength to hold him down. Then, suddenly, in a gigantic explosion, the Focke-Wulfe disintegrated, badly injuring two of our firemen with splinters. The rest went over the top of our heads as we knelt on the German.

A little later, during his interrogation, I asked why he was making such a fuss, lying there on the ground, and he answered, "I was trying to tell that idiot"—pointing at me—"that there was a fifty-kilo bomb still in my aircraft." Oberleutnant Heinz Setzer thought he was in France and took me for a Frenchman.

The curtain had not yet fallen on this drama. A bobby appeared and informed me, "There's another one down half a mile short of the runway!" I drove with him through the dark lanes and came to a farm-house surrounded by orchards. Inside sat a German pilot, badly injured about the head, drinking tea with a bewildered elderly couple. Oberfeldwebel Otto Schultz, seeing the West Malling flare path, had tried to pull off an emergency landing. The lights went out at the last moment and Schultz crashed into the apple trees. He, like his comrades, had lost himself completely in the hazy weather, and believed he was in France.

In the hospital Schultz showed me a photo of his pretty wife and two lovely blond-haired children. What a sad mess the world was in—and it was less than five years since my first night flight in the peaceful, starry sky of Singapore.

BIBLIOGRAPHY

Blake, Lewis. *Red Alert*. Published by the author. London: 1982.

Brookes, Andrew J. *Fighter Squadron at War*. Ian Allan, Ltd.: London.

Clayton, Aileen. *The Enemy Is Listening*. New York: Ballantine, 1982.

Collier, Basil. *The Defence of the United Kingdom*. London: Her Majesty's Stationery Office, 1957.

Collier, Richard. *The City That Would Not Die*. New York: Dutton, 1960.

Churchill, Winston S. *The Second World War*. Vol. 1. London: Cassell, 1948.

————. *The Second World War*. Vol. 3. London: Cassell, 1950.

————. *Their Finest Hour*. Boston: Houghton Mifflin, 1949.

His Majesty's Stationery Office. *Front Line 1940–1941*. London, 1942.

Horley, Ronald T. "Occurrences 1939–45." Private memoirs. By kind permission of Patrick Langrishe.

Kee, Robert, and Smith, Joanna. *We'll Meet Again*. London: Dent, 1984.

Price, Alfred. *Instruments of Darkness*. London: William Kimber, 1967.

Rawnsley, C. F., and Wright, Robert. *Night Fighter*. London: Collins, 1957; Corgi Books, 1959.

Richards, Denis. *Royal Air Force 1939–45*. Vol. 1. London: Her Majesty's Stationery Office, 1953.

Shirer, William L. *The Rise and Fall of the Third Reich*. London: Pan Books, 1964.

Stahl, Peter W. *The Diving Eagle*. London: William Kimber, 1984.

Terraine, John. *The Right of the Line*. London: Hodder and Stoughton, 1985.

Wakefield, Kenneth. *The First Pathfinders*. London: William Kimber, 1981.

Wallington, Neil. *Fireman!* London: David & Charles, 1979.

————. *Firemen at War*. London: David & Charles, 1981.

Wood, Derek, and Dempster, Derek. *The Narrow Margin*. London: Hutchinson, 1961.

INDEX

DATE DUE

DATE DUE			
JAN 1 1 1990			
FEB 3 1990			
FEB 2 4 1990			
MAR 2 8 1990			
DEC - 3 1996			
NOV 2 0 2003			
GAYLORD			PRINTED IN U.S.A.